THERAPY WITH YOUNG MEN

The Routledge Series on Counseling and Psychotherapy With Boys and Men

SERIES EDITOR

Mark S. Kiselica
The College of New Jersey

ADVISORY BOARD

VOLUMES IN THIS SERIES

Volume 1: *Counseling Troubled Boys: A Guidebook for Professionals*
Mark S. Kiselica, Matt Englar-Carlson, and
Arthur M. Horne, editors

Volume 2: *BAM! Boys Advocacy and Mentoring: A Leader's Guide to Facilitating Strengths-Based Groups for Boys—Helping Boys Make Better Contact by Making Better Contact With Them*
Peter Motorola, Howard Hiton, and Stephen Grant

Volume 3: *Counseling Fathers*
Chen Z. Oren and Dora Chase Oren, editors

Volume 4: *Counseling Boys and Men With ADHD*
George Kapalka

Volume 5: *Culturally Responsive Counseling With Asian American Men*
William Liu, Derek Kenji Iwamoto, and
Mark H. Chae, editors

THERAPY WITH YOUNG MEN

16–24 Year Olds in Treatment

DAVE VERHAAGEN

Routledge
Taylor & Francis Group
New York   London

Routledge
Taylor & Francis Group
270 Madison Avenue
New York, NY 10016

Routledge
Taylor & Francis Group
27 Church Road
Hove, East Sussex BN3 2FA

© 2010 by Taylor and Francis Group, LLC
Routledge is an imprint of Taylor & Francis Group, an Informa business

Printed in the United States of America on acid-free paper
10 9 8 7 6 5 4 3 2 1

International Standard Book Number: 978-0-415-80446-2 (Hardback) 978-0-415-80447-9 (Paperback)

Library of Congress Cataloging-in-Publication Data

Verhaagen, David Allan.
  Therapy with young men : 16-24 year olds in treatment / by Dave Verhaagen.
    p. ; cm.
  Includes bibliographical references and index.
  ISBN 978-0-415-80446-2 (hardback : alk. paper) -- ISBN 978-0-415-80447-9 (pbk. : alk. paper)
  1. Cognitive therapy for teenagers. 2. Teenage boys--Mental health. 3. Young men--Mental health. I. Title.
    [DNLM: 1. Cognitive Therapy--methods. 2. Adolescent. 3. Men--psychology. 4. Professional-Patient Relations. 5. Young Adult. WM 425.5.C6 V511t 2010]

RJ505.C63V47 2010
618.92'891425--dc22   2009053530

Visit the Taylor & Francis Web site at
http://www.taylorandfrancis.com

and the Routledge Web site at
http://www.routledgementalhealth.com

To Christy & Abbey,
my beautiful, amazing daughters.

Contents

About the Author

Dave Verhaagen is a licensed psychologist who earned his PhD in psychology from the University of North Carolina at Chapel Hill. He is board certified (ABPP) in clinical child and adolescent psychology and has consulted with organizations across the country. He has served as clinical director for three mental health agencies, and he is currently a managing partner and CEO of Southeast Psych, a large psychology group practice in Charlotte, NC. He is the author or coauthor of five other books, including *Sexually Aggressive Youth: A Guide to Comprehensive Residential Treatment, Assessing and Managing Violence Risk in Juveniles*, and *Parenting the Millennial Generation*. His work has been featured several times in *USA Today, Newsweek*, and dozens of newspapers around the country. He is a popular speaker at local, state, and national conferences. He is married to Ellen and they have two daughters, Christy and Abbey.

Introduction

A few years back, I attended a conference presented by a nationally recognized therapist. During the Q&A, a member of the audience asked how his model and techniques could be applied to difficult, nontalkative, adolescent males.

The man didn't pause for a moment. He simply answered, "You just have to take what you can get."

At that moment, I knew I was going to write this book. All day, I see difficult, nontalkative adolescents and young men, and I would never "just take what I could get." I want the therapy experience to be an extraordinary experience for them.

Not too long ago, I told the chair of a university's psychology department that my specialty was therapy with young men.

"God bless you!" she replied, as if I had sneezed, then followed it with, "I can't imagine...," her voice trailing off, as if I had just told her I worked on an oil rig or inside Chernobyl. She said it with some sort of mixture of pity and admiration, suggesting that she thought it was something that someone needed to do, just not her.

"I really enjoy it. I think it's fun," I said.

"That's great," she responded, as if she couldn't believe such a thing were possible.

These two moments highlight two hopes for you as a therapist who works with adolescent boys and young men. First, I want the experience to be *extraordinary*, not just something that you put up with or take what you can get. I hope you finish this book with a model and a toolbox full of techniques that make the experience more effective, but I also hope you come to the final chapter with a strong sense of calling to these clients. I hope it is an extraordinary experience for you and your clients.

Second, it's my hope that you have *fun*, that you truly enjoy your work with these guys. I want it to be fun for you and your clients. I want it to be work that you look forward to doing every day. My hope is that it is such fun that it feels like you are cheating when you get paid to do it.

Two hopes in two words: Extraordinary fun.

I bet that wasn't what you expected when you picked up this book. It's a privilege to be a therapist. It's a huge responsibility to be involved in someone's life at such a meaningful level. Yet you can fully own the responsibility—and weight—of the whole enterprise and still thoroughly enjoy it.

As a therapist who sees young men every day, the most common desire I hear is, "I just want to be happy." Yet, for many reasons, happiness seems to elude many guys these days. A recent national survey of more than 3,000 adults by the Pew Research Center found that young adult men in their late teens and early twenties were the least happy of any group surveyed. Only 26% of these guys reported that they were very happy. What's more, the scholarly research tells us that adolescent boys and young men have the highest rates of behavioral problems, completed suicides, and drug and alcohol problems of any demographic group.

Mental health agencies that serve adolescents have long reported more males than females among their clients. Now, as the stigma associated with psychotherapy begins to fade (Chandra & Minkovitz, 2007), even therapists in private practice are seeing more adolescent boys and young men who are voluntarily seeking treatment for a range of issues.

Young men frequently come into therapy with unresolved identity issues, behavioral problems, and drug and alcohol problems. In addition, these clients tend to have greater problems in managing their emotions and successfully negotiating close interpersonal relationships. The fact that there are often many issues to address makes the therapy process more complex and more challenging. However, when done well, therapy with young men can be highly effective and quite rewarding for both therapist and client.

In this book, I'll present a comprehensive model of therapy with young men that addresses each of these concerns, beginning with the rapport and engagement process, then moving to specific ideas and skills for managing and treating commonly seen problems. The book describes a wide range of novel, effective cognitive-behavioral interventions that can readily be employed in the therapeutic process. The paradigm-shifting influence of positive psychology is also woven throughout the book.

I love the wisdom we get from both research and clinical practice. My hope is that this is a strong synthesis of both perspectives. While the tone here is intentionally familiar and relaxed, you will see that the content has solid roots in empirically validated methods that should benefit both younger and seasoned professionals. When I sat down to write the book, I realized how incongruent it felt to use a remote, scholarly, clinical tone when talking about the therapy process. Instead, I write much like I speak. At times I will tell stories; at other times, I will cite research. Some people don't like professional books with case studies, transcripts, and narrative; they just want the meat. Others don't like dry clinical texts that seem disconnected from real practice. I went for the middle ground. My hope is that you will find this to be a readable, engaging book that is packed with clinical applications and techniques. Therapy is part science, part art form. It is relational at its core. As such, I have chosen a more personal writing style for the book that hopefully captures not only the mechanics of the therapy process, but the feel of it. I will use first person throughout and draw from personal experience of more than 20,000 therapy hours.

During the year that I wrote this book, I picked three actual clients and kept a careful record of their therapy progress. Obviously, I changed names and other facts about them, but the three young men that we follow through this book are real young men. Many of the quotes and conversations are verbatim or very close, but most of the time, the interactions are shortened in the text.

Several students and young professionals did some heavy lifting on this project. Many thanks to Ryan Kelly, Caitlyn Garvey, Mara Ivey, Emma Kate Wright, Matt Laxer, and Erik Goldfield, who all did great research on topics like gender differences and similarities, therapy dropouts, normative male alexithymia, identity formation, adult attachment, locus of control, empathy, sexual identity, and stages of change. Their good work helped me immensely, and I am truly grateful to them. Edwin Flynn at Myers Park High School and Erica Deshaies from Charlotte Country Day School also went above and beyond to help me collect additional survey data that has proven to be a big part of this book, and I give them my heartfelt thanks.

I am also grateful to you, the reader, and your work with this challenging group of guys. This book is for the therapist who would never "just take what you can get." This is a model of true engagement, effective interventions, and practical guidance for everyone who wants to help adolescent boys and young men.

Dave Verhaagen
Charlotte, NC

1

The Culture of Young Men

Gabriel opens his eyes when he tastes blood, his first sign something is wrong. He doesn't know where he is. No idea. Finally, it starts to come together: He is in his jeep, somehow on the passenger's side. It's dark; it's still, no noise except the engine idling. He tries to focus, looking past the cracked windshield. The sky is sideways, the trees are sideways. He is sideways.

He wipes his face with his hand and feels it smear. He doesn't dare to look at his fingers, knowing what he'll see. Panic begins to grip him, cutting through all the shots of alcohol he had not long ago. He hears footsteps crunching leaves and twigs as they come toward him. He squints as a flashlight beam hits his eyes.

"You okay in there, sir?" the voice asks.

"I don't know," Gabriel says.

"Anybody else in the vehicle with you?" the man asks, sweeping his flashlight around the interior of the Jeep.

"I don't know," Gabriel says again.

"Have you had something to drink tonight, sir?" the man asks again.

"A little bit, probably," Gabriel says, not quite lying since he had little memory of what he had done earlier that evening. He begins to move.

"Stay still, sir. I want you to stay where you are until the paramedics get here," the man says in a detached, authoritative tone.

Gabriel's mind goes to thoughts of his parents. He is three hours away at college, but he knows they will drive to be with him, regardless of the hour. It both comforts him and embarrasses him to know he will see them soon. They had immigrated legally from Mexico 16 years ago when he was just four years old. His parents had started their own business, a supermarket that catered to their county's thriving Hispanic community, which had increased by 500% over the past decade. The business had done well—far beyond their biggest dreams—and his family had become highly respected. They sent Gabriel to a prestigious private high school and then off to a well-regarded university in the state.

Gabriel knows in this moment, even as he lay crumpled in his sideways Jeep, that his parents will be furious with him, mortified by what he had done. *You could have killed somebody! You could have killed yourself! If you can't follow the rules, then you can pay your own way!* He heard all these rants in his head before they even said them.

Though this was his first brush with big trouble, tonight had been a slow train coming. He had been drinking like a fiend for the past three years. His drinking had caused him other kinds of trouble before—a few fights, many occasions of sleeping with girls he didn't know (and the ensuing complications), and countless things he had said that he wished he could take back—but nothing of this magnitude before. He had driven with a buzz or even drunk many times, but, for some reason, he always felt safe. On this night, his apartment was less than a mile from the party. He had driven that route after partying many times before and always without incident, except for the one night he hit the sign in front of the apartment complex, but somehow got away undetected. Tonight he didn't drink any more than usual. *This shouldn't have happened*, he says to himself.

The paramedics arrive for Gabriel seven minutes later, sometime around 1 a.m. Three hours away, on the north side of Charlotte, Marlon is closing at the restaurant where he works as a food prep/dishwasher guy. He hates his job, but it's the best he could do for now. There aren't many options for an 18-year-old high school dropout with a minor criminal record, and he knows it. He yawns as he snaps plastic lids on the containers of chicken and hauls all of it into the walk-in freezer. The blast of freezing air wakes him up again a little. He sits on one of the barrels inside the walk-in and stares blankly ahead. *This job sucks*, he thinks to himself. His roommate, who is unemployed, tells him to be grateful for having a job at all. He does try to be grateful for things. He is grateful he is not in jail, grateful for the aunt who raised him, grateful he has some weed in his dresser drawer to help him get to sleep, grateful Kanye's new album is ridiculously good, grateful the bus runs till 2 a.m. on weekends. But he is *not* grateful for this job. It puts enough money in his pocket to let him have the essentials—rent, food, weed—and not much more. It is demeaning. It is beneath him. He knows that this is both true and not true. He knows he should do something with his life. At least that's what people tell him. *You have such potential*, they always say. Sometimes he thinks that's bullshit; sometimes he doesn't. He'll go home tonight, smoke up, and the thoughts will float on, as if he didn't have a care in the world. Then he'll drift to sleep and have a few hours of quiet in his head.

Before Marlon gets home, Ricky comes in the back door of his house in another part of town and creeps through the kitchen, wearing his trademark skintight pants and black hoodie. He gets to the base of the stairs with scarcely a squeak from his checkerboard sneakers, but mom and dad are sitting in the living room, arms folded, fuming.

"It's over an hour past your curfew," Dad says to the 16-year-old.

"I had to give Dan a ride home," Ricky replies, his jet-black hair covering one eye entirely.

"It doesn't take you an hour to drop your friend off," Dad snaps.

"Whatever...," Ricky says.

"Don't 'whatever' me! We called you at least five times and you never picked up or called us back!" says Dad.

"My phone died," says Ricky, "And I didn't have my charger."

"You could have used somebody else's phone. All your friends have phones," Dad says, his tone becoming increasingly frustrated.

"Sorry," Ricky says, beginning to walk up the stairs.

"Sorry? That's it? That's all you've got to say?" Dad asks, his volume rising.

Ricky shrugs his shoulders and walks up the stairs.

"You're grounded! Count on that!" Dad yells up to him.

"Fuck you!" says Ricky as he keeps walking. He goes into his room and slams the door.

It's 1 a.m. on a Saturday night, and it's a busy time for young men. Our three guys are partying, crashing, working, and cussing out parents, while others are just hanging out or gaming online or even sleeping. There's such a diversity of experience that it is nearly impossible to say what is normal. On any given Saturday night in the same town, most guys won't ever get into any trouble at all. They'll go to movies, go camping, go bowling, or go out to dinner. Others are on a literal collision course with trouble. They drink too much or experiment with drugs or have unprotected sex or drag race or get in fights or countless other things that seem destined for an unhappy ending.

Among adolescent boys and young men, ages 16–24, most drink, most have had sex, nearly half of them smoke pot on occasion, and the majority of them have done something antisocial that could have caused them big trouble had they been caught. It is true there are many guys who go through adolescence in a relatively uneventful way, never getting in much trouble, doing well in school or work, seeming free of anxiety or depression, but there are also lots of guys who have a rough time of it. They struggle with school; they make bad decisions; they get rageful or deeply depressed.

The rates of drug use, binge drinking, and behavior problems among young men are in the stratosphere. Women report higher rates of depression than men, but men kill themselves at more than four times the rate of women, usually by shooting themselves (Centers for Disease Control, 2008). When they decide to end it, they usually pick lethal means. Adolescent boys and young men are also the most likely cohort to be arrested or injured in an accident or a fight (Borum & Verhaagen, 2006; Centers for Disease Control, 2008; Marcus, 2009).

While there are big differences among young guys that vary by geography, socioeconomic status, racial background, sexual identity, religious affiliation, school size, and many other variables, there is also a somewhat unifying pervasive "guy culture" that cuts across the sub-groups. In his book, *Guyland*, sociologist Michael Kimmel says that in his countless workshops at colleges and high schools in every state of the United States and in 15 other countries, he has asked young men what words or phrases come to mind when they hear the line, "Be a man!" Here's what he says they told him, summarized in what he labels a "Real Guy's Top Ten List."

1. Boys don't cry
2. It's better to be mad than sad
3. Don't get mad—get even
4. Take it like a man
5. He who has the most toys when he dies, wins
6. Just do it
7. Size matters
8. I don't stop to ask directions
9. Nice guys finish last
10. It's all good

The underlying message, Kimmel argues, "involves never showing emotions or admitting to weakness." This "Guy Code" is "the collection of attitudes, values, and traits that together composes what it means to be a man" (Kimmel, 2008, p. 45). This closely parallels the "Boy Code" described by William Pollack in *Real Boys* a decade ago (Pollack, 1999).

Today, I watched the surveillance video from a Vallejo, CA, high school of six young men punching, kicking, even strangling a 17-year-old prep school basketball star who had the nerve to come to the aid of a young woman who was being attacked and harassed by some of the guys. They left him unconscious on the concrete. He had to be taken to the hospital and put on a ventilator with a severe brain injury. Soon after, all six of the guys, ages 16 to 26, were rounded up and charged with attempted murder.

Over and over again during the course of my career, I've seen or heard of violence committed by adolescent boys and young men. To be involved with these guys is to be exposed vicariously or directly to violence and rage. As Kimmel (2008) and Pollack (1999) have observed, the exception to the "show no emotion" rule is anger. Anger and rage are perfectly acceptable emotions for young guys. Often sadness and anxiety are associated with the effeminate and the weak, whereas anger is in the domain of the masculine and strong. Consequently, you have many exceedingly angry guys who don't mind putting that on display.

A few years back, one of my clients told me that he was in a fight club modeled after the Brad Pitt/Ed Norton movie, where guys get together to beat the crap out of each other in fighting matches. He had the busted knuckles, the swollen cheek, and the YouTube video to prove it. Since then, I've had at least three other guys who have made the same claim. This week, I saw a new client who was charged with "inciting a riot," for provoking a brawl in the high school bathroom. I've long lost count of the number of young men who have been suspended from school or arrested for some type of fighting. Even among guys who don't fight themselves, many are thrilled by watching other guys do battle. The rising popularity of "ultimate fighting," with its bloody brutality, is fueled primarily by young men who support the industry. This attests to the reality that adolescent boys and young men not only experience and inflict violence, but they often greatly enjoy it.

And where there is fighting, there is often drinking. Alcohol use is so prevalent among young men that it is the norm, even for those who can't get it legally. As they have for generations, adolescent boys drink a lot. Young adult men drink even more. A study of more than 2,500 young adults found that over one-third of young men drank "21 for 21," or rather, at least 21 drinks to celebrate their 21st birthday (Rutledge, Park, & Sher, 2008). To put it in perspective, this amount could put an average-sized guy in the hospital under the wrong sort of circumstances. Most universities have struggled with how to reduce heavy alcohol use among their students (Cremeens, Usdan, Brock-Martin, Martin, & Watkins, 2008), but the rates continue to be high, and drinking remains the norm.

Like drinking, sex is a dominant theme in young adult male culture. At the top end of this age group, more than 90% of young men have had sex. Recently, an older high school student told me he had sex five times a day on average with his girlfriend while his mother worked late. A college student told me he had sex 25 times in a three-day weekend while his roommate was out of town, and they had the apartment to themselves. Whether these stories were exaggerated or not, it still highlights the point that making these claims was important to them. The college student told me, "I'm better at sex than I am at talking, so I like to do it a lot."

There is a wide range of attitudes about sex among adolescent boys and young men. Some guys say they want to wait until they get married before they have sex, though few of them make it (Rosenbaum, 2008). Other guys have no qualms with having sex with someone they just met, though these guys are in the minority, despite the popular notion that most of them would go to bed on a first encounter. The sexual ethic of most young men falls somewhere in the middle of the two extremes of waiting until marriage or casual sex. Most want to have sex, but believe it should be part of a relationship. Still, nearly two-thirds of guys (63%) say they have engaged in a hookup, a casual sexual encounter that can include anything from intense making out to intercourse (Gute & Eshbaugh, 2008). They also draw fuzzy lines around what even constitutes sex. Compared to women, college men were more likely to think that oral sex isn't really sex and to believe that cybersex (porn, online hookups, etc.) isn't really cheating (Knox, Zusman, & McNeely, 2008). The vast majority (89–92%) of young men look at pornography, with over 40% of them viewing it on at least a weekly basis (Carroll et al., 2008; O'Reilly, Knox, & Zusman, 2007). As you might expect, significantly more men than women look at porn online. As another therapist told me, "Sex is the engine that drives these guys. If they aren't doing it, they're looking at it."

On a typical day, I see seven clients, nearly all of them adolescent boys and young men. The day after I started this chapter, I listed the clients I saw during that day and the issues we discussed in the session. Here's who I saw, beginning with my first appointment:

- Harry, a 20-year-old who had dropped out of college and was currently living in his own apartment after his parents had kicked him out of their house, coasting on his college savings, and doing nothing all day except playing online games and looking at porn. He reported he literally woke up one morning and said out loud to himself, "This has got to change."
- Devin, a 16-year-old with a long history of behavior problems who explodes in rage when his parents try to set any limits on him. Within the past month, he has punched two holes in his bedroom wall and ripped the side mirror off his mother's car.
- Chad, a high-achieving 17-year-old high school junior whose best friend had recently died of an unintentional drug overdose. Since then, he had started to have panic attacks and also began compulsively cheating on his girlfriend.
- Mike, a 21-year-old community college student and bartender who was living in an apartment with his drug-dealing brother. As the "responsible" family member, he took care of all the others, including his mother. His sense of responsibility brought him to the point of selling drugs at his own workplace for his brother in order to allow his brother to pay his share of the rent. He smokes pot on a daily basis, but says he needs it to cope with the stress of his situation.
- Cody, a 17-year-old private school student who had slid into a deep depression over the past year for no obvious reason and was no longer going to school. He also started abusing prescription painkillers recently. During the past month, he had told at least two friends that he was thinking of killing himself.
- Brett, a 16-year-old who was adopted at the age of 12 out of foster care. Though his birth mother had been found guilty of neglect when he was much younger, he had never disclosed that she had also sexually abused him until just a few months ago.
- Grant, an 18-year-old, highly intelligent young man with profound learning disabilities who had been bullied throughout middle school and early high school. Now he was seething with anger, considered himself to be an anarchist, and spent much of his waking hours ruminating about revenge.

For me, this is a typical day at the office: sex, drugs, depression, rage. Nearly every day, I hear these themes, as well as relationship troubles, identity issues, and a wide range of behavioral problems. When you work with young men, this is standard fare.

Gabriel, Marlon, and Ricky will all find their way into my office in the coming weeks. They have different personalities, different racial and cultural backgrounds, and different family experiences, but they come in with some of these same themes. They have anger and behavioral problems, poor management of their emotions, and substance issues. As we get to know them, we will see even more concerns that will need to be addressed in therapy. Some of the difficulties young men experience are obviously seen in both genders, but there are unquestionable differences in the frequency and intensity of the presenting problems of young men.

FIVE BIG DIFFERENCES BETWEEN MALES AND FEMALES

The film *(500) Days of Summer* is one of the only romantic comedies told from a male perspective. The protagonist is a young man who falls in love with a woman who ends up dumping him. In the movie, the narrator intones, "There are only two kinds of people in this world. Men and women." Over and over again, my clients have echoed these sentiments.

"I don't know if you know this, but *they* are different from us," one of my clients said with a smile on his face.

"They who?" I asked.

"Women," he said. "They're different than we are."

He said this with a tone that let me know he regarded this as a truism, something with which no reasonable person would argue. To be honest, I agreed with him. It was my assumption that men and women were different and that this wasn't a bad thing, just a fact. Many—and probably most—of the practitioners I know also think the same way. One day, one of my female colleagues who typically sees mostly female clients passed by my door with an "emo" boy who wore tight pants and had hair in his eyes as they left their session. On her way back, she stopped by my office.

"I just saw *your* client," she said jokingly.

"That's what I was thinking," I said.

"It's interesting to me how different guys and girls are, even when they have the same basic issues," she said.

Simon Baron-Cohen, the great autism researcher, argues that male brains are typically optimized for systems and female brains are optimized for empathy (Baron-Cohen, 2004). The Systemizer analyzes how systems function and tries to make the system better. By contrast, the Empathizer identifies and accurately responds to the thoughts and feelings of others, reading nonverbal cues well and caring about the feelings of others. He postulates that autism is the male Systemizer brain in overdrive, systematizing, figuring out how things work, while not tuned in to others. The research does support that males and females have different brains in many ways—and thus, different minds (Arnold, 2003; Gur, Gunning-Dixon, Bilker, & Gur, 2002; Jausovec & Jausovec, 2005; Kucian, Loenneker, Dietrich, Martin, & Von Aster, 2005; O'Boyle, Benbow, & Alexander, 1995). Neuroscientist Lise Eliot, however, says the differences are small from birth, but are amplified by social factors that produce more pronounced anatomical brain differences over time (Eliot, 2009). The fact remains, though, that by the time they reach young adulthood, men and women, probably mostly through socialization and life experience, tend to be wired differently.

I didn't consider the alternative—that men and women are not that much different—until I started to immerse myself in the research while preparing for this book. What I found is that some—though not most—researchers advance the notion of *gender similarities*. They argue that men and women really aren't that much different.

Early in the development process of this book, I tested out the material in workshops and conferences. I also asked other professionals for their thoughts about the content. While the feedback I got was overwhelmingly positive and affirmative, there was one psychologist who wrote anonymously: "I am of the opinion that viewing men and women as fundamentally different is ultimately destructive to both sexes."

I realized that what I had taken as self-evident was at least somewhat controversial. This strongly worded statement gave me some pause. In my interactions with other professionals and with clients themselves, there is a general consensus that men and women are different from each other in important ways, but clearly this is not a view shared by all.

In perspective, there is still vastly more research and inquiry about gender differences than about gender similarities. For example, with the research databases to which I have access, the keywords of "gender differences" lead "gender similarities" and similar queries by an overwhelming margin, with research on the similarities making up a fraction of a percent of the studies. Still, the fact that the similarities perspective is in the minority at the moment means nothing by itself. In fact, one of the reasons we have the scientific method is that it can illuminate new realities and new ways of seeing the world.

Janet Shibley Hyde, a professor at the University of Wisconsin–Madison, has been the chief advocate of the "gender similarities hypothesis," arguing that men and women are more similar than they are different (Hyde, 2005). She suggests that a focus on differences creates stereotypes and imposes limitations on both men and women that can have adverse consequences. For example, claiming that men are better at math skills might discourage young women from pursuing college majors or academic careers in math fields or result in young women with strong math skills being overlooked by educators. Hyde's review of 46 meta-analytic studies in which she claimed support for her gender similarities hypothesis is a powerhouse. After looking at the data for over 100 variables, including everything from various cognitive abilities like spatial perception to leadership style to self-esteem to certain social behaviors, she found that men and women are not that different from each other.

In one sense, she is correct. When considering all these variables together in a statistical stew, it is not surprising that men and women are more alike than they are different. In this case, a meta-analysis of many studies looking at various aspects of gender differences is likely to find that men and women are more the same than they are different. It would be the same if we seriously compared apples and oranges. Clearly, apples and oranges are more similar than they are different. This is almost indisputable. They are both:

Sweet in taste
Similar in size
Similar in weight
Similar in shape
Grown in orchards
Eaten by animals and humans
Readily made into fruit juice
Seed-bearing (except seedless oranges, of course)
Subject to insect damage
Subject to disease
Regarded as variations of each other in some cultures

Now certainly they have different subjective tastes, different textures to their peels, and usually different colors, but if you compare these few differences to the big list of similarities, it is apparent that these two things are remarkably alike. Dr. Scott Sandford of NASA did a tongue-in-cheek spectrometric study of this years ago and concluded that "Apples and oranges are very similar. Thus, it would appear that the comparing apples and oranges defense should no longer be considered valid. This is a somewhat startling revelation." If, after studying all the data, you also came to the conclusion that apples are more similar to oranges than they are different, you would be correct.

You also might be missing the point, depending on why this question is important to you in the first place. You wouldn't put oranges in your apple pie because the two things are so much alike, for example. With the issue of gender differences or similarities, it does matter why this question is important to you. If you are concerned with public policy, for instance, then it is wise to know that men and women are not biologically all that different when it comes to things like math ability, leadership skill, or self-esteem. However, if you are a therapist of young men, then it is good to know those relatively few but important ways that men and women tend to be different in behavioral, emotional, and relational functioning so that you can be well prepared for who walks in your door. Hyde's meta-analysis found that men and women are different in aggression and some aspects of sexual behavior, but there was no mention of studies that have found significant differences in behavioral disorders, suicidality, substance-abuse problems, or problems with emotional expressiveness. For example, in the 64 measured health risk behaviors in the Youth Risk Behavior Surveillance, there was no difference between males and females for only around 12% of the surveyed behaviors (i.e., 8 out of 64). Males engaged in 39 of the 64 risky behaviors more often than females, being more likely to do things like drink and drive, get into a fight, use harder drugs, or carry a weapon (Centers for Disease Control, 2008). From a therapist's standpoint, these are important differences that must be addressed routinely in work with adolescent boys and young men.

If we did our apples-to-oranges comparison with men and women, there are more points of similarity than difference, but *there are important differences that are borne out by the research.* Looking at the variables that are highly relevant to therapy, the research finds at least five specific gender differences. These findings are not true of all men, of course, but they tend to be characteristic differences with which therapists will often have to contend:

Males Have More Behavioral Problems

There is no dispute that young men are more physically aggressive and violent than their female counterparts. Men are approximately eight times more likely than females to commit murder, being responsible for nearly 90% of all homicides in the United States. Young men are much more likely to get in a fight, physically bully and be bullied online and in person, commit sexual offenses, be incarcerated, make threats of violence, and be both the perpetrators and victims of physical violence (Borum & Verhaagen, 2006; Burton, Hafetz, & Henninger, 2007; Feder, Levant, & Dean, 2007; Li, 2006; U.S. Public Health Service, 2001).

Young men tend to be much more impulsive than young women and more likely to engage in a whole range of risky behaviors (Chapple & Johnson, 2007; Harris, Jenkins, & Glaser, 2006). Young men also have much higher rates of gambling problems and compulsive sexual behavior than young women (Carroll et al., 2008; Desai, Maciejewski, Pantalon, & Potenza, 2005).

Males Have More Drug and Alcohol Problems

There is also no dispute that young men have more alcohol and drug use and abuse than women (Fingeret, Moeller, & Stotts, 2005; Harrell & Karim, 2008; McCabe et al., 2007; Milani, Parrott, Turner, & Fox, 2004; Nolen-Hoeksema, 2004). Not only do they tend to drink more and take more drugs, but they also tend to have more problems when they are under the influence. For example, guys are found to be more sexually disinhibited when under the influence (Hesse & Tutenges,

2008). Their higher rates of binge drinking and heavy alcohol use may put them at a higher risk for accidents as well (Good et al., 2008).

Drug and alcohol rehab programs, court-mandated substance-abuse classes, and AA programs are dominated by males. There is an understanding among mental health and substance-abuse professionals that substance-abuse and addiction treatment programs have a disproportionate number of male clients.

Men Have Higher Rates of Completed Suicide

While women tend to report more depression than men, it's also true that men tend to kill themselves much more often than women. Whether by gunshot or hanging (the two most common methods), young men typically use violent means when they try to end their lives. Not surprisingly, then, they have much higher rates of completed suicide. Being less likely to report depression and more likely to kill yourself is a bad combination.

Men are also much more likely to commit suicide following certain types of trauma, including sexual abuse (Garnefski & Diekstra, 1997). Men may report fewer upsetting emotions, but they are clearly feeling things quite intensely and don't seem well equipped to manage their distress.

Men Are More Prone to Command and Conquer

In the male-dominated worlds of online gaming and ultimate fighting, there is little doubt that guys like to command and conquer. Even in research studies where both men and women play the same competitive games, men go after more territory and fight more ferociously.

In one study where young adult males and females played a computer game where they could gain or lose territory, the men played harder and were more motivated to succeed. They played the game while being hooked up to a functional magnetic resonance imaging machine (fMRI) to show which parts of the brain are working during different activities. When the researchers examined the fMRI data, they found that the male brains had much higher activation in the brain's mesocorticolimbic center, an area known to be associated with reward, pleasures, and addiction. Not only that, but the amount of activation in that area was correlated with how much territory they gained in the game. This wasn't the case with women, however. The study concluded that successfully acquiring territory was more rewarding for men than for women (Hoeft, Watson, Kesler, Bettinger, & Reiss, 2008). One of the researchers, Allan Reiss, said, "I think it's fair to say that males tend to be more intrinsically territorial. It doesn't take a genius to figure out who historically are the conquerors and tyrants of our species—they're the males."

In social contexts, men respond more strongly and aggressively than women to threats in the face of outside competition (Van Vugt, De Cremer, & Janssen, 2007; Van Vugt & Spisak, 2008). Whether it is online or at a fraternity party, young men are much more likely than women to be competitive and territorial.

Men Have More Stigma Associated With Mental Health Treatment

Compared to women, men seek help less often for a wide range of problems, including medical issues, drug and alcohol problems, and mental health problems (McKelley & Rochlen, 2007). Men resist help for many reasons, but one of the major reasons is that they feel more stigma when asking for help and tend to view help-seeking as a sign of weakness. Specifically, men are more likely to perceive stigma associated with psychological problems and mental health treatment than females (Chandra & Minkovitz, 2006). This is unquestionably a product of how they have been socialized, but it is a difference that often must be addressed from the onset of therapy.

These are important differences and ones that must be reckoned with by therapists who see young men. Failing to acknowledge these typical differences is to risk being ill prepared for the challenges you will face when you see these guys in therapy. Not all young men will have problems with drugs or alcohol, but many will. Not all young men are impulsive or aggressive, but many are. Not all young men feel a stigma associated with mental health treatment, but many do. Whether these differences are biologically determined, culturally shaped, or both is less of the issue for a therapist. The central issue is that there are common behaviors and attitudes that young men bring into therapy, and the therapist must be ready to address them.

At the conclusion of her gender similarities study, Hyde writes, "Therapists who base their practice in the differences model should reconsider their approach on the basis of the best scientific evidence" (Hyde, 2005, p. 590). To be honest, I know of no therapists who would "base their practice in the differences model," as if to suggest any therapist automatically assumed that all girls who present in therapy have low self-esteem or all boys have behavioral problems. The best practice for all therapists is to treat each person uniquely, to listen well, to formulate specifically. No decent therapist would base his or her entire practice on a differences model.

Second, and equally important, the other side is that, while everyone is a unique individual, there are clearly some common themes that typically bring males into therapy, including behavioral problems, substance problems, and relationship struggles. Failing to be equipped for these important issues would be a huge misstep for any good therapist.

As I've noted, it is less important whether these differences are innate, environmental, or both, than it is to be ready to address them. It is also less important for us to get too deeply philosophical about whether these differences are good, bad, or neutral, or whether we should work to extinguish them. Instead, our concerns should focus on these real differences that we must be prepared to address.

One of the concerns frequently raised about the focus on gender differences is that it may create barriers for one gender—usually females—in a variety of important areas. For example, if the research suggested that men have greater aptitude for science than women, then teachers might discourage girls in these academic areas, or it may cause fewer women to pursue scientific majors or careers. This is a legitimate concern and one that should be taken seriously. However, it should not stop us from taking a look at important differences when they are relevant to our work. In my view, men and women are very different from each other in key areas that frequently emerge in therapy. Acknowledging differences does not imply that one sex is superior to the other, nor does it mean that typically ascribed traits are true of all men or all women. It simply means we need to be prepared for what we are likely to encounter in therapy with young men.

Based on my clinical experience and the bulk of the research about gender differences, I come to three conclusions:

1. Males and females are different in ways that are relevant to therapy work.
2. These differences may be biologically determined, socially constructed, or both.
3. Therapists should be aware of and be equipped to address the common issues that males bring into therapy.

While gender is an important consideration in therapy training, so is a knowledge of an individual's stage of life. Young men have different needs and issues than young boys or older men, for example. In the past, we would have seen teenagers as being adolescents and those in their 20s as being young adults, but now the boundaries between these stages of development are fuzzy. There is a huge developmental gray area of almost a decade of life between the late teens and middle 20s. I suggest 16- to 24-year-olds are neither child nor adult, but are in a stage that has been culturally constructed over the past few decades. Between the commonly accepted stages of adolescence and young adulthood lies a new stage of development.

A NEW STAGE OF DEVELOPMENT

Shortly after pleading guilty for assaulting his girlfriend, Rihanna, R&B superstar Chris Brown appeared on *Larry King Live* to give a public mea culpa. He repeatedly admitted fault and apologized. Later in the interview, he made a revealing comment. "I am not a man fully yet," said the 20-year-old.

"I still feel like a kid," a 22-year-old young man told me during a session this year. "My parents keep telling me I'm a legal adult and I know I am, but I feel like a kid. All my friends, we all feel like that."

Around the same time I heard that remark, a 16-year-old guy had the opposite complaint. "My parents treat me like a child," he said, "but I am mature enough to make my own decisions. I'm practically an adult."

With guys in their 20s who say they are kids and guys in their teens who say they are adults, this is a confusing time of life, with no clear boundaries marking either side of the territory. In the United States, the consensus is that adulthood starts at age 18, but this is hardly certain. An 18-year-old can vote, but he can't legally drink alcohol until he is 21. In most states, a 16-year-old is at the age of consent to have sex and can be charged with adult crimes and tried in adult courts. Is a 16-year-old an adult because he can legally consent to sex or be charged with adult crimes? Is the 20-year-old not yet an adult because he is not old enough to buy beer? Where adolescence ends and adulthood begins is less than obvious. And it is getting less apparent. As Chris Brown says, even 20-year-olds are not men fully yet.

It used to be that children would go through a relatively brief period of adolescence, then become full-fledged adults in the eyes of their elders and in their own eyes, but two trends have changed all that. First, the onset of puberty is occurring earlier (Bellis, Downing, & Ashton, 2006; Finlay, Jones, & Coleman, 2002). Second, the marker points that denote adulthood are getting later. The combination of these two trends has led to a much lengthier period of what has historically been called adolescence that has gone from three or four years to more than a decade.

Two generations ago, a young man might start puberty at age 14, then graduate high school at 17 or 18 and be married or off to war by age 19. Now, an adolescent boy typically starts puberty around the age of 11, graduates high school and goes off to college or even graduate school, and doesn't get married or begin a long-term committed relationship until he is around 27. Whereas a 19-year-old in 1954 was likely to call himself a man, a 23-year-old today is more likely to view himself as mostly a kid.

What this has done is create a longer stage of life that merges and blurs adolescence with young adulthood. Erikson (1968) was right when he said that the primary task of adolescence is to determine a sense of *identity* and that the primary task of young adulthood is to achieve *intimacy* with a loved one. Said a different way, these developmental stages are about establishing deep relationships with self and others.

With the line between adolescence and young adulthood becoming fuzzier, identity issues are still being worked out for many young men today well into their mid-20s. If Erikson (1968) was right, then intimacy issues cannot be fully resolved until a person has a healthy sense of personal identity. If you don't know who you are, you are not ready to have a healthy, reciprocal, intimate relationship with someone else.

According to Erikson (1968), if adolescents were allowed to explore and make their own choices—both good and bad—the teenagers would end up resolving their sense of identity. They would know who they were, what they were about, and where they fit in. If they were not allowed to explore and make their own choices, then they would likely have a poorly resolved, poorly integrated sense of self.

In the stage that follows identity formation, Erikson (1968) proposed that the next major developmental crisis was finding intimacy. For him, it was broader than just finding a mate. This stage is really about self in context with others, which includes intimate partners, but also issues relating to work and family. The central questions for a young man during this time of life were about whether he would settle down into a family and a focused career or whether he would continue to live as a single, unattached person with no commitments.

As young adults stay in school longer, marry later, and stay at jobs for shorter periods of time, we are seeing this developmental stage of intimacy versus isolation getting resolved later in life, usually in the late 20s or early 30s on average. At the same time, we have individuals in their early to mid-20s who are still exploring fundamental issues of identity. There is little question that we are now seeing adolescence begin earlier and end later.

Some may argue that adolescence is just getting extended upward, but I would suggest that the stage Erikson (1968) considered adolescence is now occurring far earlier, and the stage that he considered young adulthood is happening far later. We now have 16- to 24-year-olds who are neither teen nor adult. They have the capacity for self-determination and autonomy, but neither see themselves as nor function like independent adults. They are still cared for by parents, yet expected by society to be fully responsible for their actions.

Parents are involved with their young adults in ways that they had not in past decades. Those in higher education consistently affirm that the notion of the "helicopter parent" is absolutely true. Parents are calling deans and department chairs to complain about their child's supposed unfair treatment by professors; they are e-mailing professors with excuses for why their child failed to turn in an assignment; they are contacting campus directors in attempts to resolve roommate conflicts. Historically, these are issues that have been resolved by the students themselves. Now parents are inserting themselves into these situations with increasing frequency. In many ways, young adults are being parented well into their mid-20s.

These young people are now living between adolescence and adulthood, still being cared for and raised by parents, but with greater freedoms and more options. Arnett (2006) suggests five main features of these individuals, whom he calls *emerging adults*:

Identity explorations: a time in life to figure out who you are and where you fit in, especially in relationships and work

Instability: an inherently unstable time of life, with changes in relationships, living situation, and work

Self-focus: a period of life where the individual is more self-involved than in other stages

In-between: a time when a person feels neither like an adult nor an adolescent

Possibilities: a stage of life full of hope and opportunity

Arnett has studied emerging adulthood for the past decade and a half (Arnett, 1994, 1997, 1998, 2000, 2001, 2003) and notes that in response to the question, "Do you feel that you have reached adulthood?" the majority of 18- to 25-year-olds answer, "Yes *and* no." When asked what the criteria for adulthood would be, the top three answers across regions and ethnic groups are: accepting responsibility for yourself, making independent decisions, and becoming financially independent. Arnett notes that these three conditions occur gradually and incrementally and, for most, are not fully realized until a person's mid-20s.

Like Arnett (1994, 1997, 1998, 2000, 2001, 2003) before me, I suggest that we now have a new stage of development that sits between Erikson's (1968) conceptions of adolescence and young adulthood. While he tags it *emerging adulthood*, I refer to it as the *pre-adult stage*, but we are talking about the same notion that there is a new stage of development that is not a generational difference but one that will be enduring for generations to come. If adolescence is about identity—figuring out who you are and where you fit in—and young adulthood is mostly about how you manage intimate relationships, then this new stage of pre-adulthood that fits between these stages is about responsibility, taking ownership for your own life.

In Eriksonian terms, the developmental crisis might be phrased, "Responsibility versus Diversion." Those who don't complete this developmental task of learning how to be a responsible adult will find themselves deferring the grown-up tasks of taking full ownership of their lives and, instead, will primarily seek fun, entertainment, and pleasure. Those who are successful in resolving this developmental crisis have a sense of personal responsibility that will carry them into their adulthood and serve them well in their work and relationships.

In my own research for this book, I surveyed over 150 males between the ages of 16 and 24 and asked them to rate their values and how true specific self-descriptors were for them. The highest rated value was "fun" while "fun-loving" was the second highest-rated self-description (preceded only by "loyal"). The survey confirmed my clinical observation that having fun was the greatest value of this age group. By the way, this was not a gender-specific finding; both males and females were nearly identical in their esteem for fun.

We often talk about postcollege-age adults who are still being supported by their parents and focused on having fun as being in a state of prolonged adolescence, but I am reasonably certain that a 24-year-old who still lives to party, makes few to no commitments in relationships or work, and still has his parents paying for his car insurance and cell phone is not what Erikson (1968) had in mind when he thought about that psychosocial stage. This same 24-year-old may, in fact, have a relatively clear sense of identity. He may even feel self-confident, have high regard for himself, have a strong sense of his own likes and dislikes, and know himself well. In other words, he may have resolved his identity crisis. He is no longer in a state of adolescence. However, he is not quite into adulthood, at least if that is defined as someone who is fully responsible and independent. He is out of adolescence and not yet into adulthood. Hence the term *pre-adult* seems to be the best descriptor of this stage of life. Through most of the book, I will use the term *young men* as the descriptor for these pre-adults, but I regard them as adults in training.

The benefit of regarding 16- to 24-year-olds as *pre-adults* is not to add more restrictions to them, as is our cultural instinct, but actually to add fewer and accept that these young people are in training to be responsible, independent adults. Culturally, they have been conditioned to value fun above all else, over such important values as helping others, being a good person, making an impact on the world, or being close to one's family. Fun is an important and good value, so there is nothing inherently wrong with wanting to seek it and have more of it in life. Adults across the life span tend to have more vital and rewarding lives when they have fun. In fact, in my group practice, fun is regarded so highly it is one of our four core values. The problem only comes when it is valued above all else. When fun is the dominant value well into a person's 20s, it makes it increasingly difficult for him to complete the crucial developmental tasks necessary to become an independent adult.

What I am proposing is that 16- to 24-year-old young men now occupy a previously nonexistent developmental space between adolescence and young adulthood, where the chief developmental task is to gain a sense of personal responsibility for one's life. To do this, they need more freedom, not less; they need more opportunities to manage their lives, to fail or succeed on their own; they need to prove to themselves and others that they are ready for adulthood. As therapists, we have much to offer them with all this.

2

Prelude to Therapy With Young Men

Ricky's hair, dyed jet black, hangs flat-ironed straight over his right eye and covers half his face. It takes him 45 minutes each morning to get it just right. Marlon's hair is neatly braided into tight cornrows. It is no fuss, low maintenance for a month at a time. There is an old saying that clothes make the man. This may be true, but it is definitely hair that makes the young man. It is their social signature. It says much about where they fit in—or hope to fit in—socially and how they see themselves.

Pictures of Gabriel before the accident show his hair alternately down to his chin or tied up in a small ponytail. After the accident, he shaved it down to a quarter-inch with a #2 guard on the clippers, perhaps better to tend the nicks and cuts on his scalp. He looks like a completely different person now than he did even a month ago before he nearly killed himself in the Jeep. Pre-accident, his hair signaled *party boy/ladies man*. Now it is gone, as if his identity were stripped away with it. Practically nothing is there. He has lost his place in the world, at least for this season of life.

Gabriel will come into therapy to address his charge of driving under the influence, but there are other issues that have been brewing for many years. He is explosively angry at times, prone to jealousy, hypersexual, and extremely moody. The accident has only served to make him more quick-tempered and defensive. For some, such an event is a humbling experience; for Gabriel, it is a wound to his pride and a "shit hand" that life has dealt him.

Like Gabriel, Ricky is an angry guy, chronically annoyed and irritated. He says he is "pissed at the world" most of the time. While sullen

and defiant with his parents, Ricky is also depressed from years of struggle with his sexual orientation. He feels sad, angry, and anxious—sometimes all at the same time. He started cutting himself last year because
he felt so lousy, but no one has noticed because he always wears long
sleeves, even in the summer.

Marlon doesn't seem as angry as Gabriel or as distressed as Ricky. In
fact, he does not seem to feel much of anything. When he feels backed
into a corner, he can "freak out" and has actually gotten a resisting-
arrest charge when he was picked up once for a minor offense. He lost
control of himself and felt bad about it later, apologizing to the officer at
the station where he was booked, photographed, and fingerprinted. Day
to day, Marlon has little motivation or joy in life. He's socially anxious
and still smokes pot every day to manage his stress, despite two citations
for possession. Upon first meeting, he is friendly and polite. He smiles in
a cordial way, but, except for his aunt, he has no real relationships and
no real attachments.

These are the common themes you will often hear in your therapy
with young men. They have behavioral difficulties, substance problems,
poor emotional management, and relationship conflicts. They are full
of anger and rage or seem emotionally disconnected from themselves.
They get into trouble with the law or with parents; they can be aggressive and violent.

Despite this, they are often reluctant to seek or accept help. They
prefer to keep their feelings inside or deal with things on their own.
To be effective as a therapist, you must be especially skilled at forming
a quick alliance and have the skills to deliver on the promise of being
helpful. You also have to be prepared to deal with some specific challenges in your work with young men.

UNIQUE CHALLENGES IN THERAPY
WITH YOUNG MEN

There is no question that young men can be tough clients. Right off the
bat, you are often at a disadvantage because young men are typically
referred for what concerns others and not what concerns them. Not
surprisingly, young men are encouraged or coerced to go to therapy for
things like drug use, anger problems, and rule breaking. These squeaky
wheel behaviors cause parents, teachers, and others much alarm, but
may not be a source of concern for the young man himself.

One client may come in because his parents don't like his anger outbursts or bad attitude, but he doesn't think these things are much of a
problem. Other clients come in for other problems that are concerns for
those around them, but not for themselves personally. Parents may find
paraphernalia in a 17-year-old boy's car. When they investigate further,
they find that he smokes pot every day on the way to school. They are
greatly concerned, but the young man may not be troubled by this at all.

In fact, he is likely to be more disturbed by the parental intrusion and insistence on therapy than he is with the drug use.

One client of mine had been suspended twice in a month for fighting. The school staff and his parents were upset by this and wanted him to "get help," but he was of the opinion that the school was overreacting and being too strict on him. He did not see the need for any sort of change, even though the adults around him were worried for him.

This is even true with older clients. A 20-year-old college student bombed out of school because of his drinking. His parents were alarmed, citing a family history of alcoholism and previous episodes of binge drinking. They urged him to go see a therapist. Once he came in the door, he maintained that his drinking was well within the normal bounds of a typical college student. They insisted that he participate in therapy and made it a condition of his return home.

These and other examples are typical of how young men are often referred for what concerns others and not as often for what concerns them. Obviously, this poses some challenges from the outset of therapy.

A second challenge stems from the first. If young men are often referred for what troubles their significant others and not what concerns them, then it follows that a therapist who develops a successful working alliance with them may do so around goals other than the ones that brought them in the door, at least initially. If the young man with a marijuana pipe in his car doesn't see his drug use as a problem but, once engaged in therapy, is willing to talk about his struggles with anxiety or some significant relationship concerns, then you now have both a good outcome and a bit of a dilemma. The parents are expecting work on the drug use, while the client himself is wanting to work on his social anxiety. You now have a potential lack of alignment between the client's goals and the goals of those who referred him—and who are usually footing the bill.

Ricky, our 16-year-old emo boy with hair that hung into his eyes, gauged earrings, tight-fitting clothes, and checkerboard shoes came into therapy because his parents were frustrated with his disrespect and isolation. He was rude to them and defiant. He wouldn't communicate with them at all much of the time, except by cussing them out. He agreed to come in, but only on the terms that it was individual therapy and not family therapy and that information shared in the session wouldn't be shared with the parents. They consented to this.

After all of this had been worked out, he told me that there was something that he needed to talk about. Tears welled up in his eyes.

"So, I'm gay...," he said, his voice trailing off.

We talked about how his struggles related to his sexual identity had caused him some serious depression over the past few years that came out mostly as isolation and anger. He said he managed it with drug use and "trying not to think about it."

Within weeks, Ricky did well in therapy. His depression lifted. His drug use, which was mostly hidden to his parents, stopped. He was able to tell some close friends that he was gay and got a positive response. But the truth was that he was still noncommunicative with his parents, still rude to them on occasion, and still outright defiant on other occasions. Even with my suggestions, he resisted involving them in the therapy process or even allowing us to talk much about his relationship with them.

"If they come in here," he said, "it will make this about what they want to talk about and not what I want to talk about."

For Ricky, the therapy experience was a big success, but for his parents, it was a clear failure. They had not achieved their goal of a better relationship with him. This is a considerable challenge because for them to continue to support therapy financially and emotionally, they have to see some benefit. I can't tell them what that benefit is, and Ricky is not ready to share it with them himself.

One more example: Kirk was a 19-year-old college freshman when I met him. He went off to a large university, but he did not fit in well there, got discouraged with the whole college experience, and stopped going to class sometime around mid-October. His parents had no clue about any of this until the end of the semester, when they discovered that he had failed every class. They insisted that he see a therapist. Their stated goal: Figure out why this happened, then fix it so it won't happen again next semester. He agreed to come to therapy, but when he began to process what was going on, it became clear to him that he wasn't sure that he wanted to be in college at all—not just at the university where he was enrolled, but anywhere. He thought he might need a year or two to work and figure out what he really wanted to do. His parents were adamant that he stay on the college track, however. This, of course, set up a clear lack of alignment between his parents' goals and his goals. With young men who are still being supported by their parents, whether they are of legal age or not, there are often inherent challenges because what they want can be quite different from what their parents want.

Another unique challenge is that young men are typically less open to help initially. Their view of therapy is less positive than that of their female peers. While there is evidence that attitudes toward therapy are shifting and becoming more positive, it is still true that young men are more reluctant to have a favorable view of therapy from the outset. I reviewed the early session notes of a random sample of 100 of my adolescent and young adult male clients from the past three years and found that 72% of them did not come into therapy willingly on the first session. During my agency days, I am certain this percentage would have been even higher. Among my recent clients, the first session frequently had notations like, "Said parents forced him to come in," and "Said he would come in for only one session." However, after the first session, a full 95% of these clients had agreed to come back for more. As I will emphasize repeatedly, the first and second sessions are essential in your work with young men. Unless you work for an agency where your clients are mandated to see you, you will typically not have the opportunity to build trust and rapport past one or two sessions. Most young men come in under duress or as a favor to a loved one. As a rule, they are typically less open to help initially.

Any time you work with minors, you have some thorny confidentiality issues that can arise in therapy. However, this is especially true in the case of young men, since they have higher rates of aggression, alcohol and drug use, completed suicides, and general risk-taking behavior. At what point does an adolescent boy's risk taking warrant a breach of confidentiality? At what point does his drug use require notifying his parents? What if you find out he is having unprotected sex or is selling marijuana or getting into drunken fights? What if you find out that he had been drinking and driving the previous weekend?

The same is true even if a young man is of majority age. Are you compelled to let the parents of a 20-year-old know if he has a gun in his room, even if he has no intention of using it? What if he says he did cocaine at a party? Should you tell if you know he has been breaking into neighbors' houses during the day and stealing from them?

As with all clients, you have to make judgments about what constitutes imminent harm or danger, balancing out the need to preserve confidentiality with the needs for safety. With young men, these judgment calls are more frequent, and the stakes are often much higher because the behaviors are so risky and alarming.

Therapy with young men poses some unique challenges because they are typically referred for what concerns others and not what concerns them. They are usually less open to help initially, and if they do get engaged in therapy, there is often a lack of alignment between their goals and the goals of those who referred them, and there can be some especially thorny confidentiality issues.

IMPORTANT THEORETICAL INFLUENCES

To have a strong therapeutic model that holds together well and gets results, we need to have a solid theoretical foundation. This book draws heavily from three perspectives in psychology that all integrate nicely. Together, they offer a comprehensive model of therapy that suits the needs of young men well. These are the three perspectives:

1. Motivational interviewing
2. Cognitive-behavioral therapy (CBT)
3. Positive psychology

The spirit of motivational interviewing is necessary for engagement and rapport with young men in therapy. The cognitive-behavioral skills and strategies provide the tools for helping them make important life changes. Positive psychology sets the tone, direction, and emotional frame for the entire enterprise.

Motivational Interviewing

William Miller originally developed motivational interviewing as a counseling approach for problem drinking, especially for those who were typically considered resistant to treatment (Miller & Rollnick, 2002). The model was pioneered to help individuals with alcohol problems who were often court-ordered or compelled by some external reason to participate in therapy. These clients would typically come in with arms folded, scowling and defensive, but would often leave fully onboard with the counseling process and willing to make changes in their lives.

Since its inception, motivational interviewing has been applied to a wide range of problem behaviors, mental health issues, and special client populations with great success (Miller & Rollnick, 2002). Like cognitive-behavioral therapy's well-tested methods that demonstrated strong efficacy in the research literature, motivational interviewing is also regarded as an empirically supported treatment. The research is highly favorable to motivational interviewing, suggesting that it works well, often in a fairly short amount of time.

Simply put, motivational interviewing is a style of therapy that helps clients look at their own internal motivations and reasons for making a change. This is accomplished by exploring the client's ambivalence about the area of concern, looking closely at both what is good about it and what is not so good about it, all from the client's perspective. In other words, the client is not told what is bad about his problem behavior nor given reasons to stop doing it. It's his responsibility—not the therapist's—to articulate the good and the bad of it. The therapist guides this process in a way that is nonconfrontational and nonjudgmental. Therapy and counseling using this approach feels much more like a collaboration than a hierarchical, authoritative relationship. The four core principles of motivational interviewing that shape its tone and focus are:

Express empathy: Derived from the early work of Carl Rogers, this well-researched principle has become a key component of good counseling practice for the past 40 years. Motivational interviewing puts the principle front and center, emphasizing it as an essential element of helping people make difficult changes. This is accomplished by "skillful reflective listening." Miller and Rollnick (2002) emphasize the need to accept the client in an unconditional manner and suggest that it is this process of acceptance that actually facilitates the person's ability to change.

Develop discrepancy: In motivational interviewing, a person is viewed as being more likely to change when he sees a gap between what he is doing and what he wants or values. For example, a client may be cheating on his girlfriend, but see himself as a person of honesty and integrity. Another client may be partying all night during the week and missing his classes, but truly desiring a college degree. There is a discrepancy between what he is doing and how he sees himself, what he values, or what he wants. The therapist's job is to gently expose that discrepancy, not to make a case for what should be changed. In fact, it is the client's job—not the therapist's—to "present the arguments for change." The therapist helps highlight the discrepancies that will drive the client to make important changes. When this is done well, the client increases his drive to close the discrepancy without feeling pressured by the therapist.

Roll with resistance: In the motivational interviewing framework, one of the worst things that can happen in the therapy session is for the therapist to argue for change while the client argues against it. Yet, even seasoned and skillful therapists find themselves trying to convince resistant clients that they really do need to stop smoking marijuana or start respecting their parents or change some other problematic behavior. Young men, especially, tend to dig in their heels when they feel lectured or coerced by parents, girlfriends, or others. The therapist's arguments for change often have the opposite effect and end up causing the person to become even more resistant.

The better option, practitioners of motivational interviewing would suggest, is to roll with resistance. When a client is reluctant to make a change, the therapist gives feedback about how much it makes sense to be hesitant to make such a major life change. When the client is ambivalent—a key concept in motivational interviewing—the therapist explores both sides of the dilemma without pressure or judgment. When resistance surfaces, it's a signal for the therapist to change gears and go in a different direction. The therapist wants the client talking less about what changes he won't or can't make and more about what changes he wants to make in his life. When resistance to change comes up in the session, the therapist rolls away from the topic and shifts focus.

Support self-efficacy: For therapists who use motivational interviewing, the message they send to the client is that he alone has the capacity and ability to make the change. The therapist takes the position that he or she is a helper, a guide, a support, but not the one who makes the change. The client alone is the one who can make the change happen.

In many respects, the main issue here is bolstering the client's confidence. Motivational interviewing takes the position that clients are able to make important changes in their lives, even with very difficult issues. When a person wants to make the change but cannot, the issue is framed as a crisis of confidence, not a lack of ability. Clients who believe they can make these changes tend to take more steps of action and see more improvements in their lives.

Motivational interviewing, when done well, is absolutely brilliant at building rapport, establishing treatment alliance, and engaging even highly resistant clients. Motivational interviewing becomes the front door of therapy and sets the general tone and approach for all that follows.

More than any other treatment framework or model, motivational interviewing has been by far the most helpful in my work with resistant male clients. However, what I am going to present in the coming chapters is not a purist's version of motivational interviewing. Instead, I have taken the spirit and essence of Miller and Rollnick's model (2002) and applied it specifically to work with young men. I have found accurate empathy to be an essential element of good therapy, as well as the need to develop discrepancies between personal values and choices. I also gladly roll with resistance, especially in the early stages of the process, because I know that it will pay off therapeutically.

Where I tend to differ with the motivational interviewing model is on the emphasis on self-efficacy. As a principle, I absolutely support *self-determination* in therapy (i.e., a young man's right and ability to control the direction of his own life), but *self-efficacy* implies that the client can solve the problem and does not require "expert" knowledge or assistance. In many cases this is true, but in some cases, it is not. I understand how this principle evolved from its early roots with problem drinkers and its rejection of authoritarian treatments. However, as the model has been applied to a range of psychological difficulties, the argument for self-efficacy weakens.

Take a problem with severe anxiety, for example. A young man who is having panic attacks or social anxiety may have absolutely no idea about what he can do to solve this problem. In fact, he may have notions about it that are completely wrong. He may want to avoid situations that trigger the anxiety when he needs to have a willingness to go into them. He may work hard to keep from having certain anxious thoughts when he needs to have the skills to manage those thoughts instead. Whether it is anxiety, depression, anger outbursts, relationship problems, or dozens of other concerns, a client cannot always be relied upon to come up with his own solutions. He may need skills and information to make the changes he desires in his life.

From a motivational interviewing standpoint, the concern with teaching these skills or providing this information is that it may change the dynamic of the relationship and create a hierarchy (i.e., expert/recipient roles). In doing so, the concern is that you may not only undermine a client's internal motivation, but also hurt his confidence in solving his own problems. In practice, however, I am confident that skillful clinicians can create a collaborative, nonauthoritarian tone in therapy and still provide information when it is lacking and teach skills when they are missing.

Motivational interviewing is by nature a "directive" method for helping a person change. While it shares much of its DNA with Carl Rogers's person-centered approach, the model stands in contrast to Rogers's nondirective stance (Rogers, 1951, 1961). But motivational interviewing is directive only insofar as it targets the client's ambivalence about his problem. For those who are ready and willing to change, however, it offers little in the way of specific techniques or strategies. In motivational interviewing, a person's ability to change is seen as mostly a matter of personal confidence to take the necessary steps. While it is consistent with motivational interviewing to offer advice or direction when it is requested, there is little within the framework that gives clinicians much guidance about building needed skills. It is here where I differ the most with the pure motivational interviewing model. I believe it is necessary to have a toolbox full of skills that you can offer your clients when the time is right. That's where cognitive-behavioral therapy fits into this framework.

Motivational interviewing wisely acknowledges that it can be the pervading model throughout therapy, a prelude to other therapy work, or a fallback option if you hit a roadblock. In work with young men, I propose that the basic framework of motivational interviewing is most typically the prelude to the cognitive-behavioral work, while its respectful attitude and tone continues to saturate the therapy time.

Cognitive-Behavioral Therapy

There is no tradition in psychology with a stronger research base than cognitive-behavioral therapy (CBT). With applications ranging from the treatment of depression and anxiety to relationship problems and substance abuse, the CBT model is robust, versatile, and powerful (Butler, Chapman, Forman, & Beck, 2006; Hofmann & Smits, 2008; Klein, Jacobs, & Reinecke, 2007; Magill & Ray, 2009; Smits, Berry, Tart, & Powers, 2008).

Since the motivational interviewing model is an effective way to begin therapy with young men but doesn't offer much in the way of specific tools to help them manage their difficulties, CBT is often an effective next step. CBT provides cognitive tools in ways that can be readily understood and used by these clients. While there are many kinds of CBT therapies, they are all conceptually connected by interventions that target thoughts and actions to help reduce the symptoms of problems. This type of therapy frequently makes use of rehearsal, role-playing, and homework to strengthen the newly acquired skills. One of the many benefits of CBT is that it also tends to involve behavioral goal setting in ways that are measureable and make it easier to assess whether progress is being made.

I'm not the first to integrate motivational interviewing and CBT. For example, Sampl and Kadden (2001) provide a detailed, effective group curriculum for adolescent substance abusers. What I will present, however, are some new and unique interventions that are well suited to therapy with young men. These strategies are specifically targeted at the common difficulties young men in therapy are experiencing. As you will see, motivational interviewing and CBT integrate nicely as a model of therapy for young men.

Positive Psychology

A paradigm shift has come from the influence of positive psychology, championed by Martin Seligman (2004). In contrast to traditional clinical psychology approaches that focus on pathology and what is wrong with a person, positive psychology looks at what is right with a person. Rather than examining how to alleviate depression, for example, positive psychology might look at how to boost happiness or increase optimism. This isn't merely a hair-splitting distinction; it is a fundamentally different focus. Instead of mental illness, the focus is on mental wellness. Instead of reducing the effects of psychopathology, the focus is on increasing the benefits of happiness.

The positive psychology model has caught fire with the general public. Thousands of self-help positive psychology books have been written in the past couple of years. Universities have even begun offering courses on happiness. The resonance of positive psychology is that it offers a more accessible, more hopeful way to receive the benefits of psychology. Throughout this book, you'll see the influence of that perspective, especially as we talk about issues related to identity formation and relationships.

Years ago, when I was the clinical director for a large community agency that served highly aggressive adolescents, I first began hearing about the importance of what we were calling "protective factors" for at-risk teenagers. For decades, we had known about the risk factors, such things as abuse, neglect, difficult temperament, neurological problems, growing up in high-crime areas, and so on, but this was the first time we all starting thinking about the other side of the equation. Perhaps there were protective factors that could offset the risks. The early research was encouraging, so we joined the effort and began to look at the role of strengths in helping violent kids stay out of trouble, stay in school, and make progress toward their treatment goals.

We had over 100 clients that had to go through a formal certification process to be a part of our program. They were served in a full continuum of treatment options ranging from outpatient and in-home support on the low end to group homes and secure residential on the high end. Each client was rated for all the known research-based risk factors and protective factors. We also completed monthly behavior ratings on standardized checklists and tracked their progress toward each treatment goal.

What the research had said up to that point was that the sum of the protective factors minus the sum of the risk factors best predicted outcome. In other words, if a client had 12 known protective factors and 3 known risk factors, then he would have a score of +9. According to the research, the higher the score, the more likely the client was to have favorable outcomes like staying in school, staying out of trouble, and remaining at home with the family. By contrast, if a client had 5 protective factors, but 15 risk factors, his score of −10 would predict trouble for him.

I accepted this premise, but there was one claim the research made that just did not seem right. The research declared that the risk and protective factors were not weighted according to how much impact they had on the client's functioning. It wasn't the weight of the factors, but the sum of all the factors that best predicted outcome. I found it hard to accept that something like attachment problems would carry as much weight as something like having a shy or withdrawn temperament in the final analysis. I was so convinced that I had a group of 10 licensed clinicians assign a weight (1–3) to each known risk factor. We used both the weighted formula and the unweighted formula and we tracked our clients' data for more than a year.

What we found surprised me. The weighted formula was no better at predicting the outcome than the unweighted formula. In other words, I was wrong. It wasn't the weight of the protective factors themselves; it was the sum of all of them together. The higher the number of the simple formula (protective factors minus risk factors), the more likely a client was to do well during that year; the lower the number (especially when it went into the negative), the more likely he was to do poorly.

It was a powerful, elegantly simple prediction model. It also made the case that the presence of protective factors could offset the damage done by risk factors. A teenager with many strikes against him could still do well. It began to help us make sense of why some kids from high-risk situations beat the odds and why others did not.

Most importantly, the resiliency framework focused on the positive side of the equation. Most of the risk factors were set. They were things that had occurred in the past (abuse, neglect, exposure to toxins in the womb, history of delinquency, etc.), were mostly unchangeable aspects of the child (low IQ, chronic health problems, difficult temperament, attachment difficulties), or were contextual problems that often had little promise of being different (living in a high-crime neighborhood, court involvement, antisocial siblings). By contrast, the protective factors were often aspects that could change in response to intervention. There were 21 protective factors that had research support. Here's just a sampling of those that could potentially be added or enhanced in treatment: improving his connection to family, creating a more positive tone for family communication, developing better social skills, and increasing skills to cope with stress. In addition, a therapist can encourage other activities that are known to be protective factors, such as involvement in positive group activities (sports, youth group, theater, clubs, etc.) and educational support services that can increase interest and achievement in school. Involvement in group activities with healthy peers, positive school bonding, and improvements in academic functioning (especially reading) are all known to be protective factors.

Of the 21 protective factors, 18 of them could change a little bit or a lot. That should be extremely encouraging to anyone who has worked with high-risk clients. If it is true that adding protective factors can tip the scale toward a more positive outcome for a client with many challenges against him, then this perspective brings a great deal of hope. A client may not be able to change his past, his internal wiring, or even some of his current circumstances, but he can add skills and supports that can increase his chances of doing well in life.

In the resiliency research, there is often a distinction between internal and external protective factors. Internal protective factors would be things like empathy, remorse, attachment, and sense of humor. External factors would include involvement in extracurricular activities, going to a school with high academic standards, and having positive friends. Some researchers conceptualize resiliency as the internal factors only, arguing that true resiliency is seated within the individual and not his context. We didn't accept that premise, believing that resiliency is the sum of his personal qualities and the factors around him that helped him deal with adversity. However, when I developed a study for this current project, I chose to test out only the factors that could be directly observed by the therapist during sessions. I tested out only eight protective factors that would reasonably be associated with therapy outcomes. Several therapists were asked to rate up to 10 of their current young adult male clients who were between the ages of 16 and 24. They rated a total of 63 clients who were 18 years old on average and had been seen an average of 13 sessions. The study found that four specific protective factors were the best predictors of positive outcomes in therapy with young men:

1. Ability to talk about feelings openly and honestly
2. Ability to show empathy and compassion
3. Ability to set and keep realistic personal goals
4. Belief that good choices lead to good outcomes

Together, these four protective factors have a highly significant relationship with therapy progress for young men ($r = .78$). Here is a brief description of each of the four factors:

Can talk about feelings openly and honestly: The ability to talk openly and honestly about emotions is the bedrock of what has been called "emotional intelligence." This trait has been associated with a whole range of positive outcomes in the research literature, including success in school and vocation, healthy relationships, and general life functioning and adjustment.

Shows empathy and compassion: Not surprisingly, empathic people do better in relationships. Those with greater empathy tend to connect with others more and bully and intimidate less. People with higher degrees of empathy and compassion are much more likely to engage in prosocial behaviors like helping others than those who have more deficits in these key areas.

Can set and keep realistic personal goals: People who do well in life often set and keep personal goals. The act of having a goal is not necessarily a protective factor because the goal needs to be realistic. If a high school senior who is not even on the school basketball team has a goal of playing professional basketball, then just having that goal is not helpful. Those who set and keep good goals have more positive persistence, higher frustration tolerance, and greater delay of gratification, all qualities that tend to bode well for a person's life.

Believes good choices lead to good outcomes: Locus of control refers to the degree to which individuals believe they control the course of their lives. A young man with an external locus of control sees himself as being at the mercy of outside forces, luck, or circumstances. By contrast, a person with an internal locus of control tends to believe his good choices lead to more options and better outcomes, while his bad choices lead to fewer options and worse outcomes. When I was in graduate school, one of my professors told me, "You will almost always get a significant result if you have a locus-of-control measure in your research." He wasn't being cynical; he was just expressing the importance of the concept of locus of control. Individuals with an external locus of control believe that their lives are ruled by bad luck and outside events, while individuals with an internal locus of control believe that the choices they make determine the general direction of their lives. They believe that bad decisions generally lead to bad results and that good choices lead to good outcomes. Having an internal locus of control has tremendous benefits for a person. It leads to such outcomes as better school performance, greater social action, better health management, and more self-efficacy.

In the study, the therapists rated each client on the various protective factors. The ratings were on a 5-point scale that ranged from strongly disagree (−2) to strongly agree (+2). The therapists also rated each client on five dimensions of therapy process, and outcome:

1. Uses *therapy time* effectively
2. Has established good *rapport* in therapy
3. Has a strong *commitment* to therapy
4. Follows through on therapy *agreements* and homework
5. Has made positive *changes* in his life since therapy began

There were three significant findings that emerged from this study that can be helpful in our work with young men in therapy. Bear in mind that all of these findings are correlations, which indicates relationships between variables but offers no assurance that one variable causes another one. For example, there is a correlation between male gender and aggression, but it would not be fair to say that male gender causes aggression. However, it is important to know that the relationship exists. In this present study, I am not making the claim that one variable or set of variables causes the other, but the relationships between the two pieces of data are meaningful. The study found these three big relationships:

There is a strong correlation between the combined protective factors and the combined therapy variables. When I totaled these four protective factors together as one composite variable and also summed all the therapy factors together as another composite variable, the relationship between these two composite scores was strong and highly significant ($r = .78$). Practically speaking, this means that young men who have these four more protective factors tend to do better in therapy. With more of the four protective factors comes the likelihood a young man will use the therapy time effectively, establish good rapport, commit to the therapy process, follow through on therapy agreements, and make positive changes in his life.

There is a high correlation between emotional expression, therapeutic rapport, and commitment to therapy. Young men who are able to talk about their feelings in open and honest ways tend to establish better rapport with their therapists. In the present study, I found a high correlation ($r = .72$) between these two variables, which is not at all surprising. Much of rapport often comes from the ease with which we can talk about emotional content. Guys who are constricted and tight-lipped obviously create greater challenges in building rapport than those who are pretty open and emotionally expressive. It's no shock at all that a young man's ability to talk about his feelings openly and honestly is strongly associated with therapy progress because possessing this core feature of emotional intelligence is likely to make the therapy process smoother and less taxing for him and his therapist.

The current study also found that the ability to talk about feelings openly and honestly was related to a client's *commitment* to therapy ($r = .72$). Those clients who talked about feelings freely not only had better rapport, but were more committed to coming to therapy. They were more likely to stick with the process and work toward mutually agreed-upon goals. These young men were less likely to drop out of therapy before their objectives were met, which makes the enterprise much more rewarding for therapist and client alike.

With such a high correlation, there is a good chance a therapist will be able to predict which clients will complete therapy almost from the time they begin therapy. It seems that the ease with which a young man shares emotionally lines up with whether he connects with this therapist (and vice versa) and whether he will stick with his therapy. By contrast, clients who do not talk about their feelings easily may need more work on this skill early in the therapy process to increase their chances of staying with it.

There is a significant correlation between locus of control and therapy outcome. Of all the protective factors that were part of this current study, one best predicted whether a client made positive changes in his life after beginning therapy: whether he believes good choices lead to good outcomes.

This simple measure of internal locus of control is significantly related to making healthy life changes ($r = .64$). If a young man believes in a cause and effect between the decisions he makes and how his life turns out, then it follows that he will also benefit more from therapy. He already sees himself as being in charge of his life; therapy just gives him the tools, insight, and direction to achieving his goals.

Many clients come in believing bad luck or other people—mean teachers, unfair parents, biased employers, conniving females—determine how life goes for them. What the current study finds is that these young men are less likely to benefit from therapy than those who believe they chart their own course. On the other hand, the smart money is on those who believe they determine their own destiny by the choices they make. As one of my clients said, "People always wish me good luck, but I make my own luck."

PROTECTIVE FACTORS IN PRACTICE

Resiliency research seems to always yield highly practical information that readily translates to practice. The same is true from this current study. The three big findings of the study lead to three specific implications for therapy with young men.

Assess Protective Factors Early in Therapy

If these four protective factors predict the process and outcome of therapy with young men, then it makes good sense to assess them early in the therapy process. Three of them—talking openly and honestly about feelings, having realistic goals, and locus of control—can be readily assessed by at least the second conversation. Empathy may take a few sessions more in some cases to get a truly accurate read. Here are some good prompts or questions you might consider to assess each of the four protective factors:

Talks about feelings openly and honestly
- Tell me a time when you felt really happy (sad, angry, worried).
- What do you do when you get worried?
- Do you often share what you are feeling with other people?

Shows empathy and compassion
- Tell me your opinion about people in general. Are they basically good or bad? Do you tend to like most people or not?
- When have you felt sorry or concerned for someone else?

- Can you tell me a time when you helped someone out when they were having a hard time?

Can set and keep realistic personal goals
- Tell me a time when you wanted something and really went after it.
- Have you ever had a goal that was hard to accomplish, but you finally achieved it?
- What would you like to be doing three years from now?

Believes good choices lead to good outcomes
- Tell me about a big decision you made and how it turned out for you.
- Do you feel like luck is a big factor in how things turn out for you?
- Why do you think life turns out well for some people and not for others?

These questions may provide you with a lot of information about these four protective factors, but some of them are best judged by observation. It's far better to see a person spontaneously show empathy in the conversation than to ask about it, for example. But either by direct questioning or through observation, it is good to assess these traits early in the therapy relationship.

Compensate for Weak Areas

One of the most encouraging aspects of the resiliency research is that many of these protective factors can be developed. A weakness may never be a strength, but it can stop being a drag on a person's functioning. Take locus of control as an example. The research indicates that a person's control orientation can change in response to therapeutic education. A person can move up the scale from a highly external control orientation to at least a mild or moderate internal control orientation. There is also evidence that a person can develop greater empathy after being taught how to take perspective or after having experiences with underprivileged individuals. In fact, nearly all of the protective factors can be developed in most people, at least to some extent. Absent or weak areas are not likely to become strengths, but they can at least be neutral or average for many people.

Make Existing Strengths Stronger

An analysis of the Gallup Organization's database of over 2 million individuals found that people are likely and able to grow more in their strengths than in their areas of weakness (Buckingham & Clifton, 2001). If someone is good at expressing empathy, for example, but has a poor ability to set and keep personal goals, the odds are that he is more likely to improve his ability to become even more empathic than he is to become more goal-driven.

From a strengths-based perspective, you would focus more on the area of strength than on the area of weakness. What is right with a person becomes more important than what is wrong with a person. Helping him change involves a greater emphasis on fortifying his strengths than becoming well-rounded in his weaknesses. This thinking applies to all of the young man's traits and skills, not just the four protective factors we have discussed here. These four areas are important, though, because they have a relationship to how well a young man does in therapy.

Be mindful to build on each client's strengths in therapy. In the study, I found a significant relationship ($r = .67$) between the number of strengths for each person (i.e., the protective factors that were rated with positive numbers) and the composite score for therapy progress. An individual with more positive assets is apt to do better in therapy, so use his strengths to his advantage. First identify them, then build on them. Work on making the strong areas stronger whenever possible.

QUALITIES OF GREAT THERAPISTS

What you do is important in therapy. Having a framework and being equipped with techniques to address the common issues you will face is essential. What is more important than what you do, however, is who you are. Some may dispute this, arguing that therapy can be effective with lock-step techniques and strategies. In my experience, however, there is no way you can get around the reality that much of therapy rests with the individual characteristics of the therapist.

There are masters in nearly every field of practice and study. In many cases, their mastery is on display. A master actor's work is on the stage or screen for people to see. A master mechanic's work can be readily inspected. A master chef's work can be tasted and savored. A master musician's work can be recorded and appreciated for years to come.

There are master therapists, too, but their work is harder to critique and evaluate. It happens behind closed doors and is accomplished one person—or small group of people—at a time. A person may be a good presenter, but a weak therapist, or vice versa. A person's reputation may be boosted by one vocal client or sullied by another. As with any field, it is good to know who the best practitioners are and how they do what they do.

Using peer-nominations, Skovholt & Jennings (2004) studied the common factors of "master therapists" and found that they typically are people who embrace complexity and ambiguity, are humble and self-aware, and have a strong passion for life, among other qualities. Other researchers have looked at the question by asking clients what qualities they prefer or find most helpful. There is an emerging consensus as to what qualities are found among the best therapists. Based on a review of the literature, I propose a dozen characteristics that seem to be typical of the best of the best (Ackerman & Hilsenroth, 2003; Littauer, Sexton, & Wynn, 2005; Martin, Romas, Medford, Leffert, & Hatcher, 2006; Selekman, 2005).

Authentic: This quality appears on nearly every list and in almost every study. The best therapists seem to be genuine people who come across as being thoroughly authentic. Excellent therapists are fundamentally honest. They are honest in what they say, never giving false praise or flattery. Top-drawer therapists keep their word, they hold confidences well, and they follow through on agreements. They can be trusted. They are true to themselves.

Empathetic: The very best therapists understand the feelings of others and can communicate this by how they respond. They are excellent listeners who give spot-on feedback. They get the internal experiences of others in ways that few people can.

Patient: The best therapists seem to be supremely patient, not moving too fast and not getting exasperated by setbacks or slow progress.

Spontaneous: There is a sense of fun and playfulness among the very best therapists. The sessions don't feel canned or rote. The therapist responds to the client in ways that are surprising and refreshing. There is often a sense of humor about the whole venture. The best therapists also change direction, slow down, speed up, shift focus, and change approaches as needed.

Respectful: Exceptional therapists communicate deep respect and unconditional regard for others, regardless of differences. They respect the timing and readiness of those who are in a process of making changes in their lives. They respect different worldviews, outlooks, and lifestyles.

Self-aware: It appears that the master therapists know themselves well. They know their strengths and weaknesses, and they have a deep acceptance of themselves. They also seem to have a sense of humor about themselves and don't take themselves too seriously.

Open: Excellent therapists are open to new ways of seeing the world and alternative possibilities. They understand that issues are complex and often ambiguous, and they feel comfortable with that.

Optimistic: A common theme in the research is that the best and most helpful therapists not only feel optimistic, but they exude a sense of optimism for their clients. They are hopeful, and it shows.

Intuitive: The very best therapists have strong intuition. They pick up on nuance and go with their gut much of the time. In most cases, their instincts are right on the money.

Confident: The best therapists are self-confident without being cocky. They approach life and sessions with great confidence and a sense of calm.

Warm: There is an emotional warmth about the best therapists that is not sentimental or gooey, but grounded and solid. They put you at ease and you enjoy being in their presence. They smile easily, and they can be affectionate with their words.

Interested: The very best therapists are highly curious people. They are interested in others, and they want to know more about their stories. Even after years of seemingly hearing it all before, they appreciate and enjoy the uniqueness of the individual in front of them.

The best therapists seem to have all of these traits integrated together. They can be patient, yet spontaneous. They are authentic, but are still genuinely optimistic. In some cases, these are traits that have been developed through training and practice, but for many of the best, these characteristics are simply part of their nature. It is who they are as people. If you have all or most of these qualities, you are probably in the right field.

SUMMARY

In this chapter, we started with some unique challenges that you will face in your work with young men. From there, we discussed the theoretical influences and underpinnings that will guide us in our work, including motivational interviewing, cognitive behavioral therapy, and positive psychology. Finally, we took a look at some of the personal characteristics that are true of the best therapists, the masters in our field. With this prelude, we can now focus on the processes that cause our clients to make important changes in their lives.

THERAPY TAKE-AWAYS

1. Use the principles of motivational interviewing to build rapport and lower resistance; use the tools of cognitive behavioral therapy to equip your clients with skills and strategies; use the spirit of positive psychology to keep your focus on what is good with each client.
2. Assess protective factors early in the therapy process, especially emotional intelligence, empathy, goal-setting, and locus of control.
3. Build on strengths throughout the therapy process. Address weak areas when you must, but spend as much time as possible building on the strong areas.

APPENDIX: BRIEF THERAPIST SURVEY

Rate a *current male client between the ages of 16 to 24* on the following items:

Client's Age: _____   Total Number of Sessions to Date: _____

Primary Presenting Problems (Check all that apply):
☐ Behavioral problem   ☐ Emotional problem   ☐ Substance problem
☐ Relationship problem   ☐ Other problem

Racial Background (Check only one):
☐ African American   ☐ Asian   ☐ Caucasian   ☐ Hispanic   ☐ Biracial
☐ Other

Circle the appropriate number for each item	Strongly Disagree	Disagree	Neutral	Agree	Strongly Agree
1. Can talk about feelings openly and honestly	−2	−1	0	1	2
2. Shows empathy and compassion	−2	−1	0	1	2
3. Can set and keep realistic personal goals	−2	−1	0	1	2
4. Believes good choices lead to good outcomes	−2	−1	0	1	2
5. Uses therapy time effectively	−2	−1	0	1	2
6. Has established good rapport in therapy	−2	−1	0	1	2
7. Has a strong commitment to therapy	−2	−1	0	1	2
8. Follows through on therapy agreements and homework	−2	−1	0	1	2
9. Has made positive changes in his life since therapy began	−2	−1	0	1	2

3

Setting the Stage for Change

"My aunt thought it was a good idea for me to do this," Marlon said in his first session with me. "She thinks I need to make some changes in my life."

"What do you think?" I asked.

"I don't know," he said. "I never really thought about it."

As odd as it may seem to have someone say that he had not considered making a change in his life during a therapy session, it is a surprisingly common occurrence. Many young men come into therapy under duress. Some are entirely resistant, while others just don't want to be there. We tend to think of therapy as being mostly about helping people change, but if you work with young men, you will find many of them come in without ever having seriously contemplated making a change in their lives. Marlon is a classic example. He is sitting in a therapist's office and says he has never even thought about it. To understand how to get him to the point of change, we first need to look at why anyone changes in the first place.

WHY PEOPLE CHANGE

There are a multitude of reasons for why people make life changes, including social forces and motivational factors (Orford, Hodgson, Copello, Wilton, & Slegg, 2009). There is no one reason, but there are a few consistent themes when people begin to improve some important area of their lives. For young men, here are some of the common reasons they give for making a change:

Involvement of others supporting change: As much as practitioners of motivational interviewing like me want to focus on intrinsic motivation to change, the reason most problem drinkers and those with other problem behaviors give for making a change is that it is important to those who are important to them. Whether it is a parent, a close relative, a girlfriend or boyfriend, or another close friend, the influence of these significant others is profound. Most young men come in the door the first time to a therapy appointment because of someone else's concern. Anyone who works with young men in therapy will hear time and time again that they are willing to change something because it is important to someone else.

In one sense, if a client wants to change because of the influence or concern of another person, this is a form of internal motivation. The true motivation, ultimately, is that the individual values the other person. Perhaps he wants to please his parents or doesn't want to lose his girlfriend or simply respects his friends. In any case, he places an important value on the relationship with the other person, and that person's wishes are given high regard.

Concern over consequences: Again, external factors are typically regarded as less important and potent within motivational models of change, but the truth is that clients say concern over consequences is a factor in their decisions to alter some aspect of their behavior. After a client of mine was robbed at gunpoint during a minor drug sale, he decided he needed to make some major changes in his life. When another client of mine flipped his car six times and ended up with only a busted ankle and some scratches and bruises, he took that as a sign he should stop drinking. And when one of my other clients had to pay a neighbor back over $2,000 because of some property destruction, he came to the conclusion that he needed to work on getting a better handle on his impulse control. Sometimes the consequences are plenty reason enough to start making a change.

This should not be taken for license to try to impress upon a client the consequences of failing to change, however, as this is the downfall of many therapists. When we are at our most frustrated, anxious, or undisciplined, we find it easy to revert back to attempts to lecture about the consequences. For most young men, they already know the potential risks for continuing to drink, use drugs, get into fights, shoplift, have unprotected sex, defy their parents, and nearly every other problematic behavior. Telling them what they already know is hardly ever effective, but many times the logical and natural real life consequences are hugely helpful in starting a change process.

Wanting a better life: Some individuals make changes because they don't want to experience negative consequences, but there are also individuals who decide to make changes in their lives primarily because they want positive things. One of my clients began training for a marathon because he wanted to be in better shape and accomplish a big goal. Another one of my clients stopped smoking marijuana because he realized that the girl he was interested in would only date men who didn't use drugs. Not long ago, one of my clients, a sophomore in college, told me he needed to move off campus. When I asked why, he said he wanted to get more focused so that he could have a better chance of getting into a good MBA program. His motive for leaving some negative friends behind wasn't to avoid consequences or to please his parents. Instead, he just wanted something better for himself.

If you listen carefully, some clients are telling you that their motive for changing has less to do with pleasing others around them, less to do with avoidance of consequences, and more to do with trying to make a better life for themselves. Our pathology-focused training may cause us to miss this motive for change, but it's often there. Individuals frequently make life changes—often big changes—to enhance their lives. One of the ways that positive psychology has begun to shape the practice of therapy is by helping us listen for the good, healthy, affirmative reasons people give for making a change.

Becoming aware of discrepancies: Most of us don't fully line up with our own values, beliefs, and standards. Much of the time, though, we just ignore these internal disconnects if we are able to avoid dealing with them. Pascal wrote, "We are only falsehood, duplicity, contradiction. We both conceal and disguise ourselves from ourselves." At times, though, our contradictions peek through, and we see them a little more clearly. When this happens, we either cover them back up again with our artful denial or we work to reconcile them. Many times, individuals are led to change by the realization that there is a gap between what they value or believe and how they are really behaving.

A young man who finds himself cussing out his parents when he's angry may begin to see the discrepancy between that and his value of respect for others. The inconsistency between his actions and his values may drive him to change. Another guy may hold a religious belief that sex should be saved for marriage, but find himself in a sexual relationship with his girlfriend nonetheless. At that point, he has three choices: change his beliefs, change his actions, or not think about it. Like many young men, he may initially opt to avoid thinking about it. However, when the reality of the gap between his behavior and his beliefs is unavoidable, something is going to change.

People change when they feel discrepancies in their lives. They may feel a discrepancy between where they are in life and where they want to be. They may also feel a discrepancy between who they are and who they want to be. These gaps between what is and what should be often drive the change process.

We are often a mass of contradictions. When we face those discrepancies within ourselves, it drives us to change. Sometimes individuals come into therapy with those discrepancies already exposed, but other times, it is the therapy process itself that begins to shine a light on how we are different from how we want to be.

Simple maturation: Some people change by the process of growing up. Rebellious adolescents tend to get more compliant, and crazy college students tend to settle down. Most guys who are raging in anger at their parents in high school live perfectly respectable lives in adulthood. Most who are involved in antisocial and delinquent behavior stop doing it by the time they reach their middle 20s. The same is true for most problems that typically begin in adolescence.

Mental health professionals are slow to acknowledge that many problems of adolescence and early adulthood are simply solved with age. Most people who smoke marijuana in adolescence and young adulthood are not regular substance abusers in later adulthood, for example. The majority of pot smokers just stop their use as they get older. However, not all of the problems of youth are that easily remedied, and some young men will persist with drug problems, behavioral problems, and problems with emotional regulation well into adulthood without intervention. While there are some known risk factors that help us know which individuals have a greater chance of long-term problems, the truth is that we do not know if any given person is going to have ongoing difficulty past his adolescent and young adult years.

IMPORTANCE AND CONFIDENCE

Any time a person debates making a life change for whatever reasons, there are two questions in play, whether he realizes it or not: How important is it to make the change? How confident is the person that he can make the change?

Motivational interviewing stresses the need for an ongoing assessment of these two important aspects of change (Miller & Rollnick, 2002). *Importance* refers to how crucial it is for a person to make the change. An issue like drinking or anger management may be extremely important to others around the person, but not the individual himself. To make a change, it has to be important to the person, not just to those in his life. *Confidence* refers to how convinced a person is that he could make the change. Past successes or failures and other factors may shape his confidence about stopping a negative behavior or starting a positive one.

Let's use our three clients to talk about how these two dimensions might make a difference in how you approach therapy with each of them. Table 3.1 lists one of the concerns that was raised in the first session in therapy by each client's parent or parent figure. Each client rated

TABLE 3.1 Rating Importance and Confidence for Caregiver Concerns

Client	Caregiver Concern	Importance	Confidence
Gabriel	Drinking	2	9
Marlon	Lack of direction	4	2
Ricky	Anger outbursts	7	4

the issue himself for both importance and confidence from 1 (very low) to 10 (very high) in either the first or second session.

Despite the DUI and being taken out of school, Gabriel finds the concerns about his drinking much ado about nothing. It's nothing more than typical college kid behavior, and he doesn't drink any more or less than anyone else his age, he reasons. However, if he decided he needed to quit, he could stop right away with no problem, he explains. For Gabriel, the presenting issue of problem drinking is low in importance, but he is high in confidence. Marlon does not view his lack of direction as a tremendous problem, and he is not confident he could make a change, even if he wanted to do it. Ricky is nearly exactly the opposite of Gabriel. He agrees with his parents that he needs to get a handle on his anger, but he doesn't think it is likely. For his presenting issue, he finds it to be of high importance, but he has low confidence about changing it.

It should be readily apparent that each of these guys needs a different beginning to therapy. For Gabriel, he needs work around increasing his motivation to change his problem drinking. For Marlon, he needs help with increasing his motivation to change and his confidence that he can make the change. For Ricky, he desires to make the change, but he needs help getting over his lack of confidence.

Ratings of importance and confidence are different for every client and for every issue. Gabriel, for example, may see little importance in changing his drinking, but may view improving his relationship with his girlfriend as being extremely important. Ricky may have little confidence that he can improve his anger control right now, but he may have a lot of confidence he can improve his grades. Each issue needs to be individually assessed. Often, finding the issues where there is a greater degree of importance and confidence will make the difference between whether the client is successfully engaged in therapy or not.

STAGES OF CHANGE

Because individuals vary widely on the degree of importance they place on a given issue and how confident they are about changing it, they may be at different stages of the change process when they come into therapy. Marlon, for example, said he never really thought about making a change before. Gabriel is fairly resistant to the idea that he should alter his drinking, even after the DUI and the ugly accident. Ricky has been wanting to make a change, but he is not sure if he could do it. These guys are at different stages in the change process.

The stages-of-change model, first conceptualized by Prochaska and DiClemente (1983, 1984), says that people go through invariant steps as they begin to wrestle with some problem in their lives. They begin in the *precontemplative stage*, where they really are not considering making a change in their lives. Perhaps other people are saying he should change or are expressing concern, but the individual himself is not really actively considering it. He has no intention to make a change in the foreseeable future.

The next step is the *contemplative stage*, when a person begins considering the pros and cons of making a change in his life. He feels ambivalent about the problem, seeing both the good and the bad of it, the costs of changing and the costs of not changing. He feels torn.

If he decides to make the change, he moves into the *preparation stage*, where he has decided to deal with it. He realizes he has got to do something about the problem, that the benefits of making the change—and all the emotional energy, time, and cost—are worth it. He has made his decision and begins preparing mentally, emotionally, and physically to make it happen.

The *action stage* comes next. This is where he is taking steps to make a change. He may begin to modify his behavior or change his environment to help him stop a negative behavior (e.g., drug abuse) or begin a healthy behavior (e.g., working out). This stage typically involves the most time and work to complete. In this step, a person is doing something to make the change happen. He is taking steps to manage or get rid of the problem. He may change old habits, end certain relationships, or start new routines. He is in motion. If he keeps this up for six months or more, he moves into the final phase, which is the *maintenance stage*, where he continues the change process he has started for a sustained period of time.

The stages-of-change model is helpful in thinking about any kind of problem behavior, from drug use to anger problems to health and safety concerns. Unlike other stage models, however, the stages-of-change framework does not always move progressively forward. In other words, a person may start at Stage 1 and progress all the way up to Stage 4, then retreat and be back to Stage 1 or 2 in no time at all and seemingly without warning. A guy with a drug problem may have been sober for a few weeks, dumped all his cell phone contacts, and started attending AA one week, and then be smoking marijuana again and telling everyone how it's no big deal the next. This happens frequently when working with young men. The stages-of-change model helps you assess where a client is at any given time, which, as you will see, is of critical importance in effective therapy.

LEARNING FROM THERAPY DROPOUTS

There has been a lot of research on who stays in therapy and who drops out of therapy. We can learn a lot from either group. In a meta-analysis of all the studies, we have discovered that 35% of all clients drop out of therapy prematurely (Sharf, 2007). In other words, more than one out of every three clients leaves therapy before his treatment goals are met. With such a large number, it would be good to understand the motives for dropping out.

The biggest predictor of therapy dropout is therapist-rated alliance, followed closely by client-rated alliance. Simply put, the biggest reason clients leave therapy prematurely is because there is not a strong connection between the therapist and the client. There is no emotional bond and no alignment on goals. This significant finding makes the obvious point that the working relationship is hugely important and is a critical key to the long-term success of your therapy work. While the therapy alliance evolves over time, most of the tough work of forming the alliance happens in the early stages of treatment, usually in the first and second sessions.

In the research, there are some qualities of both the client and the therapist that predict therapy alliance (Castonguay, Constantino, & Holtforth, 2006). The client characteristics that predict a positive alliance include:

- Psychological-mindedness
- Expectations for change
- Positive attachments/healthy attachment style

These three qualities are strongly correlated with a likelihood of a positive alliance in therapy. By contrast, the client qualities that predict negative alliance include:

- Emotional avoidance
- Poor attachments/unhealthy attachment styles
- Negative self-talk

There are also therapist qualities that tend to predict alliance in therapy. Three of the qualities that tend to predict positive alliance are:

- Warmth
- Flexibility
- Accurate empathy/interpretation

On the other hand, here are three therapist qualities that tend to predict a negative alliance with the client:

- Rigidity
- Criticalness
- Inappropriate self-disclosure

The quality of the therapeutic alliance is the single biggest predictor of dropout, and these qualities of both the client and the therapist are the biggest predictors of that alliance.

Not only is it important to know why clients drop out, but it is also important to know when they drop out. From a stages-of-change perspective, it appears that the majority of clients drop out in the precontemplation stage of therapy, just as you might expect. Clients who are not considering change drop out more readily. Again, this speaks to the importance of those early sessions. Many times the task is to move precontemplative to the point of becoming contemplators. There are those guys who may not budge from the precontemplative stage for awhile, but there are definitely some who might shift if approached well.

I distinctly remember one client who gave me tons of reasons why he didn't want to stop smoking pot. Each time, I tried to get him away from locking into his resistance by shifting focus, but he insistently declared that he was not going to stop. Toward the end of the session, I explained the stages-of-change model as I drew it out on the whiteboard.

"Stage 1 is where you aren't even thinking about making a change at all. Stage 2 is where you are considering a change. Stage 3 is where you have made a decision to change. Stage 4 is where you are taking action. Stage 5 is where you keep the changes for half a year or more. Where do you think you are with this right now?" I asked, fully expecting him to say he was at the first stage.

"Probably a 1.5," he said. I was caught a little off guard.

"Why a 1.5 and not a 1?" I asked.

"Because it's probably something I need to think about some more," he replied.

With that simple statement—"Probably a 1.5"—we were in business. He agreed to meet again to think about it some more, and over the next three sessions he came to make some decisions to stop his use.

In the early stages of therapy, your task is often to nudge a precontemplator up the scale just a bit, hooking him in enough to return for an honest examination of the issue. Using a motivational approach, the therapist accomplishes this nudge by skillful reflective listening, drawing out both the positive and negative aspects of the problem behavior, as well as the costs and benefits of changing and not changing.

The stages-of-change perspective is a powerful concept in your therapy work with young men. Here's a key point: *Don't treat precontemplators or contemplators like they are ready to change.* They are not. They are, at best, willing to consider making a change. As such, there is much skillful, deep work to be done in the early sessions with these guys.

If it is true that you should not treat precontemplators or contemplators like they are ready to change, this corollary is also true: *Don't treat those in the decision or action stages like they are not ready to change.* If you are really, truly getting a green light to move ahead, then go for it. Recently, I had a guy who called in after losing his temper with his girlfriend.

"I need to get my anger under control," he said in the first five minutes of the very first session.

We didn't need to do the motivational work. Instead, we needed to get moving on helping him manage his anger. In our early sessions, there was not one moment of resistance or reluctance to do the work. He genuinely wanted to get a handle on his temper and was willing to work on it. With guys like this, we skip right to the ways he can accomplish his goal.

Understanding the stages of change is a powerful tool in helping develop greater alignment with your clients and keeping them actively engaged in the therapy process. It helps you shape and pace the therapy work in a way that works optimally for each individual. With that understanding, there are some key concepts that will help you set the right tone for helping your clients make important changes in their lives.

THREE THERAPY TONE-SETTERS THAT HELP YOUNG MEN CHANGE

Down the hall from me, one of my colleagues who sees mostly older adults has attractive art on the walls and nice leather furniture in his office. The feel of the room is classy and relaxed. In my room, by contrast, there is a figurine of Master Chief from the videogame *Halo* on the shelf; there are G.I. Joes, Batman, and Superman on the floor; the art is funky and colorful. There is a wire mobile hanging from the ceiling in one corner and about a dozen little critters called Ugly Dolls on the walls. The room feels casual but has a fun energy about it. I want my clients to feel like they can get comfortable, stretch out, and literally take their shoes off if they want to do that. Many of them grab things off the bookshelf beside the stuffed chair and mess with them during the session as we talk. One of my clients accidentally broke the foot off the Master Chief as he was fidgeting with it. He apologized profusely, but it wasn't a big deal.

Even though the tone of the room where therapy takes place is somewhat important, the real tone of therapy is set by the interpersonal dynamic between the therapist and the client. You can have a great room and get no traction therapeutically; you can also have a dreadful space and see amazing things happen in therapy.

Creating the right tone in therapy is absolutely essential to the success of your work with young men. Beyond the content of what you talk about, or even the process of how you talk about it, is the *feel* of therapy. I've found that there are three considerations for setting the right tone and feel of therapy with young men. All three of these tone-setters may challenge some of your assumptions about therapy. They are different than how many of us were previously trained. Here are the three big tone-setters:

1. Prepare to add structure.
2. Be playful and fun.
3. Use stories and self-disclosure.

These three are not invariably true, because they depend on the client's needs and personality, the therapist's style, and other factors that you cannot always predict or control. Obviously, as in any relationship, some guys require more of one and less of another, much in the same way that good parents flex in order to meet the needs of their children. Some kids need more warmth; others need more firmness. In the same way, some clients need more structure; others need less playfulness. For the most part, though, these three considerations are important in setting the right tone in therapy with your young male clients.

Prepare to Add Structure

Before falling in love with psychology during my sophomore year, I went to college as a mass communications major, certain that I was going to have a career in radio. I got a job at the campus radio station, then a part-time job at a commercial station, and then a prime-time spot at a larger commercial station. Soon I was doing morning drive at a station where we had call-ins, interviews, characters, and all the rest.

My cohost (who, weirdly, also later became a psychologist) and I would finish the show at 10 a.m., then prep until about noon for the show the next day. Our rule of thumb is that we always wanted to prep the next show to be at least a B grade and hope that the guests were good, the call-ins were great, and the banter clicked enough to bring it to an A. We knew there were things that we just couldn't script or plan or predict. We prepared the best show we could, then worked our hardest to make it all come together on the air.

I carry that same attitude into therapy with young men. Many therapists simply show up with their skills and let the client set the agenda. In my experience, if you do that with young men, you are likely to have a lot of really short or really dull sessions. These guys often do not come in the door with something to talk about in the therapy hour. However, they are often glad to be structured and directed in the conversation.

Just as I did for my radio prep, I typically prep the session ahead of time, looking over the goals we set in the first session or two and reviewing our progress. If I need therapeutic materials—handouts, blank paper, etc.—I get those ready before he walks in the door. After we spend a few moments getting caught up, I'll usually ask if there is anything he wants to talk about in the hour. About 9 out of 10 times, he'll say no, and I can suggest that we work on some specific things that I've planned out. If he says yes and he has something he really needs to discuss, then we'll set the other agenda aside and focus on what he needs to process.

To contrast, here's what the early portion of two sessions might look like. First, let's take a look at a session where the client is bringing no agenda into the hour:

Dave: How was the last week for you?
Client: Pretty good.
Dave: Anything to report, good or bad?
Client: Not really. Just a regular week.
Dave: Anything you want to make sure we talk about today?
Client: No. Everything was okay.
Dave: Well, we've been talking about how you can control your anger better. How's that been this week?
Client: Good. No problem.
Dave: Great. Can we pick up there and keep working on that this time?
Client: Sure.

Don't mistake his clipped answers for lack of interest or resistance. He's fine to be in the session; he booked his own appointment and drove himself there! He's waiting for the session to begin. In other words, he is waiting for me to introduce our topic and guide our discussion. Contrast that with another session that starts nearly identically, but quickly goes in another direction:

Dave: How was the last week for you?
Client: It was alright.
Dave: What can you tell me about it?
Client: Not much, really. It was really boring.
Dave: Sometimes boring is good, I suppose.
Client: Especially for me (laughs).
Dave: Right! Well, is there anything you want to make sure we talk about today?
Client: Not too much. My girlfriend hasn't talked to me in three days, that's all. It's not that big a deal, though. She's done it before.
Dave: Three days? Could we talk about that a little?
Client: I guess so.

Like many guys, he has something to talk about, but needs to be eased into it. Notice how he responds to an inquiry about whether he has something to talk about: "Not too much. My girlfriend hasn't talked to me in three days, that's all." He sandwiches important content between "Not too much" and "It's not that big a deal, though."

So I respond by saying, "Three days?" This communicates that I hear this as a fairly big deal. Then I ask, "Could we talk about that a little?" The message here is: "I want to talk about this with you, but I'm not going to wear you out." In this session, we spent nearly the entire hour talking about his confusion and frustration with his girlfriend and set the other agenda aside until the next appointment. It would be extremely easy to miss the subtlety of this communication on his part. Young men are especially prone to hide important concerns in the middle of dismissive phrases like this.

In this case, I prepped the session, but I set the agenda aside when he had something he needed to discuss. In both instances, we had solid, therapeutic sessions. You usually can't lose if you prepare well ahead of time and are ready to structure and direct the session, especially if you can listen for the opportunity to lose the structure and let go of the direction when the time is right.

I would suggest that early in the therapy process—the first or second session—you say something like, "When we meet, I'll usually ask you something like, 'Is there anything you wanted to talk about today?' and if you have something on your mind, then we will spend as much time as we need talking about it. If you don't, then I'll always have a plan for what we can talk about." This helps socialize clients to the therapy process. Most of the time, when you ask whether he has something specific he wants to discuss, you will get a response like, "Not really," or something similar; still, it is good to ask. If he has no agenda, then be ready to structure the hour to work toward goals you have already agreed upon. You will find that some clients nearly always want to structure their own time, while others rely on you to do it. Either way, you should be ready.

In addition to being willing to structure the sessions at the beginning, you should be prepared to give a therapeutic take-away at the end. Nearly two decades ago, I had the honor of interning at The Devereux Foundation outside of Philadelphia. The director of my internship training program, Steve Pfeiffer, was a wise man who taught me many things about being a psychologist. One of the most important things he taught me was the importance of "giving gifts" in therapy.

"I always try to give my clients a gift of some kind each session," he told me and the other interns. He explained that it is a good practice for a client to walk away from the session with something that he did not have before. He called them gifts, but I have come to call them "take-aways" when I refer to them. The take-away might be different for each client and include such things as:

- A new skill
- A new insight
- An affirmation or encouragement
- A validation
- A physical gift, such as a small gratitude journal

This simple idea of therapeutic gift giving has stuck with me, and it has been a challenge for me in my practice for the past two decades.

Whenever possible, I want to give each client a take-away after each session. In most cases, it is something I can plan ahead of time, but, at other times, it is something that happens organically in the session.

Planning for this and looking for these opportunities keeps therapists sharp. When we think like this, we make every session count. It also fits well with the action-oriented relational style of young men who usually want the time to have a clear purpose and outcome. At the end of each session, I typically give a summary about the conversation and sometimes verbally underline what their take-away has been from our time together. Not only should you be prepared to structure the time, but you should also be prepared to have at least one take-away for every session.

Be Fun and Playful

Not too long ago, one of my college-age clients had me laughing so hard that I had to wipe away tears with a tissue. He was going on some extended riff about having to watch some "chick flick" with his girlfriend and his worries that his genitals would fall off for having seen the film. It was funnier than most stand-up comics that I have seen. I love it when my clients make me laugh. I also love it when I can make them laugh. For example, sometimes near the end of a session, I'll offer to fight my clients:

Dave: Thanks for talking today. So before you leave, do you wanna fight?
Client: (Smiling) Nah, that's alright.
Dave: Seriously. I might be skinny, but I'm scrappy. And I fight dirty.
Client: (Laughing)
Dave: I pull hair. I scratch. A lot of high-pitched screaming.
Client: (Laughing) Maybe next time.
Dave: Plan on it.
Client: I'll be ready for you.
Dave: Good. I usually attack from behind.

Now, granted, this is a decidedly unorthodox exchange for a therapist and his client—and not one that I would attempt with every client—but it's my strong sense that this kind of banter is a key to good rapport, as well as part of the whole therapeutic process. The desire for fun and play is a huge part of being a young man. To exclude it from the therapy process strikes me as a huge mistake. Guys might use humor to avoid intimacy at times, but they also use it to facilitate intimacy in relationships (Kiselica, 2003; Kiselica, Englar-Carlson, Horne, & Fisher, 2008). Humor, in fact, can be highly adaptive for many young men, as they use it as a constructive way to blow off stress or deal effectively with personal conflicts (Brooks & Goldstein, 2001; Kiselica, 2001).

The research tells us that young men tend to have a much cruder sense of humor than most women. They tend to joke about taboo subjects more often. Their humor can be much more biting and aggressive. Rather than try to change this, I usually just try to absorb it into our interactions. This doesn't mean that I have to approve of or endorse attitudes and statements that I find distasteful, but it does mean that I have to communicate some comfort with their humor. I've learned that I really have to roll with what I am hearing and listen not only to the serious content of what my clients are saying, but also to their attempts to be fun, funny, and playful. Usually these are opportunities to join with a client in a way that will ultimately be for their good.

Many therapists don't strike me as especially fun or playful, however. They seem to have more contemplative, quiet, or even melancholy temperaments. If this is true for you, I'm not suggesting that you try to be something that you are not. Any attempt to be a comedian will surely be met with some inner eye rolling on the part of the client if that isn't who you really are. Instead, I would suggest that you merely create a context where clients who are fun, funny, and spontaneous can express that and be fully appreciated. As simply as I can state it, you need to laugh with your clients as much as possible.

The traditional therapy session lasts 50 minutes with 10 minutes between sessions to write notes, but in our conference room, we have a video projector with two different video game systems attached to it that often beckons me to come play it. Depending on the client, there are times when I will wrap up the formal session in 45 minutes and play a game for the last 15 minutes. The downside is that it means I have to catch up with my notes at the end of the day, but the upside is that I have another way to be playful and have fun with my client. The tradeoff is worth it.

Many of you don't know Madden from Mario, so you shouldn't feel the need to take up gaming if it isn't for you. However, you may have other fun outlets and interests that you could incorporate into your time with clients. Do you like golf? Perhaps you could set up a small putting green. If you like movies, you could watch clips during sessions to generate discussion. There are so many ways you can be playful and have fun with clients. Start a chess game and play a little each time. Play cornhole (look it up). Ask for his music recommendations and listen to a few songs together.

Therapy with young men should deal with the important issues, but it should also be permeated by a sense of fun. As I shared earlier, in my survey of the values of 151 young men, their top-rated value was *fun* (mean rating of 9.1 out of 10), beating out other values like friendship (mean of 7.5), romance (7.5), and education (8.8). While we are ultimately trying to move clients away from an overriding focus on fun, it's a good idea to be fun and have fun if you want to engage your clients in the beginning. Fun is a deeply ingrained part of their culture, so if you are going to be an effective therapist with young men, it would be wise to discover ways you can make the time fun.

Use Stories and Self-Disclosure

In my training, I was taught the "90/10 rule," which states that most therapy sessions should involve the client talking 90% of the time and the therapist talking 10% of the time. This is certainly a noble idea, but it simply does not fit the needs of many clients. Some young men will talk about 25% of the time; others may talk 98% of the time. The key issue is not the percentage of how much someone talks in the session, but whether the conversation feels reciprocal and interactive. For many young men, therapy will often involve the therapist talking a fair amount.

Therapy with young men should be as fun as possible, and it should also be as compelling and stimulating as possible. There may be no better way to do that than to use stories. It is a good practice to use anecdotes or illustrations of psychological principles that help the point stick better. For example, I might tell a client about a psychological study that put children in a room with a two-way mirror and gave them one marshmallow. The researchers told each child he could have one marshmallow now, but if he waited five minutes, he could have two marshmallows. Then they kept track of the kids until they were teenagers, and guess what they found? The kids who waited and got two marshmallows did better in school and got into less trouble. I ask why this might be, which leads us to a conversation about the concept of *delay of gratification*. I then asked one client if his goal was to become "a two marshmallow kid," and this became a theme that carried across multiple sessions.

One of the reasons why books like *Blink* (Gladwell, 2005) or *Freakonomics* (Levitt & Dubner, 2009) are so popular is that they take social science research and tell them as stories. The facts and principles come through more clearly because the stories make the information more accessible and more "sticky." You can do the same thing in therapy.

Another way to use stories in therapy is to tell your own story. Self-disclosure can be an effective form of therapeutic communication, but it has to be done well. You have probably noticed that I have shared a fair amount of information about myself throughout this chapter. That is by design. Effective therapy with young men often involves a give and take of information and a willingness to be self-disclosing. I watched the editor of this *Counseling and Psychotherapy with Boys & Men* book series, Mark Kiselica, do this brilliantly in a counseling session with a young man in his 20s. Dr. Kiselica would often match information shared by the client with little self-disclosures about his own family, growing up, what sports teams he liked, and so on. The effect of it was that it not only built rapport quickly, but it communicated a critical message about the lack of hierarchy in the relationship. In his clinical work, he has found that modeling appropriate self-disclosure can help boys open up in therapy (Kiselica, 2003; Kiselica & Englar-Carlson, 2008). That has also been my own experience in working with young men.

The early days of psychotherapy were dominated by psychoanalytic models that placed an emphasis on the therapist being a blank slate, someone that the patient could project his or her issues onto. There was considerable attention paid to issues of transference and counter-transference. As such, therapists tended to take a neutral and withholding stance in the sessions. Self-disclosure of the therapist was typically off-limits, being seen as something that would interfere with and potentially contaminate the process.

As psychotherapy has evolved and been more systematically studied, the research has found that therapist self-disclosure may have its place in the therapeutic process. There is no question that it can be inappropriate if done poorly and unwisely, but it is also true that it can have significant benefits if it is done well. In addition to strengthening rapport between the client and the therapist, self-disclosure can actually increase therapeutic effectiveness. Appropriate self-disclosure can also model a level of comfort with revealing personal information that may be especially helpful to some young men who have a more difficult time with this.

The downside of all this, of course, is that inappropriate self-disclosure can actually detract from therapy or potentially even undermine it. There are some specialty areas, like chemical dependency or eating disorders, where self-disclosure is expected and even the norm. There may be some merit to this, but there are considerable risks, as well. I recently had a psychologist tell me that she used to work in a treatment program for clients with eating disorders. "Because many of the therapists there had their own histories of eating disorders, the clients were used to asking all of us if we had ever had anorexia or bulimia," she said. "If you didn't answer or said you didn't have that struggle in the past, then many of them would not open up to you. It was just the culture of the place."

I have also had other therapists tell me that they have shared information about their own past drug use or run-ins with the law, only to find this information being used against them later in the therapeutic process. So sharing that you didn't have an eating disorder might derail you in one setting, but so could sharing that you did have a substance-abuse problem in the past in another. However, if you simply refuse to talk about yourself (which is the default option for many therapists), then you stand the risk of being too remote and too impersonal for many young men. As one college student told me, "I had a therapist who would always say, 'We aren't here to talk about me. Let's talk about you instead,' whenever I asked her the most basic thing, like what she did over the weekend or whether she had ever been out of the country. It felt very uncomfortable."

To find this balance between whether to disclose or not, I suggest three S's that could serve as a guide for you. Self-disclosure should be:

- *Sparse*: The first rule of thumb is that therapists should disclose personal information infrequently. If you find yourself sharing about yourself most sessions, then you probably need to reconsider how much you are talking about yourself.

- *Strategic*: The next guiding principle is that you should share personal information if you have a clear strategy for how the disclosure might be used in the session. Is it to further rapport? Is it to model appropriate self-disclosure? Is it to deepen a therapeutic moment or idea? Before you share, be clear in your own mind why you are revealing this information.
- *Supportive*: The purpose of the self-disclosure should always be to support the client and the therapeutic process. If there is even a twinge of self-indulgence in it, you should keep the thoughts to yourself. Any self-revelation should be for the good of the client and serve the process of moving you closer to your treatment goals.

Over the years, there are two big issues that I have elected to share with some clients. I have had significant sleep problems for 30 years. My troubled sleep is such a big part of my life that when I got married about 20 years ago, many of my friends told stories at my rehearsal dinner about how the only time they had ever seen me mad or out of sorts was when my sleep was disturbed. The second issue I have talked about in therapy is the intense panic attacks I had when I was kid. They followed a major car accident that seriously injured me and my brother. The panic attacks lasted for about a year until, in prepsychologist fashion, I tried to put myself in situations where I tried to have the panic attacks and talk myself through them.

I have not shared this information with all of my clients (not even close), but I have shared it with some when I thought it would be helpful to them. I have also chosen to disclose what I have *not* struggled with in my life if I thought it was for the benefit of the client. For example, I have had some clients who have told me that no one understands their depression. In some instances, I have told them that I have never experienced severe depression and do not know what it is like on a personal level. From there, I try to use that as an opportunity to build empathy by asking them if they could help me understand it better. This does nothing for some clients, but the honest acknowledgement is helpful to many others.

I have also used examples from my personal life as therapeutic metaphors when the time is right. A few years back, I was getting the groceries out of the back of our car. Like most guys, I tried to get all the plastic grocery bags on one arm. I took one step back where the concrete pad of our garage is about an inch higher than the driveway. My ankle twisted and I hit the ground hard, groceries flying, soup and vegetable cans rolling down to the street. It was a bad twist, the kind that makes your whole body shake in pain. I taped my ankle up and was walking on it again in a couple of days. After a week or two, it didn't feel like it had even been sprained. Months later, I was out walking my dogs. Another dog and owner came toward us and I stepped off the sidewalk to let them pass. I stepped on a small utility cover hidden in the grass. The next thing I know—Bam!—I'm on the ground again in pain. I found out that once you have a bad sprain, you are more vulnerable to do it again. I have used this metaphor for clients who are in recovery from addictions or those who have old habits in their relationships. You are vulnerable in your weak spots, even months and years later. The bit of self-disclosure in the form of a story makes the point stick better.

Another form of self-disclosure is revealing your internal process in the here and now by sharing your reactions, your feelings, and your opinions with your client. We have known for quite awhile that a therapist's ability to be genuine is a big predictor of positive therapy outcomes. Therapists who are inauthentic in the slightest will tend to be rejected by adolescent boys and young men, who are typically already skeptical of therapy.

With this in mind, young men tend to value honest, straightforward communication. They want to know what you think and where you stand. They want the feedback. Young men tend to be extremely uncomfortable with the blank-slate therapist or the counselor who simply does reflective listening and never voices an opinion or position. Instead, they typically respond better when they believe the communication is on the level.

During my third session with a client who was having to make an important decision about whether to drop out of college or not, I asked him if it would be better for us to air out his concerns and keep looking at all the angles, or if it would be better for him if I gave an opinion. I made it clear to him that I was more than happy to keep my opinions to myself. He said, "Just talking it out hasn't helped me in the past. I would rather just hear what you have to say." I gave him my opinion, which he accepted, and we were able to move quickly toward wrapping up.

Since I typically take a more motivational approach and try to draw a client to the point of making his own decisions, I am not fast with an opinion. However, I have come to see that if you use a motivational approach well early in the therapy process, it builds such a solid foundation in the relationship that you can offer reactions and opinions later (as early as the third or fourth session, usually) that don't undermine the relationship or compromise his self-efficacy.

I had a recent example of this when an 18-year-old client told me that he was having unprotected sex with his girlfriend at her request. I asked him what he thought about this, and he expressed a lot of ambivalence, saying that it was more pleasurable, but he was worried about her getting pregnant, that he wanted to make her happy, but he didn't want to have a child, and so on. After discussing this for awhile, he said, "I guess I should just make her happy." Normally, in a pure motivational model, I would roll away from that and not get him to lock into that answer and keep processing it, but we had a solid enough relationship where I felt like I could offer some direction.

"Would it be helpful for me to offer an opinion about this, or would you prefer that I didn't?" I asked.

"No, I'd like to hear what you think," he said.

"I know you want to be a good boyfriend and have a good relationship," I said. "But it seems this may be one of those times when you have to make a decision that is tough to make, but might be better for everyone in the long run."

"I know," he said, "That's what I have been thinking." He said this as if he had not just made a completely contradictory statement a few moments earlier. "I just need to talk to her about it again."

In the next session, he said that he had talked to her about it and that she had been mildly upset by it, but agreed to let him start using protection. "I just needed someone to tell me that," he said. He needed the nudge.

You can also be self-disclosing not just with your personal revelations or by expressing your opinions, but also with your emotional reactions. One study found that clients in therapy for trauma issues were more satisfied with therapists who were more self-disclosing when the clients expressed intense emotions, especially anger, than they were with therapists who maintained neutral expression and showed no emotion (Dalenberg, 2004). Another study found that therapists who expressed their own feelings of frustration or annoyance when their clients got hostile were more effective at resolving the anger compared to those therapists who did not reveal their feelings during these moments (Hill et al., 2003). This research challenges the assumptions that it is best to hold back on your emotions when your client is provocative or hostile. Instead, it may be a good idea to have genuine reactions in your sessions. As a therapist, you can react in emotionally honest ways without being judgmental. Young men usually value this form of communication.

You can self-disclose in a number of ways in therapy, like personal revelations, opinions, and honest emotional reactions. These decisions to disclose your actions, your thoughts, your feelings—or not to disclose these things—are important moments in the therapeutic process. Simply declining to talk about yourself or to give direct reactions may solve some problems, but it may create others and strip you of an important tool in helping your client. Like most parts of therapy, hitting the right balance is an art form that requires wisdom, experience, and ongoing judgment calls. In therapy with young men, self-disclosure is often a powerful part of the helping process.

Creating the right tone and feel is essential to good therapy with young men, so be ready to structure the conversation, to be playful and fun, and to use stories and self-disclosure. These three tone-setting ingredients will usually lead to satisfying and productive therapy sessions.

THERAPY TAKE-AWAYS

1. Assess what stage of change a person is in when he starts the therapy process and do not assume that precontemplators or contemplators are ready to make a change. Take a close look at *importance* and *confidence* for making a change.
2. Use structure, playfulness, and stories to set the right tone in therapy with young men.
3. When you use personal stories and self-disclosure in therapy, make sure that they are sparse, strategic, and supportive to have the most impact.

4

Principles and Pitfalls

Gabriel, Ricky, and Marlon have just a few things in common. All have been using drugs or alcohol to some extent. All have some history of breaking the rules. All of them have some trouble with anger at times. Beyond that, the similarities stop. They have different personalities, different family histories, different ways of managing their thoughts and feelings, different needs, and different worldviews.

As we have seen, there are frequent themes that are likely to emerge in therapy with young men. They often present with behavioral problems, higher rates of substance problems, and feel greater stigma around seeking help, among other concerns. However, among young men, there is a wide range of difference. Some guys in therapy do not have any significant behavior problems; some have never even experimented with any drugs; others are highly tuned into their emotions. Because of this, there is no fixed, lockstep approach to therapy with young men, especially after the first two sessions. However, there are some guiding principles that inform the tone and approach to therapy with adolescent boys and young men.

THE CASE MODEL

The four guiding principles are *collaborate, align, steer,* and *encourage.* Together, they form the acronym CASE. The CASE model is easy to keep in mind and shapes the decisions you make as a therapist from start to finish.

Collaborate

Marlon was exceedingly polite to me from the first time I met him. He stood and shook my hand when I greeted him and called me "sir" whenever possible. Being polite is a good trait, but he interacted with me the way he was raised to treat those in authority. It was in the middle of the first session with Marlon when this exchange happened:

"So your aunt raised you since middle school?" I asked, clarifying what he had been telling me about his earlier years.

"Yes, sir," he said.

"And she is still pretty involved in your life," I reflected.

"Yes, sir," he said again.

"Got it. By the way, I appreciate you being polite, but you don't need to call me sir," I said.

"It was just how I was raised," he said.

"I understand. It's respectful. It's a good way to be," I said. "But we usually call people in authority 'sir,' and I'm not in any authority over you. I want to make sure you know I see us as being on the same level with each other."

"That's fine," he said as he nodded, then we picked up the conversation from where we were before.

For me to break our flow deliberately, it had to be something really important. But, in my estimation, one of the more important tasks in the early sessions is establishing that I am not in an authority role. Certainly there are more reasons to call someone "sir" other than the fact that he is in authority over you; we say it to our elders and to strangers who provide us with services, for example. But I wanted to use it as an opportunity to spell out the nature of our relationship. There is no hierarchy here, I was announcing. I am not the boss. Instead, this relationship will be all about collaboration.

Rather than attempting to establish myself as an expert or authority figure, I begin with the key principle that therapy with a young man is a cooperative partnership. We are on the same team, working toward the same goals. Therapy with adolescent boys and young men is most successful when it is nonhierarchical and nonauthoritarian. There should be no battle for control and no attempts to assert power, at least not on the part of the therapist. This message should be sent loud and clear in the first two sessions. When necessary, it may need to be reiterated later in the process, as well. It will make all the difference in your work.

Align

As we learned from our discussion of therapy dropouts, the best predictor of whether a client will stop coming before his treatment goals are met is the strength of the alliance between the client and therapist. As much as possible, you want to stay in the game in those first two critical sessions. The best way to do that is to quickly form an alliance with your client. You do this by claiming him as your client, understanding him well, and helping him meet his goals. Before the first session, he may not have even been able to articulate his goals, but by the end of the session, you will have hopefully made it clear that you are working on his behalf toward objectives he has said will make his life better.

The first part of alignment is claiming your client. He may have walked in believing you are an agent of his parents or the agency or some other authority, but he needs to walk out knowing you represent him, his needs, his best interest. Some models of therapy with adolescents regard the family or the parents as the principal client, whereas I do not. I believe the young man is your client. Family therapy and parent consultation are often important and necessary parts of the treatment regimen for some adolescent (Selekman, 2005; Sells, 1998; Smith, Sells, Rodman, & Reynolds, 2006). What I am describing, however, is a model of individual therapy for adolescent boys and young men, or, as I have called them previously, pre-adult males. If you are aligned with his parents, you may not be able to be fully aligned with him, at least not in some instances. The first order of business in forming an alignment is being clear with yourself that he is your client.

To be clear, there are many times when a family therapist needs to be involved in helping the young man get better. For the family therapist, the family is the client. However, when you are doing individual work with a young man, he should clearly be understood by all parties—parents, family members, outside agencies—to be your client.

Claiming your client is a cognitive and behavioral process, but the next parts of alignment involve mostly affective processes. To fully align, you have to be well attuned to your client. Becoming attuned in therapy is complex and nuanced, but ultimately it involves a unique rhythm with each unique individual. As you tune in closely to nonverbal communication, speaking style, comfort level, sense of humor, intellectual level, and areas of interest, you try to align your style and approach to fit the client's, not the other way around. What this means is that you need to be willing and able to adjust as needed. Some clients need to move quickly; others need you to move slowly. Some like banter and joking, while others are put off by it. Each client requires an adjustment. This is not to say that the therapist is a chameleon, changing with every social interaction. However, it does mean that the therapist is constantly seeking attunement, the way any good attachment figure does.

Attunement is a dance that requires subtle moves and corrections almost constantly, especially in the beginning sessions of therapy. You may find yourself fully attuned with your client at the beginning of a session and out of phase with him at the end. Somewhere in the middle, it got out of rhythm through some nonverbal communication or a poorly timed comment. I recall one session where a client said he was going to cut his hair short for the summer. I made a comment that this made good sense during the hot humid months. I noticed we got out of phase at the moment I made that comment. I have no idea why, but he reacted negatively to it in a real, though almost imperceptible way. Perhaps he thought I was saying I didn't like his current look. Perhaps he was thinking I had missed the point about why he wanted to cut his hair. Maybe he thought I sounded like his parents. I still have no idea. My point is that it is easy to get out of alignment with a client with just minor missteps.

Despite your best efforts, you will have many slipups with your clients. There is no need to get hypervigilant or anxious about this. It's going to happen. You'll have a neutral facial expression when he was expecting more emotion—or you'll show emotion and it will make him self-conscious. You'll make a joke that falls flat. You'll look away at the wrong time. There are a hundred ways to mess up. The good news is that you can be in attunement, then get out of phase, but you can also be out of attunement and get back in sync. You can have little therapeutic ruptures that can be repaired. In fact, there is evidence that this "rupture-repair" sequence can actually improve the long-term alliance in therapy (Constantino et al., 2002; Castonguay et al., 2006; Stiles et al., 2004).

Attunement in therapy is paradoxical. It requires a lot of energy and focus, but never feels pressured. It is intense, but entirely relaxed. The therapist leads, yet takes his cues from his client. This is the art of therapy that can never be fully captured by manualized, lockstep approaches. Becoming attuned is really about forming an honest, authentic attachment.

Becoming attuned to your client will ultimately open the door to the most important part of alignment: experiencing and expressing *accurate empathy*. The best way to align with your client is to understand him well. You understand him and he feels it. You do this most effectively by using reflective listening skills. My goal is usually to give around three reflections for every open question I ask, though this varies from client to client, depending on their response styles. The quality of the reflection is also important. While there is plenty of room for *simple reflections* (e.g., "So your anger gets out of control very quickly"), there is evidence that more *complex reflections* (e.g., "So your anger gets out of control very quickly, but you're open to new ideas about how to manage it better") may have more impact (Tollison et al., 2008).

Aligning with your client begins by claiming him as your client in your thoughts and actions. When that happens, you are freed up to become attuned to him as you build a bond of trust and authentic attachment. From there, you explore and consider the world through his eyes, giving you increasingly more accurate empathy. When you have done these things well, you have laid an exceptional foundation for helping him.

Steer

During a supervision session, a young therapist told me about her difficult 16-year-old client who wouldn't give her eye contact and sat slouched back in the chair. She felt like she had tried everything to engage him and still he seemed bored out of his mind and resentful.

"How do you start the session?" I asked.

"I try a little chitchat to ease into it," she began. "Then I ask him what he would like to talk about today and he says, 'Nothing,' or 'I don't know' or something like that. I ask if he would like to talk about school or his parents or whatever and he says, 'Not really.' I feel like we are completely stuck."

This is the typical lament of counselors who work with young men. After lots of attempts to find a handle, they often feel like they are getting nowhere. Many therapists are trained in client-centered models that work best when the client charts the course. For many individuals who come to therapy, this is a good fit, but for many young men, this approach quickly stalls out.

The alternative is to be client-centered but therapist-directed. This is usually essential in the first two sessions because they will chart your course for the rest of therapy. From that point forward, you should steer each session along the path you have established in those earlier meetings. Instead of fishing for what he wants to talk about or even asking if he would like to talk about specific issues or topics, you propose the agenda for the session. You guide it and direct it throughout the entire therapy process.

There is a subtle but important distinction between the need to be nonauthoritarian (i.e., collaborate) and the need to steer the therapy process. With young men, *therapy is steered and directed as a service to the client*. For example, if you hired a personal trainer, he would guide you and keep you on track, but he would not be your boss. The two of you would establish what your goals would be, then you would work together to meet them, with him guiding the process. It is not about authority and hierarchy, but about what roles each of you play in the relationship.

In therapy, the same process happens: mutual determination of goals with direction and instruction from the therapist as needed. If a client wanted to generate the focus for the session, you would go with that, but those times are rare. Most of the time, he will usually want you to guide your time together. He is looking to you for direction. Your best bet is to provide it.

Providing direction can be surprisingly subtle. Much of the time, it involves drawing out a certain type of talk from your clients. Motivational interviewing places a strong emphasis on eliciting and listening carefully for "change talk," the kind of speech that favors positive movement. In a motivational interviewing framework, there are four kinds of change talk:

1. *Disadvantages of the status quo*: when the client talks about the negative aspects of his current situation
2. *Advantages of change*: when the client talks about the potential good things that could come with making a change
3. *Optimism for change*: when the client expresses confidence that he could make a change if he really wanted to do it
4. *Intention to change*: when the client says he is willing or committed to making a change in his life

Motivational interviewing stresses the importance of listening for any of these forms of change talk and drawing out these pro-change comments, while avoiding or rolling away from any resistant or anti-change talk. Good therapists who use motivational approaches are alert to these sometimes subtle communications and focus on the opportunities for change.

Here is a brief hypothetical interaction that illustrates the difference between keying in on the pro-change talk or missing it. This is what it might look like to miss the change talk:

Client: I don't see the big deal about weed. It's a natural substance. It's a lot safer than alcohol, and alcohol is legal. It doesn't make sense to me why people think it's such a bad thing.
Therapist: How many other people see it doesn't really line up with how you see it.
Client: Exactly.
Therapist: So how does it fit into your life right now?
Client: Just whenever. Some days, it's just once. Other days, it's a couple of times. It just depends.
Therapist: When do you usually smoke during the day?
Client: At night after everyone goes to bed. I just smoke, then go watch some TV and fall asleep.
Therapist: So it's part of your evening ritual, part of going to bed.
Client: Yeah, but I don't really need to do it to get to sleep. I could stop if I had to and still get to sleep.
Therapist: So how does it help you besides that in the evening?
Client: Just to chill out. It makes my TV shows more interesting, too.
Therapist: You feel like it makes the evening a better experience.
Client: Pretty much. It's just a good way to end the day. It's something to look forward to.

The therapist here in this made-up bit of dialogue is doing a decent job of reflective listening and keeping the focus on the area of concern, but he missed the change talk. When the client says, "I could stop if I had to and still get to sleep," he is expressing some change talk. In this case, he is showing some optimism for change, that he could change if he really had to or wanted to do it. That would be the direction for the therapist to take the conversation by reflecting back what he has said and exploring his confidence to make a change. Let's take the conversation from that point and move it forward with a focus on the change talk:

Client: Yeah, but I don't really need to do it to get to sleep. I could stop if I had to and still get to sleep.
Therapist: You feel like you could stop if you put your mind to it.
Client: Absolutely.
Therapist: It really seems to be such a big part of your nighttime routine, but you still feel like you could change it.

Client: Oh yeah, if I had to. It would be tough for a few days, but I definitely could do it.

Therapist: Tell me how you are so confident about that.

Client: I've done it before. I went for two weeks without it this past summer when my family was on vacation.

The focus on the change talk shifts the direction of the conversation and opens up other chances to move him toward change. Drawing out that subtle change talk is a big part of helping him get closer to making that decision.

Encourage

Therapists as long ago as Adler recognized the importance of encouragement in helping people get better (Adler, 1956). But as therapy became more focused on technique, this essential component got neglected in the literature. In my view, all clients need encouragement—direct affirmation and optimism—from their therapists, but none more so than young men. Nearly all men (96%) who have come to therapy report that they were influenced to attend by someone else, and over a third acknowledge that they would have not sought help at all if it were not for this nudge (Cusack, Deane, Wilson, & Ciarrochi, 2004). Men are less likely to have favorable opinions of therapy and seeking outside help in general than women, and men with gender-role conflicts tend to have a more negative set of expectations about therapy (Schaub & Williams, 2007). When young men come into therapy, they are much more likely to expect that it is not going to be a good experience for them. Many are afraid it will be seen as a sign of weakness, or they fear that they will be pushed emotionally beyond what they would like.

Because of this, it is essential for them to leave the first two sessions of therapy feeling encouraged. In general, young men do not feel encouraged after having unburdened themselves to someone else, nor do they tend to feel encouraged by having someone listen well to them. Instead, they tend to feel encouraged by direct affirmations. If there is one consistent thread in my practice of therapy with young men, it is the use of affirmations for the purpose of encouragement.

To be effective, affirmations have to be done honestly and with integrity. They are not flattery. A good affirmation is positive, honest, attuned feedback to the client. You should not tell a client he is a smart guy if he is not. You should not tell a client he is courageous or strong if he is not. You should only say these sorts of things when there is a core of truth to them. Your client must trust you completely to give honest feedback. If you start to flatter him, you not only run the risk of losing his trust, but you also fail him by giving him information about himself that he cannot rely upon.

To be deeply encouraging to a young man, you need to find out what personal characteristics and traits are important to him, then look for evidence of these in him. When you see these things, you let him know what you see. Saying things like, "I'm impressed by how hard you keep fighting this anxiety. You really are a pretty strong guy," can be encouraging and affirming if it has the ring of truth to it.

In my experience, there are two general areas where guys desire encouragement and affirmation: strength and likeability. Young men soak up encouragement about their strength, including emotional, moral, and intellectual strength. They also want to hear that they are likeable and desirable. In the first meeting, I work hard to like each client I see. For those clients that I don't find likeable, I tend to keep this information to myself. But for those individuals that I connect with and genuinely like, I will almost always tell them this. Without being too effusive, I may say something like, "I'm really glad you came in today. I like you a lot and I can tell I will enjoy talking to you." This accomplishes two things: It lets him know where I stand with him, and it affirms that he is a likeable person.

One caution is in order here. More than a few clients have told me that they have not felt at all encouraged by previous therapists who told them they were doing well when they were not. As one guy told me, "(My therapist) just kept saying, 'You're doing better' and 'You're improving,' but I knew I wasn't. I still felt really depressed and really anxious most of the time." In this sense, young men do not typically respond well to cheerleading or baseless claims of progress. Telling the client he is improving when he is not will put you out of attunement with your client quickly. To be encouraging, a therapist has to speak truth in a way that lets the client know you get it, you understand the depth of the struggle, you see the road ahead, and you are willing to be honest about it.

Encouragement is absolutely essential to the therapy process. Getting good at it is an art form that requires the right balance of saying enough to make an impact but not so much that it is overdone or ineffective. To do this, it has to come from an authentic place in the therapist. It can't be seen purely as a technique to build rapport. Instead, it has to flow from a mindset of genuinely trying to understand and appreciate the young man in your office.

SEVEN TRAPS THERAPISTS SHOULD AVOID

The CASE model guides us with what we should do in therapy, but it's worth considering the other side of the equation. There are definitely some traps to avoid and some things we should *not* do in our therapy with young men.

In my third meeting with Marlon, he told me that he had been selling drugs for his roommate to help pay the rent. In fact, he had been selling them at his own workplace, just outside the backdoor of the kitchen. The expression on my face probably didn't register it, but inside, my mind was whirring. I was thinking something like, "This is a really bad, really stupid idea."

I began by asking him how this started, and he explained how his roommate had talked him into it over the past few months, how his paycheck was thinner than he expected, and how he only sold when the manager was not around.

Then I tripped up.

"This sounds like a bad idea," I said. "If you got caught, you could lose your job. You could get arrested again."

Marlon just shrugged. "I only sell to people I know," he explained.

"But you could still get busted," I said. "A lot of the guys I have seen who've gotten arrested would tell you that it happens when they least expect it."

"It's alright," he assured me, dismissing the topic. "I won't do it for long."

Everything I said was right, but I had messed up. I had fallen into a trap. On the surface, it didn't seem like a major mistake, but it was clearly an error on my part. Had I fallen into this trap in an earlier session, it could have derailed us for good. As it was, we were able to recover.

Like this misstep with Marlon, there are a few big traps you can fall into or that can tangle you up in therapy. They have caught me many times over the years and made me wish for a do-over with some clients. The more I have become aware of these danger zones, though, the more I have been able to avoid them.

Gabriel, Ricky, and Marlon all pulled me toward one or more of these traps. I dodged them with Gabriel and Ricky, but I stepped right into a couple with Marlon. Maybe it was because he didn't have any other male figure in his life and I felt the need to be like his dad and act like an authority figure, teach him, and try to get him to shape up. When I found myself getting caught in the trap, I was able to get out in time to salvage the relationship and stay in the game. With other clients in the past, though, I haven't been as successful in getting myself out of the mess that I had stepped in. I'll share some successes and failures in avoiding seven big therapeutic traps.

Being the Boss

With Gabriel, I had the invitation to screw up right off the bat. His mom, well-intentioned as she was, all but ordered me to do it. She was a forceful woman who knew what she wanted me to do.

"I want you to tell him that he cannot drink and drive again!" she said during my first meeting with them. "He needs to hear it from you!"

Honestly, this sounds like a reasonable request from a parent. After all, Gabriel nearly killed himself and was facing serious DUI charges. It makes good sense that I would tell him he cannot drink and drive again. I very much wanted him never to drink and drive again. But I had to resist the urge—and instruction—to tell him what to do. If I didn't hold back, I would become another authority, another parent. Fortunately, I didn't follow orders.

One of the biggest stylistic traps that can trip up a therapist of young men is being the boss. You become the boss when you posture yourself in an authority role: scolding, instructing, preaching. Many young men, including Gabriel, enter therapy with the expectation that it will be another adult lecture, sort of like going to the vice principal's office or checking in with a probation officer. Because of this, you have to work extra hard not to get caught in this trap. Right from the beginning, it needs to be clear to your client that you don't want to be his mom or dad, that you are not going to wrestle with him for control or authority. Instead, the message you want to send to your client is that he should be the boss of his own life and that he can be a good boss.

This doesn't mean you are not directive. As you've seen, being directive is often essential to good therapy with adolescent boys and young men. Being directive does not mean being the boss, however. When you try to be the boss of your client, you tell them what to do as if you were an authority figure: Don't ever drink and drive again. Obey your parents. Stop skipping school. Follow the rules. No doubt, all are wise things to do, but when you try to be the boss of your client, you undercut the change process and you get caught in a sticky trap that may derail you in a big way.

Being in a Hurry

Years ago, I had a client who came in a month before he was to ship off for his freshman year at college. He had a serious drinking problem, and his parents had decided that they were going to set the limit on him by not paying for college until he came to counseling. Unfortunately, they waited until July to put the hammer down.

In the first session, this young man, Jake, came in with arms folded and a scowl, insistent that he didn't need to be there. His father, a big, hot-headed man, started with a litany of Jake's alcohol problems: He drank at least five days a week, got drunk at least three times a week, had gotten into numerous fights and altercations when drunk, had driven home drunk on a few occasions, and had at least two blackouts in the past three months. All of this had apparently been going on for the past year or more.

Jake did not dispute any of these facts. He just thought all of this was normal for guys his age. According to him, he did not drink any more than any of his friends, and none of them were being hauled off to see a counselor. He liked to drink, he freely admitted, but he didn't have a drinking problem.

"I'm not going to pay for you to go off to college just to party," his dad said, his face getting redder as he spoke. "You're not taking this seriously!"

Jake just rolled his eyes and slouched down into his chair. "There isn't a problem," he muttered under his breath.

Three things quickly became apparent to me: First, Jake did, in fact, have a serious drinking problem. Second, his father would not accept anything less than getting this fixed before he went off to college in three weeks. And third, Jake had no interest in any of this.

The perfect storm of all this raised my anxiety. Here was a serious issue that needed to be addressed in a short amount of time with someone who wasn't willing to work. He made it clear from the first meeting that he "had to come" to therapy, but felt like it was a waste of time.

Before I had any training or experience with motivational models of therapy, my approach to this situation was much like other therapists I knew in similar situations: I started pedaling hard and fast. I started trying to convince him that he had a problem, that it was likely to cause him trouble in college, that we really needed to get to work because the time was short.

As Monty Roberts, the fabled horse whisperer, said of his work, "If you act like you've only got fifteen minutes, it'll take all day. Act like you've got all day and it'll take fifteen minutes." For Jake, it was more like, "If you act like you've got three weeks, it will take all year." Despite—or maybe because of—my pleading for us to move forward, Jake refused to budge.

It's so easy for therapists to be in a hurry, especially in situations like this. There is often a sense of urgency that this serious problem needs to be corrected right away. As therapists, we give the instinctively human response: We panic. It's easy to see why so many therapists fall into this trap in their work with young men. The behaviors—drug use, drinking, aggression, and the like—are genuinely concerning and the stakes are high. Nonetheless, it is still a trap to be in too much of a hurry.

Being the Expert

Over the years of working with young men, I have learned a lot about alcohol and marijuana. I know how many drinks will get the average-sized guy drunk; I know how marijuana tends to affect motivation and memory. I know the biological processes of addiction. But, for the most part, I've learned to keep this information to myself in my therapy work. That wasn't always the case, though. It certainly wasn't the case with Jake.

With Jake, I found myself being the expert much of the time. Perhaps if he knew more about how dangerous binge drinking could be or the signs of alcoholism, he would reconsider his use. Maybe the issue was that he lacked the right information, having been misinformed or misled by his peers. If I could disabuse him of some of his misconceptions about drinking, he might quit or at least cut down. So I set out to give him the right information with the hopes that it would set him straight.

Of course, it didn't. In fact, it didn't make a dent in his thinking or his behavior. Despite a meager track record of success in using this approach, many therapists still find themselves acting like conduits of expert information, especially on matters related to drinking or drug use. It rarely works, and it usually thwarts the progress of therapy. Being the expert can be great if you are teaching a course, consulting with parents, or even supervising other professionals. In therapy with young men, though, it's usually just a trap you need to avoid.

Being Pushy

It won't surprise you to know that Jake failed out of college his first semester. He got a 0.4 GPA (that's right, a 0.4, not a 4.0) because he got a C in his flag football P.E. class and failed everything else. He returned to my office, tail a little between his legs, with angry dad in tow who was hitting the couch again, furious with Jake for his colossal screwup. This time, Jake's tack was not to deny that there had been a problem, but that he had learned his lesson and it was all behind him.

"I didn't know what college was going to be like," he said, "but now I do. I know what to expect this time."

"You've got to knock off all this partying," his dad demanded. "That's what killed you."

"I can handle it," he said. "That's not the problem."

"Well, what was the problem then?" his dad asked, his face getting red again.

"I just didn't take it that seriously," Jake said, perhaps not realizing how infuriating this would be to his dad.

"So I just paid thousands of dollars for you to not take it seriously? That's just great!" his dad roared. "Just great!"

During this round, I knew I had more than three or four sessions to work, so I didn't try to move so fast. But because Jake was so resistant, I felt like I really had to crash through his denial. In the next session, when he gave me his "It's not a problem" mantra, I gave him my "Clearly it is" retort, complete with a review of his recent screwup and statistics about drinking and research about what predicts ongoing drinking problems. I was not only the expert, but I was a pushy expert. His protests and rationalizations did not deter me. I had to break through. The more resistant he became, the more forceful I got in my display of facts and appeals for him to change.

Again, you won't be surprised to learn that he returned to college and failed out once again. All my pushing, expert knowledge, and forcefulness were for naught. Some may argue that I needed to push more, to be even more forceful. I would argue exactly the opposite. Being pushy is a huge trap that has sidelined many well-intentioned therapists.

Being Critical

The step beyond being the expert is being pushy. There is also a step beyond being pushy. It's when you become openly critical of your client. You are disapproving, even a little chastising. When Jake told me that he had driven after he had a little too much to drink on a few occasions,

I felt the need to go on record with him to express my disapproval. He wasn't just doing something that was affecting him; he was also doing something that could affect other people.

Of course, I was right. Drinking and driving is a ridiculously bad and selfish thing to do. It's also bad to disrespect your parents, hit your girlfriend, sell drugs, have sex with a girl who has passed out, or shoplift. As a therapist, you should see these things as morally wrong. Therapists are moral beings and therapy is, in many respects, a moral enterprise. The question is not whether these things and dozens of other behaviors are wrong (they clearly are), but how you respond to them.

When I criticized Jake, I did not gain ground therapeutically. I did not make him any less likely to drink and drive in the future. I may have eased my conscience or expressed some sense of personal outrage, but I didn't advance the cause of getting him to do this any less in the future. I don't have to endorse the behavior, dismiss it, or minimize it, but when I start to criticize, I fall into a trap that shuts my client down and makes the therapy process far less effective.

Being Too Certain Too Soon

You recall that when Ricky's parents first came in, they portrayed him as a spoiled brat of a kid. The issue was that he had no respect for authority. However, when Ricky himself came in, it became apparent that there was so much more to him, and things were much more complex than his parents had originally portrayed them to be.

Ricky is a perfect example of the pitfalls of being too certain too soon of what the problem is. If you merely take his parents' perspective, you would simply see an oppositional-defiant adolescent who needed to work on his behavior and attitude toward his parents. You might even do a skillful job at getting him on board with therapy goals and perhaps even get him to agree to do some work on having a better attitude. But you would probably be off the mark. This is not to say that he couldn't stand some help with his crappy attitude. It would almost certainly be good for him to do that. The problem is that you would miss so much of him, including the more important issues that need to be addressed.

Seasoned therapists may, in some respects, be more vulnerable to this. They have seen so many clients that, over time, they start to see patterns: This is an Asperger's kid who needs social skills training. This is an ADHD boy who needs work on being able to stop and think. This is a bipolar young man who needs help with coping skills and emotional regulation. They've seen it before, and it's easy just to fit the client in front of them into one of the types of clients they know so well. While there is some benefit to this, there is also a danger of missing so much, even if we are right about the diagnostic category. Being too certain too soon is a trap that can snag sharp young therapists and well-practiced clinicians alike.

Being Too Much in the Box

Gabriel is back in my office, and he is complaining about the AA meetings he is being forced to attend. I like AA, and I've seen it be helpful to many of my clients, but right now it's not working for him.

"You have to say you're an alcoholic," he explains. "I'm not alcoholic, I just got into a freakin' car wreck."

Gabriel may or may not be an alcoholic, but like many clients, he resists being labeled. If I insist that he accept the term, I will likely lose my connection with him. Instead, we will just focus on the drinking behavior itself and leave the label for later.

Not only do we as therapists sometimes err when we automatically put clients into neat little boxes in our heads (as in the previous trap), but we also can get tripped up by making them accept our labels. In some circles, for instance, it is absolutely essential for a problem-drinking client to acknowledge that he is an "alcoholic" before he can really progress in treatment. In some programs, a client who has acted-out sexually must say that he is a "sex offender" before work can advance. A young man with wild mood swings must call himself "bipolar" before the treating professionals are comfortable with him leaving the hospital. It isn't whether these labels or others like them—"addict," "Asperger's," "ADHD," to name just a few at the beginning of the alphabet—aren't helpful. In many cases, they can be extremely helpful in allowing clients to understand their difficulties and manage their condition. The point here, though, is that rigid insistence on a label early in the treatment process just gunks up all your momentum if the client isn't ready to accept it.

For some, having a label can be liberating and even validating. I had one client who said it was "awesome" that someone finally told him he had Asperger's because it completely explained 20 years of not fitting in, misreading cues, and getting fixated on odd interests. At the same time, I have had some other clients with the same struggles who would be deeply offended and put off by the label.

It is not that labels or diagnostic terms are bad, but they should not be required for treatment to progress. If they are helpful to the client, then use them, but if they are not, then hold back. When in doubt, hold back.

With Jake, I was pretty certain he was an alcoholic from the first session, but my desire for him to own that label didn't do him any good. He wasn't ready to accept this, and he didn't find it helpful. In fact, he didn't even agree that it was true. It would have been better for me to have kept this label to myself.

It's possible that there wasn't much I could have done to help Jake, but my guess is that I could have helped him a lot more if I hadn't kept stepping into all these traps. Since I have started using a motivational approach, I haven't tripped up as much, and I've been more helpful to my clients. Sometimes knowing what not to do is as important as knowing what to do. We all stumble in our therapy work from time to time, but knowing these traps can help you steer clear of them and stay in the game.

THERAPY TAKE-AWAYS

1. Use the CASE Model in therapy with young men: collaborate, align, steer, and encourage.
2. Draw out as much *change talk* from your client as possible and get away from resistance talk.
3. Avoid common pitfalls like being the boss, being in a hurry, being the expert, being pushy, being critical, being too certain too soon, or being too much "in the box."

5

Beginning Therapy
The First Sessions

The first time I met Gabriel, we barely spoke to each other. He sat in the room and listened to his parents rattle off his list of sins and transgressions (almost literally in those terms). He barely said a word. With Ricky, his parents came in first without him, and he came in by himself for the second session. And with Marlon, he came in by himself for the first appointment, and I never met his aunt who had referred him. Therapy started for each of them in three different ways: attending with parents, attending alone after the parents had met privately first, or attending alone with no parent meeting. All three are legitimate ways to start, but require slightly different approaches.

Starting off therapy well is absolutely essential in your work with young men. The parent meeting and the first two meetings directly with the client are probably the most important of any sessions of the entire process. Because some young men are still living with their parents and may be legally minors, the first session is usually with parents, either with or without the client himself. It is usually optimal for the parents to come to the first session if they are still supporting him, regardless of the young man's age, whenever this is possible. In some instances, this isn't possible, or the young man is completely autonomous and independent, so the first session will obviously involve just the client himself. I will give a framework for three initial sessions: the client and parent together, the parents only, and the client only. In addition, I will also give some detailed thoughts about the second direct contact with the client himself.

THE FIRST SESSION: PARENTS ONLY

Ricky's parents came in without him during the first session. They wanted to give me their perspective and also check me out to see if they felt like I could be helpful to their son.

"He just won't talk to us at all," his mother said, her tone revealing years of frustration with her son. "I'd be surprised if he talks with you either."

This is a common concern of many parents. They worry that because their son won't talk with them that he won't talk with the therapist. It seldom happens that a client refuses to talk, but it's understandable why parents who have been frozen out by their son would have this worry. Like Ricky's mom and dad, many parents want to come in first so that they can talk freely without fear of upsetting their son in front of the therapist and potentially spoiling the therapy relationship. This is often a wise idea and should be left to their discretion whether to invite their son to the first session or not. Whether he comes or not, the content and coverage is essentially the same, but the tone may be different. In either case, you will want to get the following information during that first visit:

- *Current concerns*: What brought them here? What are they most concerned about for their son?
- *Relevant history*: How long has this been going on? What was he like as a younger kid? As an earlier adolescent? What do I need to know about the family history? Have there been other issues before this?
- *Strengths*: What are his strengths? What does he do well? What are his most positive personal qualities? Where are his passions?
- *Their goals*: What are the parents' goals for therapy? How would they know if we were making progress or had accomplished these goals?
- *Identifying my client*: Are the parents on board with the fact that he will be my client and not them? What if he does not want to work on these goals but wants to work on other goals? Would they still support the therapy?
- *Defining my role and approach*: Are the parents okay with the notion that a therapist or counselor of young men is more like a guide or a coach than a parent or another authority figure? Are they okay with a more motivational model that involves taking an honest look at the issues rather than trying to convince or persuade him? Are they in support of an approach that involves us working on the issues he is motivated to work on, even if those are different than the issues they want him to work on?
- *Confidentiality and information sharing*: Are the parents okay with you being able to talk confidentially with their son? If they share information with you, are they okay with you acknowledging that you got it? If he consents, would they like to get some kind of general update (where we are in the process, his level of engagement, etc.)?

This is a lot to cover in one session, but it is possible to do it all if you stay on point. There are parents who are so hurt or confused or angry that they will want to go into elaborate detail about various incidents or interactions. At times, the information they want to share is important and valuable, but at other times, it is simply reinforcing a point that has already been made—he is defiant, he doesn't listen, he makes impulsive decisions, he doesn't work up to his potential, and so on. I would suggest you politely keep the conversation moving forward to ensure that you hit all your necessary marks. You can do this in a way that does not seem overly brisk or insensitive, especially if you employ good reflective listening skills and let them know you have really heard their concerns.

As I've already stressed, one of the most important outcomes of this first session is a clarification of who is really your client. For a more motivational approach to work, it has to be clear to everyone that you are not an agent working on behalf of the parents. You work *for* the young man, though you certainly will work *with* the parents, which is the opposite of how many therapists see their work, especially with adolescents. The young man is the client. His goals—informed by the parents' input and directed by the therapist—are the accepted goals of therapy. Once this is clarified, you are set to go to work with the young man himself.

THE FIRST SESSION: PARENTS AND CLIENT TOGETHER

Often the parents want to meet with the therapist and their son in the first meeting. I typically suggest this and use it as an opportunity to set the correct tone for the therapy relationship and work out the boundaries with everyone in the room at the same time. In my view, this is the optimal first session whenever it can be achieved.

This is how I started the therapy relationship with Gabriel: I greeted him and his parents in the waiting room. He wore a dress shirt buttoned to the top, tucked crookedly into jeans. It was immediately apparent his parents had made him dress up for the appointment. He shook my hand, looking to the side, smiling slightly and falsely, as you might if you were meeting your parole officer. His parents shook my hand in turn, both looking politely resolute. They followed me back into my office and we shut the door.

"It's good to meet you all," I began. "Gabriel, if you are okay with it, I would love to spend some time talking with your parents first."

"Naw, that's good," he said, scanning the room.

"I just don't want it to feel like we are talking about you like you aren't in the room," I explained.

"It's all good," he said, rolling his head onto the back of the stuffed chair where he was sitting. He stared at the ceiling.

I turned to his parents who were holding hands on the couch, both sitting forward, their eyes trained intensely on me. My initial impression was that these were determined, confident people who were used to getting things done. Unlike some parents who seemed angry or trem-ulous or resigned, they registered none of these things. They were here to make things happen.

"Tell me what's going on," I directed them.

"You want the long version or the short version?" his father began.

"Either one. We've got time for whichever one you prefer," I said.

"I'll start with the short version. He was away at Wake Forest. He got drunk at a party and drove back to his apartment. He went off the road. The police came. He was arrested and charged with a DUI. That's why we are here."

"How long ago was this?" I asked

"About two weeks ago," his mother said. "We took him out of school and he is back at home for now."

"Any trouble like this before?" I asked.

"Not like this," his father said. "But when he was in high school, we did have a few times when he would come home and we knew he had been drinking. He got into a fight once at a party and the police were called, but nobody got arrested."

"He's been a good boy mostly," said his mom. "He did well in school. He works hard. He's good."

Gabriel rolled his eyes and shifted a little in his seat. His parents told me their story, of how they had started their own business, how they struggled in the early days to provide for their family, how Gabriel's grandfather had trouble with alcohol and his uncle had some undiag-nosed mental illness. Father spoke concisely, almost in bullet points; mother told stories and elaborated, often to the dismay of Gabriel, who seemed slightly perturbed by her.

During this time, Gabriel didn't speak one word. He didn't correct them or challenge their accounts of his past. He just sat there. To a fly-on-the-wall observer, he was as passive as he could be.

Let me put this session on pause to make a point: With some clients, I want them talking right out of the gate, but for others, I just want them there, soaking it in, even if it is passive-looking on the surface. Gabriel was one of those guys. I didn't want to give him a chance to tell me he didn't want to be there or didn't need the help. He already told me that in the waiting room by how he greeted me. I wanted him to be quiet, without a chance to verbalize his resistance. This is a key point that I don't want you to miss. Don't get a resistant young man talking in front of his parents. If possible, just let him hang out with no pressure the first time you meet.

Toward the end of this session, I wanted to make sure Gabriel's par-ents felt heard, but that it was also clear that he was going to be my client. This requires a bit of finesse, but it usually can be done in a straightforward manner. I began by asking them what they hoped he would get from the therapy experience.

"I think I understand where things stand now," I said. "So with all that you have told me, what would you like for him to get out of this?"

"I just want this kind of thing never to happen again," his mother started.

I saw Gabriel shift in his seat, his mouth tensing. If I could see into his head, the thoughts would likely be, "It won't. We don't need to be here." But he said nothing.

"We want him to make good decisions so he can have a good and happy life," his father added. "That's really what we want."

"Thanks, that is good for me to know," I said. "Today gives me the chance to meet all of you and for you to meet me. In my work, much of how well this goes has to do with how good a fit this is between Gabriel and me." I turned my attention to Gabriel. "If you are open to it, I would like to have a meeting where just you and I talk and take an honest look at some of these things."

He nodded in the affirmative.

"The first time you come in here," I explained, "you are doing it because your parents wanted you in here, but after today, it will be your choice whether to come or not."

I could sense his parents tensing up, very uncomfortable with me giving him this choice. But this moment—either in the parents' presence or with him alone—is vitally important. He must be given the chance to consent to coming in. For this to work, he must be my client. He must be the one to choose to participate. He does not have to say he wants to come or enjoys being in therapy, just that he is willing to do it. Many of my best clients over the years came in reluctantly, resistant to being in therapy, then consented to coming back and ended up saying it was a good experience for them. To get there, though, it must be his decision. His parents may want him to come back, but he has to make that choice himself.

The first session with the parents and client together becomes a bit of a metaprocess where the parents and I are exchanging important pieces of information, while at the same time, I am telegraphing my style, approach, and intentions to the client himself. For me, the most important part of the parent meeting is getting them on board with me. I want them to meet me, get a sense of my style, and feel comfortable with how I work. I rarely take their agenda as the final word for treatment direction, however, and I let them know this. For therapy to work, I explain, their son ultimately has to set the agenda. I want their blessing, in a sense, more than I want their guidance.

I rarely have problems with parents that come in during the first session with their son. It is those parents who just send their 20-year-old son in to see me by himself that usually end up having the most concerns. They don't know me, can't possibly trust me, and don't see where things are going. These are the parents that send the frustrated e-mails ("He still hasn't gotten a job." "He's very mean to his younger brother."). As a therapist, your job gets easier when parents understand how you work and where you are going; they need to have some basic feedback loop so that they know things are moving somewhere. And you also need to be honest when there isn't any forward movement. They may not be entitled to hear confidential information, but as the ones who are paying for a service, they should know if there is at least some promise of the service being beneficial.

The intent of having clients present but not talking much in the first session is to reduce resistance. Getting those resistant guys in the door is often hard to accomplish. You want them there to check you out and get somewhat comfortable, but not opening their mouth enough to dig into their resistance, especially not in front of their parents. At the same time, you want the parents to be heard and also socialized to the way you do therapy. There is a great deal of process happening in that first meeting.

In some cases, you may have clients who are engaged in the process right away. They are friendly, open, agreeable. You sense no resistance to participating in counseling. In fact, in some instances, they may have actually requested the therapy (which is true of about 5%–10% of my clients). If so, there is no need to keep them quiet or disengaged in the first session. Get them interacting right away. The more eager and engaged clients need to be talking for most of the first session. This is an aspect of the art of therapy that requires flexibility and the ability to read the moment well. For the guys who are ready to talk, you still want to hit most of the same beats as before, but your primary source of information is the client himself. You will collect information about what is going on now, the relevant history, strengths, and all the rest. You still need to work out the bounds of confidentiality and information sharing. Those same elements still need to be covered, but with the client talking more than listening. The parents are there for moral support and supplemental facts.

Here is a key point: *Don't assume that your client is going to be resistant, but be ready for it.* If he doesn't want to be there, then try to keep him quiet and observant. If he is open and willing, then get him talking and participating. Make your judgment call on the fly, beginning with your impressions of him in the waiting room.

In your work as a therapist with young men, you take a posture that is different from that of his parents. To be successful, you have to work hard not to be in a role of authority with your clients. Their parents, by contrast, have been authorities. In some cases, they have done a good job with this; in other instances, they have failed, either being too authoritarian or too hands-off. Regardless, they have been in the authority role for 16 or more years.

Because of this fundamental role difference, it is important to acknowledge that the roles are different and should remain so. For example, in Gabriel's case, even though he is of majority age, his parents have used their authority to pull him out of school, cut off his financial support, berate and lecture him, and insist that he come to therapy. That is perfectly within their right to set these limits and exert their authority. This is their role, but it is not your role. Conversely, it is your role to be the therapist and not the authority. Keeping these role boundaries clear and well-defined is important. Because of the differences in roles and responsibilities, you need to be alert to three potential dangers and potentially address them head-on in the first session:

Being Co-Opted Into the Parent Role

For Gabriel, his parents play a critical role in helping him get better. They have set firm limits with him and insisted that he seek help. As we discussed in Chapter 4, one of the biggest traps you can fall into as a therapist is to be the boss. Gabriel's mom very much wanted to co-opt me into being a third parent. Simply stated, that's not my job; it is her job. I'm glad she is up to the task, but it is not my role, nor should it be so.

Trying to Move Parents to Be Therapists

There are many times when parents behave in decidedly "nontherapeutic" ways. Gabriel's mom, for instance, likes to lecture and threaten, two things that I would never want to do with him. While I intend to coach her to back off in some respects, it is not fair or good for me to ask her to operate like a therapist. She needs to be the parent, even if her approach could be better.

I am in favor of teaching parents therapeutic skills, such as reflective listening, anger de-escalation, or limit setting, but there is a big difference between equipping parents with skills and asking them to behave like therapists. Trying to get them to be therapists is like expecting them to cease being in an authority role, which is not reasonable and also not wise much of the time, especially with the younger half of this client population.

Nagging and punishing parents are an unpleasant part of your young man's reality, but a part that may ultimately be necessary to help him make some changes in his life. In some ways, these parents may help you move your client forward. There is also no question that many parents have serious problems and deficits that need to be addressed. In those cases, it is best to refer them to a colleague for their own therapy.

You can direct parents to respond in more helpful ways, but don't try to strip them of their right and ability to be parents. Let them set limits, give consequences, and all the other things parents do, then deal with your client on how he is going to respond to the hand he has been dealt.

Good Cop/Bad Cop

A final danger is in letting the parents set the limits and give the consequences, but colluding with your client over how bad and unfair it all is. Some guys would like to spend much of their therapy time complaining about how unreasonable their parents are, then try to draw you into taking up their side. You become the good cop, the parents become the bad cop. The problem with this, of course, is that you are sending a message undermining the parents' judgment and authority.

Trust me, you will be frequently misquoted when you work with young men. Your active listening will be taken as agreement. A stray comment will be amplified and restated. You and your words will be used as ammunition against parents ("Verhaagen agrees with me about this."). It is best to be mindful of this and not give your clients any more material to work with than what they will already have with your nods, reflections, and offhand remarks. You don't have to support all parental decisions or responses, but neither should you throw them under the bus.

Don't let yourself become a parent; don't try to make the parents into therapists; and don't position yourself as the good cop against the parents' role as bad cop. Be a therapist with no authority and let the parents keep their authority. It all works better that way.

FIRST SESSION WITH THE CLIENT

Whether it is following a "parents only" meeting or the very first session, the first appointment with the client alone is a key moment in your therapy work. We often think of building rapport as something that happens over many weeks or even months, but the truth is that the majority of rapport building is going to happen in the first 15–30 minutes of your individual meeting with your client.

Marlon's aunt had urged him to come in and had paid for the first session, but she thought it was best for him to come in by himself because "he's an adult now." Even though Marlon had been living with his aunt and was being supported financially by her, I never met her during the entire time I worked with him.

Marlon came in 10 minutes late for our first meeting together, saying he had gotten lost. Actually, it was his friend who had driven him that morning who had gotten lost. Marlon didn't have his driver's license and generally took the bus to get back and forth from work.

He wore black baggy pants and a white t-shirt. His hair was braided down into tight cornrows; he had a little goatee; and he had earrings in each ear. In the waiting room, he slouched with his legs stretched out far in front of him, his eyes closed after less than a minute in the chair, but he stood up sharp and greeted me politely with a warm smile. Once we came back to my office, he sat much more formally than before, almost as if he were in a job interview.

"I'm glad it worked out for you to come in today," I said.

"Thank you," he said in reply, his eyes darting from my face to the floor, then back again.

"I would just like to get to know you a little first. Is that good?" I asked.

"Yeah. Whatever you want," he said. This may sound like a disengaged client, but there was no tone in his voice signaling resistance. He was clearly uncomfortable from the start, but was telling me he was willing to be a part of the conversation. We were able to move ahead with the first session, which has four parts: rapport-building, socializing, assessing, and integrating.

Part 1: Rapport-Building

As I typically do, I asked Marlon several rapport-building questions in the first session with him. During this part of the session, I also ask a few questions about his basic sense of identity and his social relationships. Below are the questions I asked him and the intent behind each one. Each question had one or more follow-up questions to help clarify or build some momentum.

Question	Purpose
What kinds of things do you really enjoy?	*Rapport building, beginning with a nonthreatening, nonpathology focus. Spend as much time here as you can.*
What are you good at?	*Continuing with rapport building; looking for strengths.*
If you were filling out an online profile and it asked for three words that best described you, what would you say about yourself?	*Looking at identity; asking for self-description. This is often a surprisingly tough question for many young men; Marlon had an extremely hard time answering this one.*
Tell me the first names of a few friends and tell me a little bit about them.	*Social connectedness; general sense of peer group. I usually ask for first names only, because asking for full names often makes some clients unnecessarily suspicious.*
If I were to ask (two or three names of friends) to describe you, what would they say?	*Identity again, but from an outside perspective; also a bit of perspective taking.*

After Marlon's response to a few questions, I would also make some connections between us. For example, he said he liked video games, so I told him I shared this interest, and we talked for awhile about what games and platforms we liked the most. He also mentioned a few artists and bands he enjoyed, and while I didn't like the ones he mentioned, we were able to talk about our mutual appreciation and love for music.

This is a typical beginning for me. I ask some relatively nonthreatening questions about likes, strengths, basic self-concept, and friendships. This should be the lengthiest part of the first client session, with no sense of being in a rush. It should not feel like small talk, either, but a time when you are genuinely getting to know him. This may sound a bit paradoxical: The session should really have a lot of energy but move at a leisurely pace. You should not be overeager or overly enthusiastic, because that comes across falsely, but you should be fully engaged, looking for opportunities to laugh, make connections, and find ways to appreciate and enjoy him as a person.

Again, I cannot emphasize enough the importance of this first part of the first session. The client is rapidly forming his impressions of you and the therapy experience. How you begin—and how you end—will make a huge difference in whether he wants to return to see you.

Part 2: Socializing to Therapy

At this point, I would advise you to pause here and explain a few things. Even for a client who has seen other therapists in the past, it is good practice to make sure you orient and socialize him to the process. I don't start with this because it would make for a very flat opening, but I usually put this in the middle and use it to give information about how therapy works and also to transition to the more personal questions.

These are typically the things I say at this point in the session, but you obviously have to do it in a way that works best for you and your style:

Defining your role: "Have you ever talked to a person like me before? You probably know I am a psychologist (counselor, psychiatrist, therapist, etc.), and I help guys your age meet their personal goals."

Describing your style: "The way I do that is just like you've already seen. I tend to be straightforward and on the level. It may not be like what you've seen on TV or what you might expect. Hopefully it will feel more like a regular conversation."

Posing the questions to be addressed: "Today, we really have to answer two questions. First, is this is a good match for the two of us to meet? In this work, a lot of this is really about personality and how well it clicks. If it isn't a good match for you, I want you to have the freedom to say that or say you need to think about it at the end. The second question is whether there are some things you are wanting or willing to work on with me. If so, we will figure out what that looks like together."

Claiming your client: "You probably know that I met with your parents and they gave me their perspective on things. That doesn't necessarily mean that I take their point of view. I really need to hear your take on things and how you see it. The bottom line is that if we are going to meet after today, then I will work for you."

Reducing stigma: "Some people have the idea that you have to be crazy or something like that to see a psychologist, but most of the people that I see are really pretty normal people who may have an area or two that they want to improve." (Note: This is a total judgment call about how to say this, depending on the client's presenting issues, your work setting, and your style, but it usually should be addressed early in the process.)

Bounds of confidentiality: "You may already know this, but everything we talk about is between us. It doesn't leave the room. The only exception to that is if you tell me you are getting ready to do something to hurt or kill yourself or someone else." (For clients under 18, I would also add a clause about my requirement to report the abuse of a minor.)

Permission to give parents progress reports: "Even though we can talk confidentially, if we decide to meet together, I would love to have your permission to give your parents an update from time to time, just so they know whether we are moving forward and working on things. I won't share anything without your knowledge and permission, however."

Addressing the authority issue: "The way this usually works is that I might suggest some things for us to talk about or bring up some questions, but you can also bring up anything you want to talk about. I will make some suggestions about where we should go, but ultimately, you're in charge. I don't have any authority over your life nor do I want any."

Permission to ask more personal questions: "If you're okay with it, I would like to ask you some more personal questions. If there is anything you don't want to talk about, then you can just tell me that, and we can just move on to something else. Are you good with that?"

With some clients, this part of the session is very straightforward and moves quickly, but with others, there is a need for more elaboration, give and take, or clarification. All of this serves to socialize your client not only to therapy in general, but how you do therapy in particular. For guys who have been in therapy or counseling with other clinicians, this information is still important to distinguish you from what they have experienced before.

Part 3: Assessing His Needs

Assuming you have permission to move ahead, I use the last part of the first session to assess what he needs. I typically ask these questions, regardless of what information I have already received from parents or from the initial referral call. This pattern deviates from the usual "So what brings you in today?" questions asked in other first sessions. Adding this structure tends to work better with young men than asking extremely open questions at the beginning.

In this part of the session, you will need to assess emotional functioning, drug and alcohol use, family relationships, social supports, behavioral functioning, school/work functioning, and other important areas.

If you assess each of these areas, it is likely you will cover the problem that brought him in initially, as well as any other areas that might be of concern. While it is possible some important information will slip the net, you will have a good starting point. Here's a basic outline of the final phase of the first session:

Question	Purpose
I want to ask you about four emotions: happy, sad, angry, worried. From 1 to 10, with 10 being the most, how happy have you been on average in the past month? With 10 being really sad, depressed or down, how sad have you been on average in the past month? With 10 being really angry, mad, pissed off, how mad have you been? And with 10 being really worried, anxious, nervous, how worried have you been?	*Assessing recent emotional functioning. It is also good to get not only the average, but also the range during the past month.*
Of those last three emotions—sad, angry, worried—which of those do you feel the most frequently? Which one do you feel the most intensely when you do feel it?	*Continuing to assess emotional functioning. Don't assume that the highest number given with the first set of questions is necessarily the one they feel most frequently or most intensely.*
I'd like to ask you about your drug use and drinking, if you are okay with that. Remember you can tell me if you don't feel comfortable answering. During the past week or month, how often have you had something to drink? How often do you smoke pot? What other drugs have you tried over the past year, even once?	*Assessing substance use. May require multiple follow-ups, depending on initial answers. Follow-ups may include: When you drink, how often do you get drunk? Has your drinking (or drug use) ever caused you any trouble (trouble with the law, fights, unplanned sex, conflict with others, school or work trouble, etc.)?*
Tell me who is in your family and how you get along with each person.	*Assessing family relationships, including family conflicts and family strengths.*
Besides close friends and family, do you have any other significant relationships in your life?	*Assessing social support and other people who are important to the client, including girlfriends (or boyfriends), coaches, mentors, teachers, and so on.*
Have you gotten into any trouble? Have you had any problems with your behavior?	*Assessing behavioral functioning.*

Question	Purpose
Tell me about school (or work). How do you like it? How do you do there?	*Assessing academic or vocational functioning.*
Tell me anything else about you that would be good for me to know.	*May not generate any new facts, but it is well worth asking because it will occasionally yield some very important information.*

Marlon's responses let me know that he smoked pot daily and had been arrested twice for minor drug charges and one time for resisting arrest. He had not graduated from high school and was not on course to finish. Until three months ago, he had been living with his aunt and had been abandoned by his mother when he was 2 years old. He had never met his father. He also told me that he felt highly anxious in social situations. He told me a great deal in a short amount of time. Our pace seemed slow and almost leisurely, but he revealed a lot about himself in about a half hour.

Marlon came in for the first session by himself, while I actually met Ricky in the second session, following an initial meeting with his parents. He knew that I had met with them, but I didn't tell him what we had discussed, except to acknowledge we had talked. His parents told me that they were frustrated because he was disrespectful and noncommunicative. Their goals were for him to be more courteous and compliant, neither of which are bad goals. However, they were far from what he needed to talk about.

Ricky sat in the waiting room with his mother, his hair covering both eyes. He had his iPod playing so loudly that I could hear the song a few feet away from him. I shook his hand, and he followed me back to my office. He was initially reluctant to talk, but I made it clear that I was representing his interests and was not an agent of his parents. I told him that his parents understood this and had consented to it. With that, he began to open up, and he disclosed a remarkable amount of information during the third part of our initial session:

- He was moderately depressed (7 on a scale of 10) for most of the past year.
- He had been suicidal at least twice in the past year, but was not currently.
- He had cut himself a few times when he became emotionally overwhelmed.
- He smoked marijuana about three times a week.
- He almost never drank and got sick when he did.
- He had tried mushrooms twice and painkillers three times in the past year.
- He feels badly about himself most of the time.

- He had angry outbursts with parents, but not with peers or anyone else. He did not like losing control of his anger.
- He did not like either of his parents very much and had not for the past two years.
- He was gay and had a boyfriend, but had not told his parents. His friends and most of his peers at school all knew and were accepting, but he was unsure how his parents would react. He didn't consider this to be a problem, but was wondering how he would come out to them.
- He was not motivated to improve his relationship with his parents. He said he did not like them and did not want to be close with them. He did say he wished they did not fight as much, however, since he found this stressful.
- His grades were mixed this year, but he was not concerned.

This was a lot for him to share in one meeting. To wrap this up, we needed to put it all together in a way that made sense to him and served as a guide for me. This brought us to the final part of our first session.

Part 4: Integrating the Information

"You've told me a lot today, which I really appreciate," I said. "Let me see if I can organize some of this into a few categories." I picked up my whiteboard and began writing what I had heard. I sketched out five words or phrases on the board, as seen in Figure 5.1. I showed him the board after I was done writing, and he examined it for a few moments. He nodded his head.

"Yeah, that looks about right," he said.

"Now let's see how these things might fit together," I said. I started with depression and asked him, "When you feel depressed, does that cause you to feel badly about yourself?"

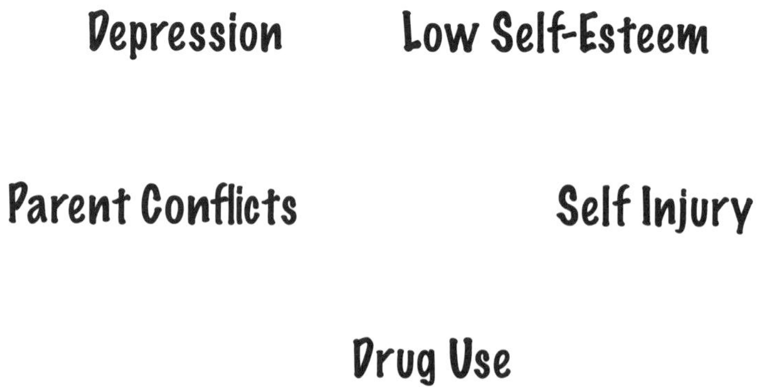

Depression   Low Self-Esteem

Parent Conflicts   Self Injury

Drug Use

Figure 5.1   Whiteboard 1.

"Yeah, definitely," he said. I drew an arrow from the word "Depression" to the phrase "Low Self-Esteem." He seemed to quickly understand how this was going to work.

"And when you are depressed, does that cause you to hurt yourself?" I asked.

"Sometimes. Yes," he replied. I drew another arrowed line.

"And when you are depressed, does that cause you to smoke weed?" I asked.

"Yeah, I guess so," he said. I drew a line connecting the two.

"And when you are depressed, does that cause you to have conflict or fights with your parents?" I asked.

"Not really," he said. I didn't draw a line connecting those two.

I started with the next area, low self-esteem, and went around the board again. Then I did it for each of the other areas. The whole process took me a little more than five minutes but gave me an enormous amount of information.

I call this the *problem map*, though I never use this term with my clients. The problem map accomplishes three things: It lets me assess what is going on with him in a more thorough way that will guide me in the coming sessions; it lets him know I hear him; and it lets both of us see the interconnection of the issues he faces. For guys who come in with multiple problems and concerns (which tend to be the majority of clients), it is a good way of doing collaborative treatment planning.

After we finished drawing all the connections, we studied the board together. Then I asked him a simple question: "If you could drop just one thing from the board, what would it be?"

"The self-esteem thing, I guess," he said.

"Why is that?"

"It would probably change the most stuff for me," he said.

I put a little star beside self-esteem. The finished product is shown in Figure 5.2. When you first look at it, the whole thing seems like a big tangle, so it takes a while to sort it all out. One of the first things that struck me was that parent conflicts caused all of the other things, but was not the result of any of them. I reflected that back to him and we discussed it for awhile. He pointed out that his drug use was caused by three of the other issues, but did not cause any of the others, so we discussed that briefly, too. This exercise gave us plenty to talk about, and none of it was generated from my previous conversation with his parents. I didn't say, "Your parents told me...," even once during the entire hour, which is usually my goal in the first session. The content of our discussion came entirely from him.

The problem map succeeds as an early assessment tool, an alliance-building tool, and as a therapeutic tool. If done well, you have completed your treatment plan and virtually guaranteed at least a beginning measure of commitment to the therapy process.

These four parts are a lot to cover in one session, but it can be done. However, it is wise to be flexible. If the rapport building goes longer,

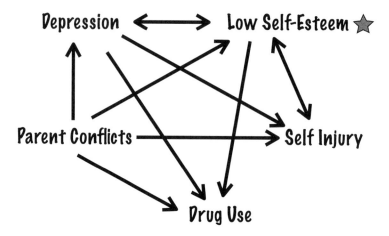

Figure 5.2   Whiteboard 2.

or if it takes longer to assess his needs, then this may carry over into a second session. As a rule of thumb, it is best not to rush the process. Use two sessions to cover all four of these parts if that works best.

NEXT SESSIONS

In the coming sessions, it is best to structure the time for most clients. Based on the information you collected from your problem map in the first or second session, you can suggest a direction for each of the following sessions. For subsequent appointments, I recommend you structure your time together in four parts: prompting since the last session, recapping the last session, offering the opportunity for him to set the agenda, and finally, giving direction for the agenda if he does not. To help me recall it, I use the acronym PROD: prompt, review, offer, direct.

Part 1: Prompt

Start the follow-up sessions with an invitation to give you an update since the last visit. It's usually best to phrase it as a prompt rather than a question to increase your chances of getting a reply of any substance. Here are some prompts you could consider:

- "Give me good news and bad news about your life since the last time."
- "Tell me something interesting that's happened recently."
- "Let me hear the highlights from the past week."

Many times, you will not get much from this, but it will give him the opportunity to share any significant events—good or bad—that may have happened since the last session. On some occasions, your client will tell you something important that may need to be discussed at length, and it may even consume the entire session. One guy told me a friend of his had gone to the hospital over the weekend because of alcohol poisoning. Another said he had reason to worry that his girlfriend might be pregnant. Still another shared that his parents had decided to get a divorce. In each case, we put the agenda aside and discussed the concern at length. I've had this happen hundreds of times, so you don't want to miss these opportunities.

Part 2: Review

After he has had the chance to give you any update, the next step is to briefly summarize and recap the last session. The reason for doing this is to rehearse the previously covered information and provide some continuity between sessions. You might say things like:

- "In our last meeting, we discussed some good ways and poor ways to cope with stress. How did you do with that this week?"
- "Last time we talked about your intense anxiety in new social situations. Can we keep going with that?"
- "Last week you said you were going to write out a list of things you were grateful for in your life. Were you able to do that?"
- "We have been thinking through pros and cons of your current relationship. Have you given that any more thought since last time?"

You recap by asking questions that rehearse the previously discussed information, give an opportunity for further discussion, review homework, or check to see if the client is practicing the newly acquired skills or strategies.

Part 3: Offer

After you recap, you extend an offer to talk about anything that has been on the client's mind since the last session. In most cases, this will be the shortest part of the session. You will simply ask, "Is there anything you want to make sure we talk about today?" If he brings up something, then take as much time as needed to discuss it thoroughly. Most of the time, though, he will tell you there isn't anything in particular that he wants to discuss, and you will move on to what will usually be the heart of session.

Part 4: Direct

After you have discovered what has happened since the last visit, reviewed the previous session, and given him an opportunity to discuss any issue of his choice, you will usually still have the majority of your session time left. During this remaining time, you should propose a topic for discussion. The topic should be in line with the previously established goals. You would say something like, "Last time, we talked about how to understand and sort out your feelings. Today, I want to suggest we talk about ways you can cope with those intense feelings of anxiety you have been having. Is that good with you?"

If you get his consent, then move forward on the selected topic. If he declines, then have at least one backup plan ready. There may be times when you propose a topic that he is not ready to discuss or is not in the mood to revisit. The young man may not be ready to process a past trauma, or he might be tired of talking about a relationship conflict, for example. If so, do not try to persuade him to discuss it. Simply suggest an alternative.

To direct the sessions effectively, you need to be well prepared each time. You should know the active goals and the progress toward each one. Keeping good notes is an essential part of being prepared. It is a good practice to write your suggestions for what to cover during the next session at the end of each note.

The beginning sessions of therapy are absolutely vital in your work with each client. It is here where you establish rapport, assess needs, and make a change plan together. Once that is all done, you can move on to directly addressing his primary concerns and objectives. If you follow this framework, you should be able to make significant progress with most clients in four to five appointments. More work will be needed for many young men, but you can make a strong impact in just a handful of sessions.

THERAPY TAKE-AWAYS

1. Depending on the needs of the client, be prepared for the first session to be either with him and his parents together, his parents alone, or him alone. Be ready for each possibility.
2. In your first meeting with the young man, build rapport, socialize him to the therapy process, assess his needs, and then integrate the information using the problem map.
3. In subsequent sessions, use PROD: prompt, review, offer, and direct.

6

Identity Formation in Therapy

When Ricky was in seventh grade, he used to come home after a day of being verbally beaten up by his classmates and spit at himself in the mirror. This shocking gesture underscored how badly he felt about himself. He was literally dripping with self-loathing.

"I hated myself," he told me.

He hated how he looked, how he acted, how he thought and felt. He hated everything about himself. Now, for the first time since middle school, he was willing to start rebuilding a healthy sense of self.

Many young guys come into the pre-adult stage with a healthy foundation of identity, having clarified their values, beliefs, and self-descriptions. Others, like Ricky, get hung up somewhere along the way and have an unresolved, unformed sense of self. If you listen carefully, you will typically hear guys with identity issues talk about the wounds of middle school.

One of my clients told me, "I feel like I am that kid with the stick legs, the wavy hair that sticks out in front of my face and is always saying something stupid, just like how I was in middle school." What was most striking about this comment was that it was coming from a 20-year-old guy who was a scholarship athlete at a nationally ranked university, had close friends and a girlfriend, and looked almost nothing like he did 7 years earlier. And yet inside, he felt very much like the dorky kid he used to be. I've heard this kind of comment so many times, I've almost learned to anticipate it. Some guys get stuck in middle school in their own heads.

For many young men, the experience of middle school is fairly traumatic and does a lot to wound them. With their bodies and minds changing rapidly, they are not only emotionally raw, but they are beginning that important first step of identity formation. Questions about who they are, how they are accepted, and where they fit in are stirred up in them. During this time of life, negative comments—especially comments about appearance and masculinity—can hit them hard. Guys who are picked on about these things are vulnerable to carrying these notions about themselves forward for years and using all kinds of strategies to protect themselves from feeling like the dorky middle school kid.

Early adolescence begins the work of identity formation, so middle school boys are trying desperately to figure out their place in the world. According to Erikson (1968), young teenagers who can explore and make their own choices will end up resolving their sense of identity. They will know who they are, what they are about, and where they fit in. If they are not allowed to explore and make their own choices, then they will likely have a poorly resolved, poorly integrated sense of self. Beside the role of the parents, factors like temperament, neurological and psychological issues, health concerns, siblings, and the influence of peers all play a role in how solid a young man's foundation of identity becomes. Identity formation is complex, but remarkably important.

THE FOUNDATION OF IDENTITY

Before beginning therapy on one of the big areas of concern, such as substance use, behavioral problems, or an emotional difficulty, it is often wise to make sure you are building on a solid base. Without a solid foundation of identity, the therapy work is not likely to stick.

Because of this, it is essential to assess identity formation early in the therapy process and help a young man build a solid sense of himself. After assessing needs and building rapport, you must be certain you have addressed identity formation before diving into the other concerns.

Each of our three young men is different in their stage of identity formation. Marlon has very little sense of identity formation and has done practically none of the developmental work he needs to do to have a clear sense of himself. By contrast, Gabriel has a very solid sense of himself, but he also has incorporated some malignantly narcissistic elements into his personality. Ricky has done some work on forming his identity, but he has a highly damaged sense of self.

All three need some work on their identity formation. Marlon needs help *building* a sense of self. Gabriel needs help *reforming* some aspects of himself. Ricky needs help *repairing* his sense of himself. Marlon is not likely to make any gains until he can explore and take on some definition in his self-concept. The work must almost certainly start with building his sense of self before going any further. Gabriel and Ricky have enough sense of self to begin working on the other issues early in the therapy process, but it would be wise to incorporate identity themes in the treatment plan. Gabriel can control his drinking and remain a narcissist, but other issues will continue or develop if his narcissism isn't addressed. Ricky can be more compliant and still feel terrible about himself, resulting in ongoing depression and troubled relationships. Tackling identity issues early in the therapy process will usually result in a better outcome. To do that, these are the three central questions you should be asking yourself early in the therapy process:

1. To what degree can he define himself (values, beliefs, personal traits, strengths, weaknesses)?
2. What aspects of his self-concept are healthy?
3. What aspects of his self-concept are unhealthy?

If he cannot define himself at all, then the answers to the other two questions become less certain. However, you can be reasonably certain that a young man who has no ability to define himself has a globally unhealthy self-concept that may need to be built almost from the ground up in therapy.

ASSESSING LOCUS OF CONTROL

"I have the worst—and I mean the *worst*—luck of any person I have ever known," said Gabriel to explain his DUI. In his mind, the issue was not that he was drinking and driving, but simply that he had been unlucky. The belief known as *external locus of control*—that your life is ruled by luck and outside circumstances—is often unyielding, even in the face of other evidence. Not long ago, I saw a client who had been arrested seven times—three of them for felonies—and he said he was just unlucky and the unfair target of police. It didn't matter to him that his arrests for drug possession and sales, use of a weapon in a robbery, and all the rest were done of his own free will over a period of three years and in several cities. I have had other clients who attribute their relationship troubles to the fact that mentally unstable girls are mysteriously attracted to them. All the issues are with the girls, not with them. The major problem with having an external locus of control is that it prevents new learning and growth. If all your troubles are the product of forces outside of yourself and beyond your control, you are not likely to make the changes you need to make.

By contrast, having an *internal locus of control* leads to a whole range of good outcomes. These include higher academic achievement, increased treatment participation, greater help-seeking behaviors, more favorable treatment outcomes, better overall physical health, healthier psychological adjustment, reduced suicide risk, and greater job motivation and performance (Carden, Bryant, & Moss, 2004; Gale, Batty, & Deary, 2008; Lauer, de Man, Marquez, & Ades, 2008; Ng, Sorensen, & Eby, 2006; Page & Scalora, 2004; Shepherd, Fitch, Owen, & Marshall,

2006). It seems that if you believe you make your own luck, your "luck" will indeed be better.

Locus of control is a fundamental part of identity because it speaks to the most basic question of whether a person is in charge of his own life or not. Do you run your life, or is it ruled by luck and forces beyond your control? If you feel in control of your own life, then you are better able to shape who you are and where you are going (Cote & Levine, 2002). A solid sense of identity is best built on an internal locus of control.

It is important to assess locus of control during the early sessions of therapy. While there are some quick instruments that can help determine a person's control orientation, an even simpler way to do it is to explain the concept, then draw a line with "Outside Forces" on one end and "Personal Choices" on the other. After you do this, you explain the two ends of the spectrum in a little more detail and then say, "Draw an X at the spot where control is in your own life." In my experience, this quick exercise not only gives as much information as a multiquestion scale, but it also can become a springboard for further discussion.

For those young men who seem to have a more external center of control, this topic becomes the focus of our conversation. Just having the discussion about locus of control can be powerfully effective. Exposing a client to the notion that individuals with a more internal sense of control over their lives tend to do better in lots of ways can often have the benefit of moving him toward a more internal sense of control. Some may argue that people who have good luck find it easier to have an internal locus of control, but longitudinal research actually makes it clear that it is the other way around.

DISCUSSING IDENTITY STATUS

After you have adequately wrestled with the issue of where control is in his life, you can start talking about identity itself. Building on the work of Erik Erikson's (1968) psychosocial stages of development, James Marcia (1966, 1993) proposed more elaborate categories of identity status for adolescents. Adolescents have differing degrees of exploration about identity options—values, passions, worldviews, and so on—and they have differing degrees of commitment to those identity options. When those two dimensions—exploration and commitment—intersect, they produce four identity statuses.

Marcia's (1966, 1993) formulation has been helpful and has spawned a great deal of good research. However, the terms that he used, like *moratorium* and *foreclosure*, feel dated and may have different connotations now than the way they were intended. I propose using the same framework for clinical purposes, but substituting some terms for clarity. I take no credit for the conceptual framework itself, but this is how I am now referring to the four identity status categories:

No Exploration

Confused	Halted
Experimentation	Achieved

No Commitment ⟶ ⟵ Commitment

Exploration

Confused Identity

A young man is not exploring possible life choices and values, nor has he made any firm commitments to them. This is often the starting point for adolescents, but if an individual is still in this state by later adolescence or certainly young adulthood, it can be highly problematic for him. A person in this identity status is likely to be stuck in life. Erikson (1968) himself wrote, "Many a sick or desperate late adolescent, if faced with continuing conflict, would rather be nobody or somebody totally bad, or, indeed, dead" (p. 176).

Young men at this status of identity development are likely to be seen as highly unmotivated, without any sense of direction or purpose. Parents of these young men are typically frustrated by their inability or unwillingness to move forward in life. Often these young men seem like younger adolescents well into their early 20s, living at home and arguing with their parents. Despite the "What are you going to do with your life?" speeches from others, these guys seem neither contented nor discontented with their life circumstances. They often go to college (often a local community college for convenience, but not always), but don't do well academically because they fail to see the point of it, or maybe because they enrolled just to get their parents off their backs. They have nominal jobs or no jobs at all. Parents frequently give ultimatums to these guys: Get a job, go to school, stop fighting with us—or move out.

Marlon is a good example of a young man in the status of identity confusion. He lives in a rundown apartment, doesn't have a driver's license, works a job he doesn't enjoy, and is making no steps to make any changes in his life. His greatest joy in life is smoking pot every evening. He came into therapy at his aunt's urging and eventual insistence, but he was in no distress. He knows what people say: "You have so much potential, Marlon. You need to do something with your life." But that is what other people say about him; it's not what he says about himself. In his mind, if he is completely honest with himself, he is okay with how things are. For Marlon, the mediocre life you know is better than the better life you don't know.

Halted Identity

Originally, Marcia (1966, 1993) referred to this identity status as *identity foreclosure*. When you foreclose on something, you rule out or exclude a course of action, so when a young man is in identity foreclosure, he has made commitments without exploring his options and alternatives. He has decided what he wants to be or do without seriously considering any other possibilities. A better way to say this today is that his identity formation has been halted. These may be the guys who marry the first girl they seriously date or proceed down the path of working in the family business without contemplating another option. They follow in their parents' choice of religious faith and never critically evaluate it. Such young men tend to share the same values and worldview as most of their family members or significant others.

For these guys, identity is not constructed, developed, or achieved. Rather, they have a *conferred identity* that comes from taking on the goals and values of those who influence them. There is nothing inherently wrong with marrying your first love, being the next generation of Schneider & Sons Plumbing, or joining Bayview Avenue Presbyterian Church, but the larger issue is that there is commitment to the identity without exploration of the alternatives. To be fair, this can often turn out fine for an individual, especially in early adulthood. The risk is that a young man risks a developmental crisis later in life. Halted identity may very well be a key ingredient in a man's midlife crisis.

Gabriel has a conferred identity. While he has a very strong sense of himself, he also has accepted the educational goals, lifestyle, and career path articulated for him since he was young. He was to work hard in school, get into and attend a prestigious university, and upon completion of his degree, he would be a partner in the family business. Of course, there was never any doubt that he would be both a Catholic and a registered Democrat. For Gabriel, none of this was a burden; none of it was a problem. It was always his assumption that this was how it was going to be.

Identity Experimentation

Marcia (1966, 1993) originally called this status identity *moratorium*. A moratorium is some sort of delay. Adolescents and young men who are in a period of identity moratorium have yet to make a commitment, but they are highly active in exploring who they are, who they could be, and where they might be going in life. Adolescent boys are often investigating values, worldviews, and personas. Their life goals and appearance may change abruptly. All of this is developmentally normal. And while this may cause the adolescent to have some intense ups and downs with mood and behavior, the payoff is that he will most often end up with a *constructed identity* that is not based on a set of previous expectations and assumptions, but comes from an authentic exploration of personal values and self-determined goals.

The term *moratorium* is a bit of a misnomer because it implies that the process has stopped. It simply means that the commitment to a fixed identity is on hold until the options are explored. Moratorium sounds passive and on pause, but individuals in the identity-moratorium status are anything but passive. They are actively and often aggressively pursuing their options and looking at all the alternatives. This is why the term *identity experimentation* is a better fit for this identity status.

Ricky is clearly in a period of identity experimentation. He is certain that he is gay, but the other specifics are not too clear for him. Still, he is striving to figure it all out by trying on different looks, different musical preferences, different friends, different values, and just about everything else. There is an anxious, frustrated energy about him as he tries to work all of this out. If he ends up with a settled, tested sense of himself, he will likely do well later in life. If he does not land on a clear sense of self, he may have an unstable personality in his adult years. As of now, it's unclear where he will land.

Achieved Identity

At the end of exploring identity options, a person is able to come to a place where he makes a commitment to a life direction and a set of beliefs and values that will come to define his identity. When he gets there, he will have met the status of identity achievement. While he may continue to explore and sharpen his own sense of self, he has a strong, clear sense of self. For most individuals in therapy, this is the objective.

ASSESSING IDENTITY STATUS

Because identity issues are the foundation for other therapy work, it is wise to assess each client's identity status. If you accurately assess the two dimensions—the degree of identity exploration and the degree of commitment—you can get a good sense of which status category best fits each client.

I propose a semistructured professional judgment approach with the focus on asking questions about different aspects of identity. As with other parts of therapy, you should make it clear that the client has the option of not answering any question if he does not feel comfortable with it. It is also a judgment call about whether to ask some questions or not. For example, with some clients, you may risk harming trust and rapport with questions about sexual identity or religious beliefs. Other clients may talk about these issues freely and with little anxiety. Some may not feel comfortable talking about it in the first couple of sessions, but they may answer later in therapy. As always, what to ask and what not to ask requires clinical judgment and skill. Here are some sample questions for you to consider in assessing a young man's sense of identity:

- How would you describe yourself?
- How do you feel about school (or your work)?
- Where do you stand with religious or spiritual beliefs?
- What issues or ideas are important to you?

- Would you describe yourself as straight, gay, bi, or some other way?
- What kinds of things do you enjoy?
- What are you good at doing?
- What would you like to be doing in 5 years?

His answers to these and similar questions, along with appropriate follow-ups, will give you a sense of how much he is exploring his identity and how solid his commitment is to it. The ease with which he answers the questions will also give you a clue as to his degree of identity formation. You will undoubtedly have some clients, even those in their 20s, who have no idea how to answer questions like, "What three words would best describe you?" or "What are you good at doing?" Not being able to answer the questions well is as important and telling as having a ready, thoughtful response.

DIRECTING IDENTITY DEVELOPMENT

After you have a good sense of your client's identity status, you will want to guide him closer to reaching a sense of identity achievement. Obviously, this does not happen in a moment of insight; it takes time to develop. In line with the identity framework, the sequence is *explore, then commit*. Young men who have not fully explored their options may need to do so. For those who have explored their values, beliefs, passions, and sense of direction well, then they may need to begin making some commitments that will give them a focus and a sense of forward motion.

Values and Traits Survey

Following some pilot studies, I developed a 43-item survey to help facilitate identity exploration in therapy. As you have seen, I have also used it as a research instrument to help collect data for other parts of the book. Based on 15 personal values and 38 self-descriptions, the inventory asks each client to rate each value or trait from 1 (low) to 10 (high). Because I do not want therapy associated with filling out paperwork or doing tests, I typically do not ask the young man to fill out the inventory until about the third session, after the tone of therapy has already been set. I have included the inventory as an appendix to this chapter for use in your work (see Tables 6.A, 6.B, and 6.C); the numbers in bold represent the average range for each item though you will notice there are no norms yet for the temperament section. For therapy purposes, I use the survey as a springboard for discussion, focusing on the items that were rated especially high or low.

The Personal Inventory

During our first session, I asked Marlon how he would describe himself. He seemed at a loss for words, sitting silently for several moments before simply saying, "I don't know." I asked again, reframing the question slightly, suggesting he give me three words that might be true of him. Again, there was a long silence and the same response: "I don't know."

The identity questions in the first interview often yield the same answer from other clients. Many male clients simply cannot describe themselves, even in the most simplistic, concrete terms. They will say that they have no idea or that they have never thought about it. The questions seem baffling and even odd to them.

Especially for the guys who struggle with the identity questions, the process of defining themselves is essential. Without guidance and structure, they will usually be unable to do it, however. One way to facilitate this process effectively and relatively easily is through a personal inventory. This intervention uses three columns: one for personal strengths, one for weaknesses, and one for areas that are just average.

Even Marlon, who was unable to generate even one word to describe himself with the open question could do this process. I began with a standard prompt and then built from there.

"Let's do something that will give us a better sense of your strengths, your weaknesses, and things in between," I said as I made three columns down the sheet on a notepad. "This will be a list of strengths. Let's start here and work across. First, tell me some skills or personality traits that you think are above average, compared to other guys of the same age."

He looked down at the sheet, then looked at me. He thought for a moment or two. "I really have no idea," he said.

"That's fine," I said. "I am going to give you some ideas in a moment, and you can tell me what column to put them under. Before that, I want to see if anything comes to your mind. Anything that you are really good at or that really describes you well."

"I am pretty good at sports, I guess," he said.

"Good," I said and wrote that down as "Athletic" on the notepad. "What else?"

"That's all I can think of," he said.

We moved on and did the other two categories with similar results. He eked out one or two for the average column and the weakness column. From there, I took out his responses to the second part of the values and traits survey and called them out and had him sort them into the appropriate category. We omitted any terms that he wasn't sure fit him well. When we were done, we had a personal inventory that looked like this:

+	0	–
Artistic	Energetic	Affectionate
Athletic	Friendly	Competitive
Creative	Funny	Confident

+	0	–
Easygoing	Good-looking	Forgiving
Hardworking	Happy	Motivated
Honest	Kind	Organized
Independent	Likable	Self-controlled
Mature	Loyal	
Moral	Open-minded	
Patient	Optimistic	
Respectful	Reliable	
Spiritual	Religious	
	Smart	

After we went through this exercise, I had him look over the three columns while I asked him a few questions about it.

"If this were not you, how would you describe this guy?"

"Laid back, pretty decent," he said. "Probably not too close with anybody."

"If you got to know him, do you think you would like him?" I asked.

"I think so, I guess," he replied. "He seems like a good guy."

"He does to me, too," I said.

The next steps were to use this to begin identity consolidation and also let him identify some areas for self-improvement. First, we start with consolidating some of these traits into his self-concept.

"If you could only pick three or so of these traits," I said, pointing to the column of strengths, "which one of these do you think are the ones that are most important to you?"

He thought for a moment and picked three: creative, honest, and respectful. I put stars by each of them.

"When you are older and people know you as a creative, honest, and respectful person, how will that be for you?"

"I'd like that," he said.

"Would you be satisfied with that, or would you want other things to be more true of you?" I asked. It was an honest question.

"That would be good with me," he said.

"Excellent," I said. "So when you think of yourself, you can start thinking of yourself in those terms: creative, honest, respectful. Imagine what kind of man that would make you if you were consistently that kind of person. It would be pretty cool."

"Yeah, that's true," he replied.

"Now, let's keep going with this. Let's take it a step further," I said. "As a general rule, we usually can't take a weakness and make it a strength, but we can usually get it up to average. Are there one or two traits here that you would really like to get into the average column?"

He studied the list carefully and told me that he would like to be more confident and more motivated, so we circled them and drew arrows pointing them into the middle column.

"Now, is there anything in the middle that you would like to see as a strength?" I asked.

"Maybe more friendly. More happy, of course," he said.

I circled those two and pointed them to the left-hand column with little arrows.

"Now, let's put this all together," I said. "What if you were consistently creative, honest, and respectful. You were also much more confident and motivated than you are now, and you were doing better with being more friendly and happier. If all that were true, how would your life be?" I asked.

"It would be cool," he said. "I don't think I could ask for anything else."

"Let me get a sense of these four things that you would like to improve about yourself," I said. "I'm going to ask you to rate each of these on how important they are for you to improve, then how confident you are that you can improve them."

I went through them one at a time and put a fraction beside each trait he wanted to change; the top number was importance and the bottom number was confidence. He rated all of them as being important, but his confidence was low on his ability to be more self-confident and more motivated. This, of course, opened up the next level of discussion for us, as we had to talk about what gave him doubts about whether he could make these changes.

I chose Marlon for this example because he had the hardest time doing the exercise. Yet, even for him, he was able to complete it in a way that left him feeling hopeful, encouraged, and focused. For the next few sessions, I would ask him, "Name three words that best describe you," and he would reply, "Creative, honest, and respectful." I would follow up with, "Tell me two things that you are working on," and he would say, "Being more confident and more motivated." More importantly, this deepened our therapy time because it allowed us to talk about themes like his sense of self-worth and what had robbed him of motivation. It was this process, in fact, that gave him the courage to first disclose his abuse.

THE POWER OF ATTRIBUTIONS

The theme of school failure came up repeatedly in my sessions with Marlon. He wished that he hadn't dropped out and gotten the GED. He wished that he hadn't stopped going to his community college course after only three weeks. He wished he could sit down and study, even just once. The list went on. School was synonymous with failure. It was a sore spot for him, and one that he felt like he couldn't overcome. He saw the importance of education in getting ahead and getting a desirable job. His months in the restaurant kitchen had more than convinced him of that. Still, all of this couldn't move him to work harder in school, he said.

"Why do you think that is?" I asked.

"Because I'm lazy," he said.

"Lazy?" I asked. "What do you mean?"

"I'm just lazy. Like I knew I had to do a paper and I just wouldn't do it. Or I knew I was supposed to be studying for a quiz or test, and I would play video games instead," he replied.

"Are you lazy with everything? Lazy at work, too?" I asked.

"Pretty much. I'm better at work, but I'm still pretty lazy there, I guess you'd say," he said.

"When did you first start thinking of yourself as lazy?" I asked.

"I always thought that," he said. "I've always been lazy."

For Marlon, it was just a fact that he was lazy. It was a notion that was completely integrated into his sense of himself. He didn't dispute it, and he didn't challenge it. This *attribution* was assumed by Marlon to be completely true, just like him saying that he had brown eyes or stood 6 foot tall, even though laziness is a changeable and fluid construct that can vary from situation to situation. Marlon saw it as a fixed trait, something that was just part of him that could not be changed.

Therapeutically, I try to elicit these self-attributions and strengthen them when they are positive and challenge them when they are negative and maladaptive. This is a big reason for doing the values and traits survey and the personal inventory. When a young man tells me that he is a determined person, I emphasize this theme throughout our therapy time together, but when he says that he is "just an angry guy," I challenge this assumption.

I have often used the "candy wrapper" story in my sessions to talk about the psychological concept of attribution. Many years ago, there was a study where researchers handed out candy to a group of fifth-graders during recess. The psychologists counted how many candy wrappers got thrown on the ground versus thrown in the trash can or put in their pockets. Then, for the next two weeks, the researchers asked the school staff to comment on how neat and clean the classroom was (which, apparently, it was) and how this must mean that these were neat and clean kids.

The custodian left a note on the blackboard (this was in the days before whiteboards and smart boards) that said something like, "This is the cleanest classroom in the whole school! You all must be really neat and clean kids!" The principal would drop in and say things like, "Wow! Look at this classroom. You kids must be really neat and clean kids!" And the teacher would make similar comments about the kids. These remarks were not just flattery or encouragement; they were essentially saying, "This is what you are like. You are a neat and clean person." This is what we call an *attribution*.

After two weeks of these positive attributions, the researchers reappeared on the playground with a bowlful of candy and, once again, they counted the number of candy wrappers that got thrown on the ground. As you might expect, there was a huge change, with significantly more kids putting their trash in the proper receptacles.

Now here comes the most interesting part. The researchers did the same experiment in the same school with another fifth-grade class. They gave out candy, then counted the number of wrappers that hit the ground. Except this time, instead of having the teachers and others make attributions, they taught the children the importance of littering. I can imagine them showing filmstrips and having the class members all sign a no-littering pledge. You know how fifth-graders are. They are all about saying that smoking is bad and they will never do it, that they won't do drugs, that they won't drink alcohol. You can imagine that they were all over the idea of not littering. Yet, when the researchers came back with the bowl of candy two weeks later, they found no changes. The kids threw nearly as many wrappers on the ground as before.

So why did the first class change and the second class keep on littering? The first class changed because they didn't just endorse a belief or a value, but they began to see themselves differently. They were neat and clean kids. And neat and clean kids do not litter—at least not as much.

Such is the power of attributions.

The therapeutic application here is that we act in line with how we see ourselves. If a person sees himself as one who gets rejected socially, then he will be more likely to be a person who is socially rejected. Conversely, if he sees himself as someone who is socially successful and competent, then this will tend to be his experience. Attributions can be good or bad, helpful or hurtful. Either way, they are powerful.

In therapy, I use the values and traits survey and the personal inventory to begin drawing out the underlying beliefs that the clients have about themselves. I typically use these self-reports early in the therapy process, and these serve as a guide for what aspects of self-concept I will try to strengthen and which ones I will try to undermine.

BEING HAPPY THROUGH SELF-REALIZATION

Go to the bookstore or check out Amazon.com and you will find dozens of books with "happiness" in the title, all of them preaching the importance of being happy and the path to getting there. As a culture, we accept without challenge the argument that the greatest good is happiness. Sometime during the first session, I always ask parents what they want for their sons. The most common response I get is, "I just want him to be happy." Richard Layard (2006) writes in *Happiness: Lessons from a New Science* that happiness is the ultimate goal because it is self-evidently good.

While most of us assume that being extremely happy is the best possible goal a person could have, the research has found that moderately happy people tend to be better off than extremely happy people. Ed Diener, a professor at the University of Illinois, found that extremely high levels of happiness might not lead to as much psychological well-being than moderate levels of happiness. He and his colleagues looked at six different studies of happiness and life satisfaction. Their results found that the optimum level of happiness is "moderately happy" and not "extremely happy" (Oishi, Diener, & Lucas, 2007). In several of those studies, investigators found that the happiest people ended up with less education and lower income levels than moderately happy people. Extremely happy college students were very social and had a good time, but they also had lower grades than their moderately happy peers. Being extremely happy is not always for the best.

Negative emotions, like worry and even sadness, may serve good purposes for us, especially in low or moderate doses. A little worry, for example, might keep us on our toes and make our performance better in certain situations. So it's okay to be just moderately happy because other parts of life, like work and school performance and physical health, may be better off. In an interview, Diener argued that a person at a 4 might need help, but somone at an 8 might be good enough. In my non-clinical sample of young men, the average rating was indeed 8, while in the clinical sample of young men, the average rating was a 6, with some from both samples rating themselves as low as a 3. When considering averages, ranges, and standard deviations for all this data on more than 200 young men, I suggest that the optimal level of happiness based on self-report is 7–9. Whenever possible, that is the target range.

Happiness Redefined

Seligman (2004) says that true happiness comes from three major sets of life experiences: experiencing "pleasantness," being engaged in satisfying activities, and having a sense of meaning that comes from being connected to a greater whole. In other words, a person isn't happy just by having fun or feeling pleasure.

In my own study of highly effective parents, I found that one of the qualities that separated the great parents from the not so great was that the excellent parents seemed more interested in their child's character than in his or her subjective well-being (Verhaagen, 2005). In interviews, they talked more about wanting their child to be a person of integrity or honesty or compassion or other personal qualities than they did about wanting him to be happy. They were not opposed to happiness, but it was not as much a part of their expressed desires and hopes for their children. This struck me as a particularly profound finding, given our culture's focus on happiness.

We are raised with the assumption that happiness—usually defined as pleasure and comfort—is the greatest goal of life. Therapists accept this goal and focus on pain reduction, which makes good sense, since our clients are usually in emotional pain or have done things that bring pain to others. We are wired to alleviate human suffering. But to be honest, if the goal of life is to feel perpetually happy and not feel pain, then we have all failed miserably. Pain is an inescapable aspect of human existence. Worse, if pain reduction is the central goal, then it sends us down all kinds of lousy paths of pain avoidance and pleasure seeking.

However, there is something good about the desire to instill happiness. What I suggest is that we reframe the concept of *happiness* and move away from seeing it as simply feeling good and experiencing no pain. I propose that *happiness ultimately is the satisfaction that comes from living a meaningful life.* A person is truly happy when he or she has a sense of meaning and purpose. Happiness is not just sustained positive feelings or the absence of negative feelings. It is a product of living a life in line with personal values that bring meaning.

This notion is nothing new. Many of the ancient philosophers recognized this. Aristotle said that when a person acts in line with his nature and achieves his full potential, he will do good and be happy. He went a step further and said that, to become a real person, a man must realize his potential. Happiness is the ultimate goal, but it is achieved, said Aristotle, by becoming aware of one's self, one's talents, and one's direction in life. In short, he said that happiness was achieved by self-realization, a discovery of what a person was meant to be. He also argued that distressing emotions like sadness and frustration were caused by unrealized potential, which he said leads to a sense of aimlessness, and, ultimately, a poor life. While we don't have to fully buy into this simplistic notion of the source of negative emotions, it seems that he was on to something.

Some of my colleagues who are practitioners of the third-wave cognitive-behavioral therapies like Acceptance and Commitment Therapy (ACT) would take exception, saying we need to lay the "happiness agenda" aside. I like their thinking and their willingness to challenge the standard assumptions, but I see it somewhat differently. Happiness can be a good goal, provided that it is seen as a journey and not a destination. Happiness does not mean the absence of pain, because pain will always be part of that journey.

So I suggest that the movement toward happiness is good, but seeing it as merely pain avoidance and pleasure seeking is ultimately wrongheaded and may even lead to greater problems. Instead, true happiness is accomplished in a deeper way when we find a greater sense of meaning and purpose. So when a client says, "I just want to be happy," I can accept that goal, but only after we have discussed how pain and struggle may still be present and how happiness comes from knowing yourself and acting in line with your own beliefs, values, and passions.

While this is a position with which not everyone ultimately agrees, I find that most clients readily accept this way of thinking of happiness, and they are more than eager to explore it. To do that, I use a straightforward but energizing process that I described in *Parenting the Millennial Generation* (Verhaagen, 2005), which has also been written about by Harvard professor Tal Ben-Shahar (2007) in his excellent book, *Happier*. Though we use slightly different terms, we describe three circles of our life:

Passions: those things that we love, that stir us, that captivate us
Skills: those things that we do well, where we have talent or great potential
Meaning: those areas of life where we finding meaning and purpose

Imagine those circles overlapping like a Venn diagram, the center point being where all three circles overlap, as seen in Figure 6.1. The goal is to find that sweet spot in the middle, where all of these things intersect. When that happens, the person has the road map to live a happier life. It's an elegant construct that serves as a practical guide for living well.

Neither I nor Ben-Shahar (2007) have previously described this idea in the context of clinical work. I talked about the concept for use in parenting; he uses it for self-help. However, over the years, I have found that it has great utility in therapy. The influence of positive psychology here is obvious. Counseling and therapy can help in solving life problems by helping people live the life that they want.

Marlon and I took the next step in gaining a greater sense of his identity by doing this exercise. First, I showed him the three circles and explained the concept. I told him what the goal was before we started. I began by asking him to list out everything he enjoyed, whether it was something trivial or very important. Unlike the previous exercise, he found this easy to do. He gave me a strong list of about 20 things, ranging from playing basketball to cooking to designing clothing (which I had no idea he liked until we did this exercise). After we had this list, I asked him which ones he felt like he had great skill or potential in. I told him ahead of time that there are some areas of passion that you can't really be that good in, so we could skip those. On his list, things like

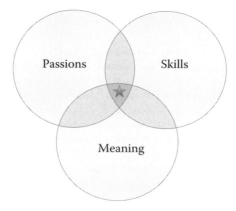

Figure 6.1   Passions, skills, and meaning.

"Hanging out with friends" and "Listening to music" were examples of those. Still, he was able to identify about seven areas of skill or potential skill, and we circled each of those. Finally, I asked him to look over the whole list again, and we would put a star by those areas that brought him a sense of meaning or purpose. Only three items got a star. When all of these steps were complete, he had just two things that were both circled (skill) and starred (meaning): designing clothing and writing lyrics. Both were creative ventures, very much in line with his core trait of creativity. We talked about ways that he could pursue these things, either as a career, a hobby, or one of each. It let us talk about what these paths might look like, what the potential obstacles would be, and how he could begin, even now, to move forward toward these.

One of the trickier tasks with this exercise is when a client ends up identifying areas that are just not practical or seem highly improbable. For example, I have had several clients of average height who are not even on their high school team identify a professional sport as their sweet spot. The dilemma is whether to encourage this or not. Therapists are of different opinions about this, since no one wants to be the guy who dissuades the next Michael Jordan or Tiger Woods from following his dreams. However, the truth is that Jordan and Woods were clearly on a path toward their dreams by the time they were 16. Much has been made about how Jordan was cut from the varsity team his sophomore year, but it was clear even at the time that he had skill and was capable of becoming an excellent athlete.

My tendency is to hit some sort of middle ground, where I don't actively discourage the dream, but I make sure that there are other reasonable alternatives to consider and pursue. There are always anecdotes of that one-in-a-million individual who overcomes the odds to become a pro ball player or successful rap artist or famous actor. I am grateful for these people and the hope they give others, but my desire is for my clients to have a sense that they can have meaningful lives without being rich or famous.

The Personal Toll of Materialism

Materialism and the desire for increasingly more and more is rampant in our culture. Kasser (2002) argues persuasively that these materialistic pursuits lead to a less happy, less self-fulfilled life. In his research, he found that "participants highly focused on materialistic values reported less self-actualization and vitality and more depression than those with less interest in those values" (p. 12). Other researchers have come to similar conclusions and have noted the link between materialism and reduced well-being (Christopher, Kuo, Abraham, Noel, & Linz, 2004; Christopher, Morgan, Marek, Keller, & Drummond, 2005; Dean, Carroll, & Yang, 2007; Kashdan & Breen, 2007). Kasser concludes, "The more materialistic values are at the center of our lives, the more our quality of life is diminished" (p. 14).

Kasser & Ryan (1996) spell out three very specific types of materialistic values that they say can ultimately do harm to a person's sense of well-being:

- *Financial success*: a focus on wealth and possessions
- *Social recognition*: a focus on fame, admiration, and social status
- *Appealing appearance*: a focus on attractiveness and image

Not only do these pursuits have a negative impact on a person's emotional well-being, but they also can adversely affect even someone's physical health. According to Kasser's (2002) research, "People who believed it is important to strive for possessions, popularity, and good looks also reported more headaches, backaches, sore muscles, and sore throats than individuals less focused on such goals" (p. 11). He found that young adults who say that financial success is a core value tend to have lower ratings of subjective well-being, higher distress, and greater difficulty adjusting to changes and stressors.

Aggressively chasing materialistic values like money, fame, and looks, it seems, may be reinforced by our culture, but these pursuits may get us far from a good, meaningful, and happy life. For our clients, it is wise for us to be aware of how these values might negatively affect their lives. When we focus on identity issues in therapy with a pursuit toward helping our clients lead happier lives, it's good for us to know that their quest for these so-called materialistic values may be ultimately dissatisfying and perhaps even harmful to them.

The Importance of Values Passion

Using the values and traits survey, I conducted a study of more than 150 young men and asked them to rate 15 values (see Table 6.A), including such things as being well educated, helping others, and being close to family, as well as 38 personal characteristics (see Table 6.B), such as being hardworking, loyal, and creative. In both cases, the ratings ranged from 1 (not important) to 10 (extremely important).

I found that the average guy rated himself as being about a 7 on a 1–10 scale for being happy. Ratings of 6–9 were in the average range for these young men. In the study, I found that the happiest guys rated their values higher and more intensely compared with those who were less happy. The happier guys saw friendship, faith, family, and all the other values as being more important. Of the 15 rated values, the happier guys rated themselves higher for each of them. In other words, *happier guys had more passion.* Happy guys were more passionate, and passionate guys were more happy.

Similarly, when I compared guys who were in therapy (N = 42) with a nonclinical sample (N = 121), I found that the therapy clients were not only less happy than the average guy, but they also rated the values as less important. Of the 15 values, those in therapy rated 12 of them lower—in some cases much lower—while the other three values (romance, helping others, taking care of the Earth) were rated equally by both groups. Guys in treatment placed less weight on personal values than their peers. There seems to be a relationship between how happy a young man is and how much passion he has for his own values. As the importance of personal values increases, so does a young man's happiness.

As part of the work in helping a young man to discover his passions, it would be a good idea to include an exploration of personal values. In particular, here are a dozen important values listed in Table 6.A for each client to explore:

1. Physical fitness
2. Friendship
3. Education
4. Career
5. Religious/spiritual faith
6. Fun
7. Romance
8. Helping others
9. Making an impact on the world
10. Being a good person
11. Close family relationships
12. Taking care of the Earth

To round out the 15 values listed in Table 6.A, there are also three so-called materialistic values associated with negative outcomes described by Kasser & Ryan (1996). It would be good to know how important these are to your client, as well:

1. Wealth
2. Attractiveness
3. Fame

In my study, being famous was by far the lowest-rated value among both the clinical and nonclinical samples. Being wealthy and attractive were in the bottom third for both samples. When these three values are rated highly by a client, you may want to bring it up later for more discussion.

Some young men come into therapy with a well-defined sense of identity, while others have barely begun this developmental task that should have been underway since middle school. For some clients, you should guide them in exploring their values and self-descriptions. For others, you need to help them act in line with their defined values. The goal for all of them is that they would discover a sense of meaning and purpose, and then move toward it with passion. For guys like Marlon, you may begin far from that ideal, but helping them to define themselves and explore their options can move them many steps closer to a sense of identity.

THERAPY TAKE-AWAYS

1. Do a personal inventory with your clients to help them identify strengths, areas that are just average, and weaknesses. Discuss it in length.
2. Use the power of attributions. Catch and challenge negative self-attributions you hear from your clients ("I'm lazy") and instill positive attributions whenever possible.
3. Help a client identify his personal passions, areas of skill, and sense of meaning. Find the areas where these three overlap.

APPENDIX: VALUES AND TRAITS SURVEY

Today's Date: _____ **Your Age:** _____ **Your Sex:** M or F

Racial Background (Circle only one): African American   Asian   Caucasian
Hispanic   Biracial   Other

Your School (optional): _____

APPENDIX TABLES

6.A   Preferences and Values

**Rate how important the following things are to you from 1 (not important) to
10 (extremely important):**

1. Being wealthy	1	2	3	4	**5**	**6**	**7**	8	9	10
2. Being physically attractive	1	2	3	4	5	**6**	**7**	**8**	9	10
3. Being physically fit	1	2	3	4	5	**6**	**7**	**8**	9	**10**
4. Having lots of friends	1	2	3	4	**5**	**6**	**7**	8	9	10
5. Being well educated	1	2	3	4	5	6	**7**	**8**	**9**	**10**
6. Having a successful career	1	2	3	4	5	6	**7**	**8**	**9**	**10**
7. Having an active spiritual or religious faith	1	**2**	**3**	**4**	5	6	7	8	9	10
8. Having fun	1	2	3	4	5	6	7	**8**	**9**	**10**
9. Being in a close romantic relationship	1	2	3	4	**5**	**6**	**7**	**8**	9	10
10. Helping others	1	2	3	4	5	**6**	**7**	**8**	**9**	10
11. Making an impact on the world around me	1	2	3	4	**5**	**6**	**7**	**8**	9	10
12. Being famous	1	**2**	**3**	**4**	**5**	6	7	8	9	10
13. Being a good person	1	2	3	4	5	6	**7**	**8**	**9**	**10**
14. Being close to my family	1	2	3	4	5	**6**	**7**	**8**	**9**	**10**
15. Taking care of the Earth and the environment	1	2	3	**4**	**5**	**6**	**7**	8	9	10

Note: Numbers in bold represent the average range for that item.

6.B   Self-Description

Rate yourself from 1 (completely not true of you) to 10 (perfectly describes you) on the following traits:

1. Affectionate	1	2	3	4	**5**	6	7	8	9	10
2. Artistic	1	**2**	3	**4**	5	6	7	8	9	10
3. Athletic	1	2	3	4	**5**	6	7	8	9	10
4. Compassionate	1	2	3	4	5	**6**	7	8	9	10
5. Competitive	1	2	3	4	5	6	7	8	9	**10**
6. Confident	1	2	3	4	**5**	6	7	8	9	10
7. Creative	1	2	3	**4**	5	6	7	8	9	10
8. Easygoing	1	2	3	4	5	6	7	8	9	**10**
9. Energetic	1	2	3	4	**5**	6	7	8	9	10
10. Forgiving	1	2	3	4	**5**	6	7	8	9	10
11. Friendly	1	2	3	4	5	6	7	8	9	**10**
12. Fun loving	1	2	3	4	5	6	7	8	9	**10**
13. Funny	1	2	3	4	5	**6**	7	8	9	10
14. Generous	1	2	3	4	5	**6**	7	8	9	10
15. Good-looking	1	2	3	4	**5**	6	7	8	9	10
16. Happy	1	2	3	4	5	6	7	8	9	10
17. Hardworking	1	2	3	4	**5**	6	7	8	9	10
18. Honest	1	2	3	4	5	**6**	7	8	9	10
19. Independent	1	2	3	4	**5**	6	7	8	9	10
20. Kind	1	2	3	4	5	**6**	7	8	9	10
21. Likeable	1	2	3	4	5	**6**	7	8	9	10
22. Logical	1	2	3	4	5	6	7	8	9	**10**
23. Loyal	1	2	3	4	5	6	7	8	9	**10**
24. Mature	1	2	3	4	5	**6**	7	8	9	10
25. Moral	1	2	3	4	5	**6**	7	8	9	10
26. Motivated	1	2	3	4	**5**	6	7	8	9	10
27. Open-minded	1	2	3	4	5	6	7	8	9	**10**
28. Optimistic	1	2	3	4	**5**	6	7	8	9	10
29. Organized	1	2	**3**	**4**	5	6	7	8	9	10
30. Passionate	1	2	3	4	5	**6**	7	8	9	10
31. Patient	1	2	3	**4**	5	6	7	8	9	10
32. Respectful	1	2	3	4	5	**6**	7	8	9	10
33. Reliable	1	2	3	4	5	**6**	7	8	9	10
34. Religious	1	**2**	3	**4**	5	6	7	8	9	10
35. Responsible	1	2	3	4	5	6	**7**	8	9	10

6.B (*Continued*) Self-Description

36. Self-controlled	1	2	3	4	**5**	**6**	7	8	9	10
37. Smart	1	2	3	4	5	6	**7**	**8**	9	10
38. Spiritual	1	**2**	**3**	**4**	5	6	7	8	9	10

Note: Numbers in bold represent the average range for that item.

6.C Temperament

Rate yourself from 1 (extremely low) to 10 (extremely high) on the following traits:

Sensitivity: disturbed by noise, light, textures, and other changes (10 = extremely sensitive)	1	2	3	4	5	6	7	8	9	10
Distractibility: easy to get off task because of external things (10 = extremely distractible)	1	2	3	4	5	6	7	8	9	10
Persistence: can stick with something, even if frustrated (10 = extremely persistent)	1	2	3	4	5	6	7	8	9	10
Regularity: regular routine, schedule, and daily habits (10 = extremely regular routine, including sleeping and eating)	1	2	3	4	5	6	7	8	9	10
Approach: at ease with new people and social situations (10 = extremely at ease with new people or situations)	1	2	3	4	5	6	7	8	9	10
Adaptability: can adjust to changes in routine or schedule (10 = extremely adaptable with changes in routine or schedule)	1	2	3	4	5	6	7	8	9	10
Intensity: strong reactions to things that happen (10 = extremely intense reactions)	1	2	3	4	5	6	7	8	9	10
Activity: amount of movement or restlessness (10 = extremely active or restless)	1	2	3	4	5	6	7	8	9	10
Mood: positive mood and outlook (10 = extremely positive mood and outlook)	1	2	3	4	5	6	7	8	9	10

·

7

Improving Emotional Intelligence

Compared to women, young men are typically not as good with what we have come to call *emotional intelligence*, the ability to understand, sort out, and manage emotions. Whether this is due to some biological differences, the impact of culture and socialization, or both, the fact remains that guys are often not as skilled with this as girls. Not only that, but many guys don't want to be skilled with it. They take pride in how they are non-emotional or in the ways they have found to avoid unpleasant feelings.

It's worth noting that the emotional deficits of the boys who typically come in for therapy may not be as common in boys who do not need therapy. Many young men are highly tuned into their feelings and extremely emotionally intelligent, and are able to maintain good relationships and manage their emotions with relative ease. By contrast, those with the greatest deficits probably experience relationship and other difficulties that result in their needing therapy. Many of the young guys who come in for therapy would best be described as emotionally avoidant. These guys don't like to think or talk about feelings. They don't like to have feelings, especially not feelings of sadness or anxiety.

"I hardly ever feel anything," was how Marlon expressed it in our second meeting. He was right. He was high on the front end and back end of the day. In the middle of day, he just kept busy with work or video games and tried not to think too much.

Gabriel was the quintessential emotionally avoidant young man, stuffing his own emotions until they would pop out in furious rages, usually directed at the women in his life. Despite the string of relationship failures, he still held out his emotionally avoidant style as superior. He described an interaction with a friend who had just been "kicked to the curb" by his girlfriend. "He was crying like a little girl," Gabriel said, "and I told him, 'Man up and put your balls back on.'"

Emo boys like Ricky represent a bit of a rebellion against this stereotype of the unfeeling male. The emo movement celebrates emotional rawness and openness. Ricky, like some other emo boys I had seen, was emotionally naked, almost reveling in rage and anxiety and deep sorrow, often to the point of emotional meltdowns and self-injury. One of my emo boys once wore a shirt that said, "If your lawn were emo, it would cut itself." I was struck by how comfortable he was in identifying himself with this.

But if you listen to Ricky, even he associates the emotional with the feminine. He explained in a later session, "I feel very comfortable with the feminine side of myself, the part of me that lets feelings out, that isn't afraid to cry or get pissed off." Even among the more emotionally expressive guys, there is often an underlying belief that emotions belong to the feminine and not the masculine.

Whether or not you believe in biologically based aspects of male emotional functioning, you must acknowledge the huge role of socialization and culture on how men develop emotionally. From an early age, boys are conditioned to inhibit their emotions. Whether from parents, peers, or pop culture, the message is clearly that boys don't cry and real men aren't emotional wimps. One recent cultural movement lamented the "feminizing of boys" in the school system, citing, among other things, attempts to get boys to be more emotionally sensitive and expressive, the clear implication being that this is not what boys regularly do.

The cumulative effect of all these messages is that, by young adulthood, many guys may inhibit their emotions to the point that it adversely affects their relationships. Levant (2008) described what he coined *normative male alexithymia*, a term that refers to men's inability to put feelings into words. Some men, he contends, have no language—internally or expressively—for emotion. Others have argued that there are no gender-specific differences in alexithymia and suggest there are major similarities in the ways that males and females experience emotions (Wester, Vogel, Pressly, & Heesacker, 2002). Alexithymia is a clinical syndrome seen in many diagnoses like eating disorders and PTSD, while normative male alexithymia is thought of as a subclinical state that has significant implications for the therapy process nonetheless. I urge caution in overextending the concept of alexithymia or even normative male alexithymia to the general population of males, but an understanding of these concepts may prove helpful in your therapy work with many young men.

PROMINENT FEATURES OF ALEXITHYMIA

Taylor and Bagby (2000) detail the prominent features of alexithymia (which literally means "lack of words for emotions") that have significant implications for clinical work. I have somewhat revised their formulation along the internal and external dimensions of the syndrome:

No Internal Language for Emotions

Alexithymic individuals have significant trouble with identifying emotions and telling the difference between one feeling and the other. In other words, all emotions feel the same. Because there is no internal language for the emotions, there is very little way of telling the difference between them. Since anger increases heart rate and constricts the stomach and so does anxiety, then anger and anxiety could be experienced as the same thing, for example.

One of the big flashes of insight for me came from Beverly James's classic *Treating Traumatized Children* (1996), in which she described the differences between how nontraumatized, traumatized, and traumatized alexithymic children respond to a stimulus. Alexithymic children would respond to nearly any emotional provocation, good or bad, in the same way: with rising panic and alarm. So if an alexithymic child scored a goal in the soccer game, his heart rate would increase, his breathing would become more rapid, his muscles would tighten, but because he could not distinguish the emotion, it would feel the same way it did when he saw his stepfather beating his mother or some other horrifying event. He would go into an alarm state and keep escalating his behavior until it was intense enough to make his body automatically numb itself.

At the time I first read this, I was working as the clinical director for an agency that served highly aggressive adolescents. Until then, we had always interpreted these events psychologically. For example, if a traumatized kid in one of our group-home or secure residential programs made a higher level or had a successful home visit, he would often follow it up with some insanely provocative behavior like assaulting a staff member or throwing a chair the following day. We would say things like, "He can't handle success. He feels like he doesn't deserve it." In other words, we gave it a psychodynamic interpretation. Yet when you would debrief with the boy, he would usually tell you he wished he could take it back and had wanted a second chance. He wanted to be successful and leave the group home, or so he claimed. Our understanding of alexithymia among traumatized children changed how we often interpreted those events. It was also a lesson in listening better to our clients and laying aside our traditional interpretations.

Alexithymic individuals have no language for emotion. Because of this, they are left with only bodily sensations and cues. And because these sensations and cues overlap so much, one emotion feels just like the next.

Impaired Internal Richness

It follows that if you don't distinguish emotions well or have much of a language for them, you probably will not have some of the internal experiences that draw from emotions, like imagination, creativity, healthy fantasy, or even much of a vivid dream life. Taylor and Bagby

(2000) talk in terms of constricted imagination and paucity of fantasy. The notion here is that alexithymic individuals lack the internal texture and richness that others have.

Think for a moment about the most emotionally alexithymic client you currently see. How does he do with recalling emotionally tinged experiences, being creative, or using his imagination? My bet is that he doesn't do any of these well at all. Of course, this has obvious implications for how far you can go with therapy.

A while back, I saw a young man who had lost both parents in the span of just two years. His father had been shot during a drug-related incident, and his mother had died of breast cancer about 18 months later. Before their deaths, the house had been full of chaos and violence, mostly due to his father's drug abuse and sales. This young man could not remember a single experience of his childhood. Not one. He had no memory of anything, good or bad. He couldn't imagine what his mother even looked like, even though he had pictures of her. He had no dreams. It was like 18 years had been erased. Unlike some others who dissociate, he gave no evidence of this. Instead, it was as if he had never encoded any emotional experiences in the first place.

Obviously, this example is an extreme, but many alexithymic clients are not far from him in their lack of inner world. They simply do not have the interior dimensions that come from fully experiencing emotions.

No External Language for Emotion

If you have no internal language for emotion, you cannot have an external language for emotion. That is, you cannot describe what you are feeling to someone else if you don't know what you are feeling yourself. This partly explains why so many therapists find work with young men immensely frustrating. Trained to elicit feeling talk, therapists get lots of "I don't know" and "Nothing" from their male clients. Sometimes this is seen as resistance when it should be more accurately described as a true deficit in being able to articulate much of anything having to do with emotion.

Externally Oriented Cognitive Style

An externally oriented cognitive style refers to a style of thinking that is overly concrete and based on what can be observed externally rather than on internal experiences and subjective feelings. Guys with this style of thinking might like going to see a good action film, but be turned off by seeing a movie that had deeper subtext or focused on relationships. They might want to spend a weekend camping or fishing with friends, but they wouldn't want to talk about emotional things. They might quickly volunteer to help a friend move, but not want to get the call from a buddy who wanted to talk about a difficult breakup.

Guys with an externally oriented thinking style believe that you can live a good life with little or no awareness of your own deepest emotions. They tend to eschew therapy and the need to "talk about feelings." When these young men do come into therapy, they would much rather describe the practical facts of their difficulties rather than dive into any emotional intricacies or nuances.

BUILDING A LANGUAGE OF EMOTION

The remedy for this is to build an internal language for emotions. I often start by talking about how men are socialized to avoid and suppress emotion, except for anger, and the impact this tends to have on them. I explain the concept of alexithymia, though I rarely if ever have used that term. It sounds like the worst kind of psychology word, and it would be nearly impossible for a person to remember it. (I would love for someone to invent a word that means the same thing but sounds like an actual word.) The concept is readily understood, even if you don't use the term.

From there, I start to build an internal, language-based framework for emotion. Among our three guys, both Gabriel and Marlon would fall into the category of normative male alexithymia. All three of them, however, could be served by some internal structuring of emotion.

I talk about primary emotions much as one would talk about primary colors. There is one primary positive emotion. Most people refer to it as *happy*, but it could also be called joy. There are three negative primary emotions. First, there is *sad*, which is also referred to as feeling down, discouraged, or depressed. Second, there is *anger*, which is also called mad, rage, or pissed off. Frustration is a variation of anger. Finally, there is *worry*, which is also related to fear, anxiety, or being nervous. I write all three of these negative emotions—sad, anger, worry—in a row near the top of the board.

For the most part, young men have a difficult time understanding their emotions and sorting them out. Most guys find it easy to feel happiness and joy, of course. They are also socialized to be comfortable with anger, but have greater trouble with the other emotions. Feeling sad and worried are the tougher emotions. There are many times when guys will feel sad, but it will come out looking like anger. The same goes for worry. There are also times when a young man will experience a mixture of emotions, like sadness and anger at the same time, and it will still come out just as anger. To sort all of this out, it can be helpful to think of the three primary negative emotions, each with its own root (cause) and anchored in some temporal (time) point.

Of the three guys, Marlon was the most disconnected from his emotions. Fear and sadness were strangers to Gabriel, but at least he felt mad and had some passion about his life. Marlon did not seem to feel anything. He was so cut off from his emotions that he seemed almost lifeless at times. We spent some early sessions talking about the role and importance of emotions. I taught him about the primary emotions, and he understood this easily. From there, I wanted to show him the roots of each of these feelings.

"Let's start with sad," I told him. "You feel sad when your grandfather dies, when your girlfriend breaks up with you, when you move to another state and leave your friends behind. In other words, you feel sad when you experience a *loss*."

He nodded with understanding. It made sense to him. I wrote the word *loss* and drew an arrow connecting it up to the word *sad*. I moved on to anger.

"You feel anger when your teacher gives you a poor grade on a group project when you put hours of work into it," I began. "You feel anger when your boss cuts your hours when you need the money. You feel anger when your aunt goes into your room and snoops around without permission."

He nodded again, but I could tell he couldn't quite see the link yet. This one was a little trickier to grasp.

"You get angry when something is unfair and out of your control to change it. In other words, there is some *injustice* in your life that makes you mad. Something is affecting you, and it usually feels like it is unfair or unjust."

He understood where I was going as I wrote the word *injustice* under the word *anger*. This, too, seemed to make sense to him. I went to the last of the primary negative emotions.

"You might feel worried when someone follows you after you leave your restaurant late at night," I said. "You might get worried when you are getting ready to take a test that will determine your whole semester grade or when your aunt isn't there when you get home from work and you don't know where she might have gone. In other words, you get worried when there is some kind of *threat*. It may be a threat to your physical safety, your future, a relationship, your reputation, another person you care about, or so on."

I wrote the word *threat* under the word *worry*. He nodded once more to let me know he was with me. We had completed the second level. There was still one level to go.

"Each of these primary emotions is connected to time in some way. I will show you what I mean," I explained. I pointed to the first column with *loss* underneath the word *sad*. "Because loss is something that has already happened, sadness is usually anchored in the *past*. The simplest way to say this is that you get sad because of a loss in the past."

I moved over to the next column with *anger* at the top and the word *injustice* below it. "And because it is usually something that affects you right now, it is an emotion rooted in the *present*. Even if it is something that actually happened in the past—like your teacher giving you a low grade or your aunt looking through your room—you feel angry because of how it affects the present moment. Anger is an emotion that results from an injustice in the present, even if it is something that has already

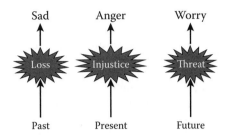

Figure 7.1   Whiteboard 1.

happened—a bad grade, a violation of privacy, a disrespect, and so on—but it affects how your life is now."

"I'm with you," he said.

I moved on to the last emotion. I pointed to the column with *worry* on top and *threat* underneath. "Worry is about what might happen," I said. "So feelings of worry are nearly always about the future. Something is a threat—to your body, your reputation, someone you care about—that may happen in the future, even the very near future."

When I was done explaining, our whiteboard looked something like Figure 7.1. This simple construction by itself is often very helpful to young men. It is not so much information as to be overwhelming, but it is enough to serve as a foundation for becoming more aware of what they are feeling. It is, in essence, a starter set for emotional intelligence.

UNDERSTANDING EMOTIONAL MASH-UPS

Using these primary emotions is helpful, but there is another critical early step in helping a young man become aware of what he is feeling. Occasionally, we have a pure emotion like anger or sadness. Much of the time, though, we are experiencing more than one emotion at a time.

Ricky is prone to this much of the time. When he can't go out, he doesn't really know what he feels; he just knows he *really* feels it. I did the same exercise with Ricky that I had done with Marlon, going through the three negative primary emotions and discussing what was underneath each one. After we talked about this simple construction of primary emotions, I pointed to the board and did something I rarely do in therapy: I asked a trick question! But at least I acknowledged it as such.

"Ricky, I am going to ask you a trick question," I said.

"Okay," he replied with just a hint of a smile.

"People often feel angry and sad at the same time, so what is the word that means angry and sad?"

"Sangry?" he said, jokingly.

"I'm so sangry!" I said with a laugh. "I guess that's as good an answer as any."

"I really don't know," he said.

"And you know why you don't know?"

"Because there isn't a word that means that?" he half-said, half-asked.

"That's right," I told him. "As much as we feel sangry, we really don't have a word for it. And that's a key part of understanding your emotions. We understand emotions by using language—either in our head or by talking or writing—and that's why people say, 'You should talk about your feelings.' Talking about it doesn't change what has happened, it just helps you process it and give it a little form so you can get a grip on it."

"I usually do feel better if I call a friend like Holly if I am really upset, even if there's nothing she can do about it," he said.

"That's right. It's not about solving the issue. It's just about using words to get a handle on what you are feeling," I explained. "So what happens if you have a mash-up or a hybrid of emotions, like *sad/angry* or *angry/worried* or even *sad/angry/worried*, and there is not a word for that blend of emotion?"

"For me, I just get more pissed off," he said.

"And, to be honest, that is what happens for most guys. We aren't great at sorting out feelings, so it just comes out as a big ball of anger or rage."

"Definitely," he said.

"So what do you do if we use words to make sense of emotions, but sometimes we don't have accurate words to describe what we are feeling?" I asked.

"I have no idea," he said.

"To be honest, you aren't alone in that. Many guys really have no idea. Let me give you a simple image that might help. If you have two or three power cords tangled up and you want to use them, what do you do first?"

"Untangle them," he said.

"Right," I replied. "The same is true with emotions. If you have two or three emotions tangled up together, you first untangle them. And to do that, you can use this," I said as I gestured back toward the board. "You can start in the top, middle, or bottom to help you figure out what you are feeling."

"Okay," he said, but I could tell he was still not sure what this really meant practically.

"Let's practice with an example," I suggested. "Give me a time when you felt more than one feeling at the same time."

He pondered for a moment. "Okay, I've got one," he began. "When these guys at school were making fun of my tight pants. This was just last week."

"And what did you feel? Sad, Angry, Worried?"

"All three," he said.

"Good example," I said. "Let's pick it apart. Why were you sad?"

"I'm not sure," he said.

"Alright, so let's go down to the next level. What was the loss?"

"I don't know," he said, then paused and thought about it some more. "I guess loss of respect."

"That sounds right," I said. "And why were you angry?"

"I wanted them to stop and I couldn't do anything about it," he replied.

"Right," I added. "That was the injustice. You are seeing how this works now. And why were you worried?"

"I guess I thought it might continue or that they might get other people involved or that one of them might take it further," he said.

"All good reasons to feel worried," I said, noting that he actually had multiple aspects for this emotion. "There you go. You untangled it and put words to it, even though there wasn't one word for the tangle of emotion that you were feeling."

"That makes a lot of sense," he said.

"It can work in a few ways. If you know what you are feeling, then it helps you figure out why. If you are not sure what you are feeling, though, you can start with the middle row—loss, injustice, or threat—and then sort out what feeling that should lead to. So you can say to yourself, 'I feel worried or anxious, where's the threat?' or you can say, 'This is a threat, so what I'm feeling is probably anxiety or worry.' Does that make sense?"

"Absolutely," he said. "I can do that."

BODY WORK

There was one more part of this to add for Ricky, but we had to wait until the next session to make sure we had enough time. We were going to work on helping him distinguish emotions by using his bodily cues. Since some of these cues are overlapping and subtle, you can't be in a hurry when you do this work. You have to move at a slow pace to really do a good job with it.

It's a simple template. Using the same four primary emotions—happy, sad, angry, worried—I asked him to think of a time when he felt each specific emotion, one at a time. I have him imagine the scene as vividly as possible and describe it to me, often with his eyes closed if he has trouble concentrating on the feelings. I ask him to describe the details of the scene, then describe the feeling he has in his body when he is imaging what happened. I push for as much detail as I can get from how he feels it physically in his body. I work to distinguish one emotion's bodily sensations from another. I nearly always begin and end with a happy memory to bookend the experience.

Most guys, even those who have trouble articulating and verbally expressing their emotions, are usually able to do this exercise. For some, it is an enjoyable experience, while others don't care for it as much. With those who seem to be getting into the exercise, I often push it a step further and have them imagine scenes when they have those hybrid emotions—*sad/angry, angry/worried,* or *sad/worried*—and go through the steps again.

The purpose of the exercise is to get these young men some practice with accessing and distinguishing their emotions. The more they can pay attention to their internal state, the greater is their ability to manage and control their feelings without resorting to stuffing or avoiding their emotions. Most clients will accept this premise and be willing to do the work. For those who don't see the need for it or view such therapy work as uncomfortable, then it would be best to skip it.

Of our three young men, all three did the body work exercises, but they had different experiences with it. Marlon found it to be relatively easy to do and enjoyed it, even though he was the least in touch with his emotions in general. Afterward, he said, "I feel really relaxed." Ricky found it more difficult to do than I had expected, but he said it was helpful. Gabriel did the exercises without complaint, but did not seem to find it that helpful, though he was the least likely of the three to give positive feedback, so it was hard to judge.

Not long ago, I saw a high school senior who had experienced the loss of both parents. His face was blank and his speech was flat. He looked less shell-shocked than he did fatigued. There was no emotional energy behind his eyes or in his speech. When it came time to do this work, he could literally access not one single memory for any of the emotions. He was completely blocked. The exercise was a complete dead end until I asked him to construct situations where he was likely to feel those feelings. He came up with something that might make him happy, and we went through the exercise. We did the same thing with sad, angry, and worried. He did it well and began to connect to his emotions. He cried through the majority of the next two sessions, which is not always a good outcome, but was significant for him. It may be that you have some clients who are not good at recalling past emotional experiences. Such clients might find it easier or safer to construct hypothetical situations where they are likely to let themselves feel some intense emotions. This is not the same as constructing memories. It has to do with using the imagination to access emotional parts of their brains that are normally inaccessible to them. For some clients, it may go nowhere, but for others, it may open up some strong emotions.

IMPROVING STRESS COPING

During one of our earlier sessions, Gabriel came in looking visibly agitated. He greeted me politely, but his face was tense and his shoulders were drawn up.

"How's your week been?" I asked.

"Alright, I guess," he said.

"Tell me a good thing that's happened since I saw you last," I asked.

"Nothing, to be honest," he said.

"Then tell me a bad thing," I pressed.

"Nothing. It's been the same," he said dismissively.

"You look tense or frustrated," I said.

"It's just the same shit it was before. Same fucking shit!" he said. Gabriel was pretty free with the cursing, but he had never said it with such anger and intensity in a session before.

"Like what?" I asked.

"Like my mother nagging me until I feel like my fucking head is going to pop off. Like court in two weeks, and I don't have a job yet to pay for fucking court costs. Like my girlfriend being a total bitch about all this. You want me to go on?" he asked rhetorically.

"Yes," I said. I could see he was surprised that I wanted to hear more of this rant.

"No car. No friends anywhere around here. All of them are at school and I am sitting at home getting bitched at 24/7 by my parents. I have no fucking idea what I am going to do next semester. I am just stressed beyond belief," he said.

"That sounds like what we should talk about today," I said.

"Fine with me," he said in a nonchalant tone.

As with many young men in therapy, we started with "nothing" but quickly found that there was a deep well of material that needed to be tapped. All of this content came gushing up in under two minutes of walking in the door. For most guys, the best move is to add some structure to this process.

"Let's start by putting everything you just mentioned on the board," I said as I grabbed for the whiteboard. I asked him to rate each stressor from 1 (low) to 10 (very high). I asked him to tell me which of the negative primary emotions—sad, angry, worried—were provoked by each stressor. Finally, I asked him to rate how much control he had over each stressor—whether he had no control, some control, or total control. The board looked like Figure 7.2.

"Just study this for a few moments and then tell me what things you notice about it," I said.

He quietly looked it over. I noticed his shoulders were less hunched, his face was less tense. The process of articulating these stressors alone had seemed to give him a little bit of relief.

"Most of it makes me mad," he said.

"Yes," I said. "What else?"

"I have at least a little control over most of it, except for my parents," he said.

"Good. So you have some measure of control over most of your stress, and your stress tends to create a lot of anger in you," I said to summarize.

"Yeah," he said.

"Let's talk about what you can do about all this. When someone is feeling overwhelmed, there are *three options to manage stress*," I explained. "First, he might be able to *reduce his stressors*."

"I don't think I can do much of that," Gabriel explained.

Stressor	1-10	S	A	W	None	Some	Total
Court	10		X	X		X	
Girlfriend	8	X	X	X		X	
Parents	9		X		X		
Money	8		X	X		X	
Car	7		X			X	
Friends	7	X	X			X	
Future	9			X		X	

Figure 7.2   Whiteboard 2.

He may be correct. While there are some people who can look over their lives and chop out some nonessential areas of stress, there are others who cannot. For example, a student who is overextended with sports, theater, clubs, and studying may need to consider what has to go. In contrast, someone in Gabriel's situation may wish to get rid of certain stressors (parents' frustration with him, pending court, questions about the future), but doesn't have that option.

Many clients will say that they have no option of reducing their stressors at first, but then they may find a few areas that can be reduced or eliminated. It's worth a little conversation to explore the possibilities, but it's also wise for the therapist to be aware that some folks feel enormous stress that they cannot reasonably stop. Gabriel was one of those guys who could not eliminate any of his bigger stressors, at least not yet.

"I agree with you. It doesn't look like you can reasonably eliminate any of these right now. There is a second option," I said to Gabriel. "*You can think about the stressors differently.*"

"I don't understand that at all," he said.

"This is a tough option, but one you can always do," I said.

"Explain it, then," he said.

I wiped the board clear and prepared to write.

"Let's take three examples and put them on the board," I said. "Tell me three of the stressors that you want to use as examples.

"The first three: court, girlfriend, and parents are as good as any," he said.

"Okay, let's talk through the *automatic thoughts* that you have first. Those are the emotionally produced thoughts that happen automatically when you are faced with the stressor," I explained.

"I don't get it," he said.

"It's like watching a cable news program and the news ticker is at the bottom. It's always crawling with information, even though it may not be the main thing you are paying attention to at the time. Automatic thoughts are those thoughts that are happening while your life is going on, but they may not be what you are aware of."

"That makes more sense," he said.

We talked through each of the three examples and pulled out the automatic thoughts for each one, and I wrote them on the board.

"Now, let's talk about *corrected thoughts* for each one," I said. I explained that a corrected thought was a rational restatement of the thought that was based on what was true and not on feelings. "Sometimes we don't know what is true or what will happen, so that just becomes part of the corrected thought," I told him.

This whole process took us about 20 minutes because he didn't find it easy to identify the automatic thoughts or to generate an alternative corrected thought. Still, with some patience and persistence, we got there, and the board looked like Figure 7.3.

"So that's what we mean by the second option, changing the meaning of the stressors. It doesn't change the stressor itself, just how you think about it," I said.

"That might help some, but I don't think I will be very good at doing that," he said.

"Like many things that we talk about, it will take practice," I said.

"I like the idea, though," he said. "I just don't know if I'll do it that much."

"We'll come back to it another time, but let's talk about the third option. The third way you can manage your stress is to *increase coping strategies*," I said.

Stressor	Automatic Thoughts	Corrected Thoughts
Court	I am going to go to jail. I am going to humiliate my family.	I don't know what is going to happen, but the lawyer says I will not go to jail. I did something wrong, but I am not responsible for how they react to this.
Girlfriend	Our relationship will never be good again. She is going to leave me.	I don't know what will happen but I am willing to work on the relationship. I don't have any real evidence that says she is going to leave me.
Parents	They will never stop nagging me. I have broken their trust forever.	This is just a temporary time of my life. I am willing to work to earn their trust back and that's all I can do.

Figure 7.3   Whiteboard 3.

"I like this one the best," he said before I could even explain it fully.

"Let's use an example of a time when you really got stressed to talk about this option. Give me a time when you felt completely over-whelmed and didn't handle it well," I said.

"I've got a good one," he said. "I've never told anyone about it before."

He told me about his last girlfriend, about the first time she broke up with him and he flew into a rage, cursing and screaming at the top of his lungs. His reaction was so intense that he embarrassed himself. Later, he swore to her that he would never do it again, but his girlfriend was so freaked out and frightened by his reaction that she agreed to get back together with him. This lasted for about three months until she dumped him again.

This time, he was sitting in his Jeep alone as she gave him the bad news over the phone, obviously not wanting to face his wrath in person. He slammed his cell phone into the windshield, cracking the glass and destroying the phone. He pounded on the steering wheel and screamed. Finally, he began to punch himself in the face, bloodying his nose and blacking his eyes. The next day, he made up a cover story about getting really drunk and falling onto the pavement near the pool of his apart-ment complex.

"That's why I said having better coping skills was my best option. I just need some good ways to handle it when shit like that happens to me," he said in concluding the story.

"That's a good way to say it," I said. "You need 'good ways' to cope."

He nodded. "I got plenty of bad ways," he said with the first hint of a smile for the entire session.

"You've definitely got ways of coping," I continued, "but they just aren't very healthy for you. Everybody copes. If you get drunk when something bad happens, you're coping. If you punch yourself in the face, you are coping. Even if you fall down on the floor in a fetal position and suck your thumb, you're coping. So the issue isn't whether you will cope, it's *how* you will cope."

I cleared the whiteboard once more and drew a line down the middle. In the right-hand column, I wrote "Poor Coping" at the top; in the left-hand column, I wrote "Good Coping." He knew where I was going, so he continued without a prompt.

"Hitting myself in the face is definitely top of the list," he said, point-ing to the poor coping side. "Busting up shit. Yelling. Getting drunk. Doing other drugs. Making threats," his words coming out faster than I could write.

"Good," I said as I wrote. "What else?"

"That's plenty," he said.

"Okay," I said, "Now how about the other column, some good ways to cope?"

He stared at me blankly. I waited.

"Give me a hint," he said with a little smile.

"Sure," I said. "You told me before you work out when you feel frustrated. That would be a good example." I wrote "Work out" on the board.

Good Coping	Poor Coping
Working out	Hitting self
Taking a shower	Breaking things
Going for run	Yelling
Playing video games	Getting drunk
Taking dog for walk	Using drugs
Listening to music	Making threats
Watching sports on TV	

Figure 7.4 Whiteboard 4.

"Right," he said. "I see where you are going. Alright, sometimes I go for a run."

I wrote "Going for run" on the board. He paused again and thought.

"Taking a shower sometimes works. Playing video games would work. Taking my dog for a walk," he said, flowing a little easier now. He paused again to think. "Listening to music. Watching sports on TV. That's about all I can think of right now."

"That's plenty," I said, as I finished writing everything he said. The board looked like Figure 7.4.

"What I am getting ready to tell you is easy to say but fairly tough to do," I told him. "Getting better at coping means you do less of these," I said as I pointed to the right column, "and more of these," I said as I gestured to the left. "Simple idea, but it takes some work."

"The big problem is that when I get stressed out, it's hard for me to think about what else I could do," he explained.

"I completely understand," I said. "This takes practice. "If you can mentally rehearse the options for good coping, you are more likely to use them when the time comes. Think of these good coping strategies as if they were on a computer drop-down menu in your head. You feel stressed and you immediately go to the drop-down and pick an option." I turned the board around and quizzed him. "Give me four options on your mental drop-down menu."

"Walk the dog. Play video games. Take a shower. Work out," he said.

"Good. And tell me one more," I said.

"Go for a run."

"Can you tell me the other two?" I asked.

"Watch sports and listen to music," he replied.

"You got them perfectly. I will ask you to list them at the beginning of our next meeting, too, if that's good with you," I said.

"That's good," he said.

"So just to recap," I said, "sometimes you can reduce your stressors, though in your case that is not going to happen right now. A second option is to think about your stressors differently by identifying automatic thoughts, then correcting those thoughts based on what is true and not on how you feel. And finally, you can deal with stress by using fewer poor ways to cope and using more good ways to cope."

"That's cool," he said. "Thanks."

For Gabriel, this was the first time he had expressed gratitude for a session. I could tell it was something he was going to use. Sometimes the simplest ideas are the most powerful, even with some of your smartest clients.

SKILLS FOR MAKING FRIENDS

If you ever get the chance to observe a group of young adult guys hanging out, you will inevitably hear them spouting off movie quotes, everything from *Borat* to *Austin Powers* to *Monty Python and the Holy Grail* to *Napoleon Dynamite* to *Office Space* to *Coming to America* or even *Scarface*. Where there is a group of guys, there will usually be movie quotes. ESPN columnist Chris McKendry says that there are five reasons why guys use movie quotes so much in conversation:

1. It's a bonding experience
2. Men can't express themselves and need the help
3. Nothing to talk about
4. Fear of intimacy
5. Quotes become part of the subconscious

The major theme here is that guys really don't know how to communicate with each other and seem to find some safe common ground with movie quotes. As a fan of movies, I have participated in this activity many times myself (my personal favorites being several Sean Connery lines), so I'm not knocking the practice. However, I think there is something to McKendry's point that men often really don't know how to relate to each other.

In my experience of seeing young men in therapy, it seems that most desire close guy friends, but they often lack the skills to take superficial joking and banter to another level. Those with close friendships know that the best relationships often involve conversations that go back and forth between silly teasing and deep sharing, sometimes within minutes of each other. There is the ability to take conversations to more authentic places and a willingness to let emotional intimacy happen.

Young men often have the silly and superficial parts down pat, but may not be good at going any further. For those guys, if they have a basic framework for deepening their relationships, they are often willing to do it. In therapy, we can equip them with a simple template and a set of skills that allows them to deepen their friendships and strengthen their relationship skills. I suggest educating them about the different kinds of social relationships, then giving them specific skills for navigating them.

There are two dimensions of friendships. The first aspect is the level of emotional depth. Some relationships are just superficial, while others have more depth. The next aspect is the length of time you know someone. Some relationships are brief and time-limited, like a college roommate or a coworker. You maintain the relationship for the period of time you are in proximity, then it drifts off after that. Other relationships are enduring and persist even when one of the individuals moves to another place or another station of life.

If you intersect these two dimensions—emotional depth and length of relationship—you have four types of relationships. A framework for thinking about these relationships can be helpful to many clients. Here are the four types of social relationships:

Acquaintances: are brief but superficial relationships. These make up the majority of all our relationships. Most people that we know in high school, college, young adulthood, or any stage of life are acquaintances. They may be people we like a lot, but we never get to know them well, and we don't keep up with them when that stage of life passes.

Buddies: are superficial but long-term relationships. These are the guys with whom you talk sports, movies, and girls. You joke with them and have a good time, but even though you may know them for many years, the relationship never goes very deep. Calling these relationships superficial is not a judgment against them. There is a big place in our lives for buddies, the guys who just want to go midnight bowling or surfing or just driving around town.

Friends: are deeper relationships that last for a season of life. For example, they may be college roommates. The relationships have depth with personal disclosure and sharing, but they may last only for a season of life. Friends also have fun like buddies do, but there is the ability to talk about personal things and real life. There is an element of trust and openness in these relationships that isn't there with acquaintances or buddies.

Brothers: are deep and enduring long-term friendships. There is openness, closeness, fun, and a sense of long-term commitment. These are the rarest of all peer relationships, and most guys would not typically have more than three people in this category. (A female in this category would rightly be called a *sister*.)

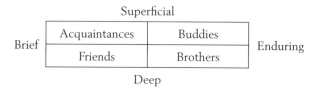

In therapy, you can use this grid to discuss examples of each and how his relationships have developed over time. You can explore whether he is content to have just buddies or whether he would like to have more true friends. You can ask if there are relationships in his life that have the potential of being like brothers. The framework allows you to explore his relationships in more detail and assess whether you need to spend more time in helping him think about and develop this important area of his life.

Deepening Relationship Skills

Brad was a freshman in college when I first met him. He was a tall, good-looking, athletic guy with an easy smile and an engaging laugh. Beneath this pleasant exterior, however, was a bundle of anxiety. Each new social interaction brought him a sense of dread or even outright terror. Every time his friends hauled him off to a party on campus, his stomach tightened up and he would start to sweat. He would usually end up going, but drank a lot so he could get relaxed enough to talk with people. Half the time, he got so drunk, he didn't even remember most of what he did the night before.

"It's the only way I can do it," he said.

"You mean drinking helps you get through it?" I asked.

"Right. I get too nervous. I can't think straight. I don't know what to say to people," he explained.

"You aren't sure what to do," I reflected.

"Yeah, that's it. I don't know what to do," he said.

I've had similar conversations like this dozens of times, socially anxious guys who don't know how to have a conversation, or boys who don't know how to talk to their girlfriends, or young men who have no idea how to resolve a basic conflict with a friend.

Years ago, I was touring a residential program in another city and the director showed me a copy of their social skills text: Dale Carnegie's *How to Win Friends and Influence People* (Carnegie, 1936/1998). At first I thought it was a joke, but the man was serious. This was the best text for helping his clients improve their social skills, he argued. After I left there, I picked up the book again and discovered that the good doctor was indeed correct. There is a reason why Dale Carnegie's little book continues to sell strongly more than 70 years since its original publication. Carnegie observed that people tend to do well socially when they show genuine interest and put the focus on the other person in conversations.

For many young men, this notion that they don't have to come up with something interesting or witty to say, but, instead, can just ask good questions and express curiosity about people, is liberating. Whether it is with friends or potential dating partners, young men often sweat the first steps of social interactions. Once relationships are established, many guys still have trouble maintaining them. Because adolescent boys and young men often struggle with relationships, social skills training is often an important and necessary part of the therapy process. Building on Carnegie's work, there are some specific skills you can teach to help improve both their confidence and competence in new relationships.

Nonverbal Skills

While there is some benefit to having an open posture, the majority of nonverbal communication comes from the head and face. Emphasize these three features:

- *Smiling*: communicates warmth and approachability
- *Nodding*: communicates interest and active listening
- *Eye contact*: communicates attention and regard

For many guys, just getting better at these three aspects of nonverbal communication can bring them one significant notch forward in their level of social skill. Often, it is good to be as direct as possible.

"You don't tend to smile when people talk to you, so they are going to make wrong assumptions about you," I told Marlon.

"They think I'm conceited," he said.

"Right. Or uninterested or bored—or boring—or cold. A bunch of things."

"I've gotten that from people before," he replied.

"So the way people signal interest or warmth early in a relationship is mostly by smiling," I explained.

As simple as it sounds, we spent the next few minutes having him practice giving me a smile—at least part of the time—as he spoke. It was unnatural and a bit of a chore for him, but it seemed to pay off. When I saw him in the waiting room before the next session, he smiled at me and it seemed genuine. I could tell it was something he had been doing.

Verbal Skills

The nonverbal skills are important, but they are extremely easy. The verbal skills take more work. As with the nonverbal skills, there are three areas to emphasize when you are building verbal skills. All of these are part of the repertoire we have come to call *active listening*.

- *Open questions*: are questions that invite the other person to talk in more detail. While a question like, "Did you watch the game this weekend?" is a closed question, asking, "What did you do this weekend?" is an open question. The single best open question is not really a question at all but an invitation to talk: "Tell me about…" You can use this stem in nearly any situation: Tell me about your weekend. Tell me about your plans for the break. Tell me about your family. Tell me about yourself. Watch sports reporters or late night hosts interview an athlete or an actor: Tell me about your strategy for the second half. Tell me what this win means to this franchise. Tell me about your new movie.
- *Follow-up questions*: are questions that come after the initial open questions. They can be open or closed, but the purpose of follow-up questions is to elaborate on the original answer and draw out more conversation. They express interest and communicate to the listener that you want him or her to keep talking. A follow-up question might be, "What did you guys do at the lake?" or "Which of your brothers are you closest to?" or "How did you learn to play the guitar?"
- *Reflections*: are when you say back to the person what he or she has just said, usually in slightly different words. Reflections are great because they communicate you are a good listener and have genuine interest in what the other person is telling you. They also let you know if you are understanding the person well. This is the hardest skill of all. It is tough to see the importance of it at first, but it is also difficult to do it well once you realize the benefit of it. All these skills require practice and rehearsal, but reflections require even more so. Reflections often begin with the word "so" or phrases such as "It sounds like…" and come after a person has responded to a question. Examples of reflections would be: "So it was just a relaxing weekend," or "It sounds like your younger brother is one of your closest friends," or "So you just taught yourself how to play." If you are out of sync with your reflection—even slightly—the person will usually tell you and let you correct your understanding of what he is saying. If a person reflects, "So you've had a pretty easy semester up to this point," and the other person says, "Well, there hasn't been a lot going on, but I wouldn't say it was easy," then it helps the listener sharpen his awareness of what is really being said.

As basic as these skills are, they can often have a profound effect on a young man's social competence and confidence. As with all the other skills, they only become useful with practice. Teach the skills, practice them, role-play, and rehearse them. Then do it again. It's like being a piano teacher or a basketball coach. Repetition brings mastery. Sometimes it is not the most thrilling part of therapy, but it can be one of the most helpful parts in the long run.

HELPING OTHERS

I hold the belief that the quality of our relationships largely determines the quality of our lives. When our relationships—with friends, family, significant others—are good, our lives tend to be good. When our relationships are struggling or stressful, our lives are usually a bit of a mess. This holds true for most, though not all, people. Healthy relationships lead to happier lives.

It's impossible to have healthy relationships, though, without the capacity to be at least somewhat empathetic and other-centered. Perhaps the best measure of this is a willingness to help others. Therapy is often accused of being a navel-gazing, self-centered venture. Those of us who have done it for awhile know better. When therapy is most effective, it turns people outward and frees them up to contribute to the lives of others in more powerful ways. One of the most rewarding aspects of therapy is watching young men move toward helping others as they get emotionally healthier.

When the time is right and you have seen significant progress in his life, ask him, "How do you think you could use what you have learned these past few months to give back to other people?" Therapy's goal is to produce healthier individuals, but its by-product should be a positive contribution to the greater good. Healthier people lead to healthier communities. Before therapy is complete, make it a regular practice to steer your clients toward making the world a little bit better by caring for other people.

THERAPY TAKE-AWAYS

1. Help your clients build an internal language for understanding emotions, especially sadness, anger, and worry. Connect these emotions to their typical roots and determine whether they are anchored to the past, present, or future.
2. List out all your clients' stressors, identify what emotions they hit, and how much control they have over each stressor. Teach ways to cope with stress and develop a list of poor ways to cope and a list of good ways to cope with stress.
3. When necessary, teach social skills, including nonverbal skills like smiling, nodding, and eye contact, as well as verbal skills like open questions, follow-up questions, and reflections.

CHAPTER

8

Sexuality Issues in Therapy

Travis was such a talented basketball player that, when he was in high school, his family had moved to another city just so he could attend a prep school that was home to a powerhouse sports program and a legendary coach. It paid off, and he was offered a scholarship for one of the best college basketball teams in the country. Now, midway through his senior year, facing almost certain draft into the professional league, he decided to come to therapy. At first, he was vague about his reason for coming in, talking about his uncertainty regarding the future and a few other stressors, but as he let his story unspool, he revealed the real reason. As a superstar athlete, one girl after another came after him, starting in his freshman year of high school when he was just 14. He slept with many of them, sometimes more than one a weekend. He didn't even have to try to get girls in bed; they all approached him. By the time he had neared the end of his college experience, he had had sex with dozens of young women, more than he could remember. Despite this, he had never been in a real relationship for longer than a month and saw no prospect of making this happen. As he looked down the road, he saw himself wealthy, well known, and all alone. "As soon as I have sex with them," he said, referring to the girls around him, "I completely lose all interest and I can't change that." Then he added a powerful line: "Sex has ruined me."

For some guys, sex has been their downfall or a source of great sorrow. Others find it to be a huge area of joy and pleasure. The one common theme for all your young adult male clients is that they are all sexual beings, whether they have had sex or not, whether they are troubled by it or love it. One day, I distinctly recall seeing three 18-year-old

139

young men in a row, all morning appointments. For each of them, the topic of sex came up during the conversation. The first guy told me he was waiting until he got married to have sex. The second guy said he "accidentally" cheated on his girlfriend—again—by having sex with one of her friends. He was terrified his girlfriend was going to find out and end the relationship. The third guy shared that he had been calling phone sex lines for the past few months and felt terrible guilt over it, but couldn't stop. Later that day, a college student expressed concern about his strong attraction to aggressive and rough sex, wondering if this might be unhealthy and a sign of a problem.

I was reminded of the incredible scope of human experience when it comes to sexuality. Young men have a broad range of attitudes, knowledge, beliefs, experiences, and behaviors. Most are exclusively heterosexual, but many are homosexual or bisexual in their orientation. Some are untroubled by sexual thoughts, feelings, and behaviors, while others struggle deeply with their sexuality. There are those who believe that sex is a sacred and spiritual experience set apart for marriage only, those who believe it is a purely physical act that is not much different than dancing or playing a sport, and still others who see it somewhere in between. Some guys think of oral sex as more intimate than intercourse, but there are plenty of others who see it as the "new goodbye kiss," with very little emotional meaning. There is nearly an unlimited range of the variations of sexual beliefs and behavior.

CONSIDERATIONS FOR THERAPISTS

The two most sensitive areas you can discuss in therapy are usually sex and drugs, with sex being far and away the most delicate. For some clients, the topic will never come up, nor should it; for others, it comes up immediately. There are young men who feel extremely uncomfortable talking about sexual issues and prefer to keep the topic private and off limits, while others want or need to discuss it with their therapist. With all that in mind, here are some important considerations related to discussing sex and sexuality.

Keep Your Voyeuristic Tendencies in Check

A few years back, I attended a conference taught by the internationally renowned trauma expert Bessell van der Kolk. He said many important things over the two-day conference, but one quote in particular stuck with me. He said, "Therapists have to keep their voyeuristic tendencies in check." This is not only great advice, but essential to good practice.

There is no question that working with young men in therapy means that sexual content will need to be discussed on occasion. Whether it is a teenager having unprotected sex, a college student who believes he is addicted to Internet porn, a young man who has come to regret his sexual conquests, or many other reasons, therapists have ample opportunity to talk about sexual content. While this is true, it is also important to check those voyeuristic impulses at the door.

A rule of thumb here is that sexual content should only be discussed under three conditions:

1. *The client brings it up and wants to discuss it.* Example: a client who is debating whether to have sex with his girlfriend and wants help making this decision.
2. *The discussion is clearly connected to a therapy goal.* Example: a client who has a goal of making better decisions but is being promiscuous and indiscriminate in his sexual behavior.
3. *Information comes out in the session that is concerning enough to warrant further discussion.* Example: a client discloses he is not using protection when he has sex with his girlfriend.

These three criteria can serve as a guide to help you decide if you should pursue further conversation about sexual content. The mere mention of sexual material is not sufficient to warrant a discussion. For example, suppose you were seeing a guy for some anxiety-related trouble, and you ask him how things have been since the last session. He recaps the weekend, saying his girlfriend came home from college and they had sex for the first time in a month, then proceeds to tell you about going out to dinner, seeing a movie, and hanging out with mutual friends. He mentions having sex as a bullet point for the weekend, not as a point of discussion. He doesn't give any indication he wants to talk about it; it is not connected to his therapy goals; he does not give you any reason to be concerned about it. In this instance, you would not bring it up or discuss it. To do so would not serve his purposes in any way.

Ask Permission Before Talking About Sexual Topics

Even if one of those three conditions is met, it is still a good idea to ask the client for permission to discuss it further. A simple question like, "Is it okay if we talk about this?" will usually suffice, provided it is clear that he has the option of saying no if he prefers not to discuss it.

This is a good practice even during times when a client brings up the topic because it communicates a respectful willingness to talk about— or not talk—about the material. I usually make a follow-up statement like, "Please let me know if you want to stop the discussion at any point and we'll talk about something else."

Permission seeking not only shows respect and regard for the young man, but also tends to increase alliance and emotional buy-in. It is especially important with sexual content, but it is good practice for any potentially sensitive subjects, including drug use, family issues, and other relationship concerns. It is good to get into the habit of asking permission before inquiring about personal matters.

Be Skeptical About Sexual Bragging

On more than one occasion, I have had clients brag about the number of sexual partners that they have had, only to find out later that they were still virgins. I've had similar experiences with clients who report extensive drug sales and gang involvement. This bragging and bravado is part of young male culture and sometimes extends into the therapy room. Years ago, one of my clients reported close to 50 sexual partners, a threesome, and other sexually adventurous behavior, but months later, he acknowledged that he had done nothing more than make out with a couple of girls.

I don't advise expressing outward skepticism when guys tell you about how successful they have been with the ladies, but I do suggest a mental bookmark that you may have just heard some inflated claims. One client of mine troubled his parents when they found condoms in the glove compartment of his car and in his bookbag. They never found out that this was part wishful thinking and part show for others. He had never been close to a sexual experience.

The reason why this is important is because it may change your course slightly and in some nuanced ways. A guy who tells you about his multiple and various sexual conquests may have less of a problem with promiscuity and more of a problem with self-esteem and self-confidence. It's a good idea not to get too locked in to an assumption that you are hearing the truth too early in the therapy process.

In every case except for the guy boasting about 50 sexual partners, I was surprised when I found out my client had lied to me. The claims didn't seem unreasonable. I am sure that I have been fooled other times and have never found out otherwise. As a rule of thumb, though, I have learned to be more skeptical of reports of anonymous and casual sex. Reports of sex in the context of a relationship, reports of cheating on girlfriends (and boyfriends), and reports of specifically named partners seem to be more credible.

One of my clients was a tall, handsome, athletic guy who worked out five times a week and was extremely well liked among his peers. Early in the therapy relationship, he told me that he always used protection and only had sex with girls he knew well, saying he had been with 8 or 10 girls. Since he had come in for issues related to some legal and behavioral trouble related to drinking and driving, the topic of sex did not come up again. However, near the end of one session, he started to shift uncomfortably in his seat.

"There is something I have been wanting to tell you," he said, "but I feel really awkward about it."

"You can tell me if it would be good for you to say it," I replied.

"I guess," he said, then took a long pause. "I've never had sex. I lied to you and I've lied to my friends, too."

He went on to explain how he had been in many situations where he had the opportunity—and the invitation—to have sex, but always stopped short of intercourse. He said he felt uncomfortable with it, not wanting to lose his virginity to "some random girl," but also felt the expectations of his peers. They teased him about his looks and called him a "man whore" because the women liked him so much. I recall being grateful we had not talked much at all about his sexual behavior, as this would have made it even more difficult for him to eventually tell me the truth. If you focus on sexual issues before the client is ready or before it is necessary, it is my strong sense you run a greater risk with young men of getting false reports and inaccurate bragging.

Respect Each Individual's Timing and Readiness to Talk About Sexual Content

Of our three young men, Gabriel talked about sexual content the most regularly and with the greatest ease. He was as comfortable talking about it as he was conversing about a sporting event or relaying the events of his past family vacation. While he felt some frustration about the fallout of his infidelity, there was no shame or embarrassment associated with his sexual behavior. His attitude was that sex was a natural part of life; it was what guys did. He neither bragged about it nor avoided talking about it.

Marlon was the opposite. It was our 10th session before he gave some indication that he had been sexually abused by a cousin when he was around 4 or 5 years old, saying only, "I don't like to be around him because of what he did." Over time, he elaborated, but with considerable effort. Beyond the abuse, the whole topic of sexuality seemed walled off. Until the abuse disclosure, there was no reason to talk about it, but even afterward, it was not something he wanted to discuss. So instead of pushing it, I completely respected that he was not yet ready and I was patient with him.

Ricky was somewhere in the between. He very much wanted to talk about the process of coming out and some aspects of his relationship with his boyfriend, but also became cryptic and slightly evasive on some topics. Over time, though, he felt more comfortable in the conversations.

Though there is considerable variability among individuals, you may find that Gabriel and Ricky are typical of college-age and high school-age clients, respectively, with the former being quite comfortable and free on the topic of sexuality and the latter being more tentative and uncomfortable. High school students are typically socialized to hide their sexual behavior from adults, while college students are socialized to talk about it openly. This extends to the therapy relationship, where college students often bring up sexual issues within the first or second session, while high school students are more guarded and uncomfortable.

Don't Assume That Your Clients Always Have Accurate Sexual Information

One of my clients told me he had been with a girl the previous weekend. "Don't worry," he said, "we were safe." I asked him what form of protection he used and he said, "We stood up while we were having sex. There's no way she could get pregnant." Most young men know a girl can still get pregnant when you stand up during sex (or have sex in the bathtub or in a variety of other mythical pregnancy-free positions or locations), but some do not. For this client, he not only had wrong information about pregnancy prevention, but also missed half the point of "safe sex," which is also the prevention of sexually transmitted diseases.

Don't assume that your clients have accurate information about sex, including issues related to pregnancy, birth control, sexually transmitted diseases, and a range of other important topics. Even some of your older clients may have incorrect information that may need to be clarified. My suggestion, though, is to only address this if some misinformation comes up naturally in the course of the conversation.

Clarify Sexual Language

The language of sex has become increasingly vague and slippery among young adults. For some guys, a hookup means oral sex or intercourse, while for others, it means nothing more than kissing and making out. Similarly, some guys say they are "talking to" a girl and they literally mean that they are just talking—in person, by phone, online, and so on. Other guys use it as a metaphor for casual sex. A while back, a client said, "I've been talking to this girl who started hanging around the coffee shop where I work." A few minutes later in the conversation, it became clear he was telling me that they were having sex.

Even the use of the term *sex* has different connotations. If a college student says, "We went back to my room, but we didn't have sex," he doesn't necessarily mean there was no sexual contact. They may have had oral sex or nearly everything short of intercourse. The phrase "we didn't have sex" doesn't necessarily tell you what did or didn't happen. So the language of hookups and sex varies from client to client and may need to be clarified if you are to get a good sense of what he means.

Be Aware That Purity Pledgers Are at No Less Risk of Having Sex

None of our three clients had ever pledged to remain a virgin until marriage. Though Gabriel was raised in the church, he never made any commitment to stay chaste. In fact, he reports having sex for the first time at the age of 14 and had never entertained the idea that he should wait, despite frequent admonitions from his priests and youth leaders.

Another client of mine named Spencer had also been raised in the church and he took the challenges to remain pure to heart. Spencer was a varsity lacrosse player who had been dating the same girl for the past six months. They both shared the same faith and went to the same church. They had made a commitment to each other to wait until marriage, and for six months, they had been successful in keeping this vow. But one night, they went further than either of them had expected, and they had sex in his car. It was unplanned so they didn't use protection. Afterward, they both felt guilty and regretful, but they had sex again the following weekend. I am confident Spencer sincerely wanted to keep his commitment to remain a virgin until he was married. It was important to him, and he had struggled with it for many months, but as with many purity pledgers, it didn't hold up.

A study by Rosenbaum (2008) of nearly 1,000 high school students who had never had sex or had taken the virginity pledge found that taking the pledge made not one bit of difference in terms of sexual behavior in the long run. She matched the students who had taken the pledge with those who had not and found that, five years later, teens who had pledged to remain a virgin until marriage had exactly 0.1 fewer sexual partners during the past year, but the same number of partners overall as those who had never made a pledge. She also found that the kids who made pledges to refrain from sex until marriage started having sex at the same age as nonpledgers. Most concerning, though, was that teens who made a pledge to remain virgins until marriage were a full 10% less likely to use a condom and generally less likely to use any other form of birth control than their peers.

When asked about making the pledge five years later, over 80% of the kids who had promised to remain chaste denied that they had even made a pledge in the first place. They didn't recall even having made the pledge—or they just lied about it. The implications for this in therapy are obvious. A young man who has made a pledge to remain a virgin may be commended for his intentions and his virtue, but the issues of sexual behavior and sexual education may still need to be addressed, especially if he is in a current relationship. As always, if he doesn't want to discuss it, then respect that, but a purity pledge should not convince you that this won't be an issue he will need to address.

REASONS FOR HAVING SEX

Of all the aspects of human behavior, sexuality is undoubtedly the most complex. When researchers asked a few hundred people why they had sex, they got 237 different answers (Meston & Buss, 2007). To take it a step further, they took those answers and gave it to a sample of over 1,500 people and had them rate how much each of these reasons had led them to have sex. When they analyzed the data, they found the reasons clustered into four big categories, each with a few subcategories.

There were *physical reasons* for having sex, including stress reduction, pleasure, physical desirability, and experience seeking. Some had *goal-directed reasons* for having sex. They used sex to gain some goal like a specific resource, social status, or revenge. Others had *emotional reasons* for having sex, like commitment and love or expression of feelings. Still others had sex because of some *sense of insecurity*. These individuals needed a boost to their self-esteem or they felt some duty or pressure to have sex or they were trying to guard their mate from being enticed away by someone else.

Men and Sex

Both men and women share some sexual motives, according to the study. They both have sex primarily because of attraction and pleasure. Men and women both gave the same top three reasons for having sex:

1. I was attracted to the person.
2. It feels good.
3. I wanted to experience the physical pleasure.

But after those top reasons, the similarities ended and the gender differences began to emerge. Among other motives, men reported having sex more often than women for these reasons:

- Stress reduction
- Experience seeking (similar to sensation seeking or thrill seeking)
- To achieve resources or social status
- For revenge
- To achieve some practical goal
- To boost their self-esteem
- Because they felt duty or pressure
- To keep their mate satisfied so as not to lose the relationship

Among young men in the 16- to 24-year-old range, most, but not all of them, have had sexual intercourse. Among the sexually experienced, they have vastly different experiences and attitudes. Some only have sex in a committed relationship; others are open to any opportunity. Some have deep hurts from past sexual trauma or bad decisions; others are free of any emotional baggage in their sex lives. Some feel inept and unskilled sexually; others feel competent and full of prowess. Some regret crossing personal standards and boundaries; others feel quite comfortable with their decisions. Some believe sex is something sacred and special; others believe it is simply a physical act. Again, there is no uniform experience, set of perceptions, or set of values among these young men in their sexuality. As a therapist, you must be prepared for the full range of sexual attitudes and experiences among your clients.

CONCEPTUALIZING SEXUALITY IN THERAPY

Because there is such a broad range, it is difficult to think conceptually about sexuality issues in therapy in a way that is meaningful and helpful to nearly all clients. Over the years, two dimensions of sexuality have emerged as most relevant. The first has to do with the degree to which someone operates within his own self-determined sexual boundaries, beliefs, and values. I refer to this as *restraint*, the ability to line up sexual behavior with personal standards. The second dimension has to do with the level of *emotional association* with sexual behavior. Some have highly negative emotional associations with sex and sexuality; they are full of shame, guilt, anxiety, fear, rage, envy, or sadness. This may be the product of sexual trauma, previous negative sexual experiences, unhealthy family messages, teasing, or other causes. By contrast, others have positive emotional associations with sex, feeling positive and joyful about it.

Restraint and emotional association are both on a continuum. For example, those high in restraint tend to keep their personal standards, while those low in restraint tend to act against their own standards, having sex in ways that are dissonant for them. But this is not an on-off switch, since most people are somewhere between complete restraint and no restraint. The same is true for the emotional association. Some may have purely positive associations with sex, while others may have purely negative connections to it, but most have somewhat mixed feelings, usually leaning in one direction or the other.

Since restraint and emotional association are both on a continuum, you can intersect these two constructs and get four quadrants, each representing a pattern of sexuality. Three of these patterns have some unique challenges that may need to be addressed:

Low Restraint

Negative Association	Compulsive	Indulgent
	Repressed	Healthy

Negative Association (left) — Positive Association (right)

High Restraint

Sexually Compulsive

Individuals who are low in restraint and negative in their emotional associations with sex are sexually compulsive. These are young men who have negative emotions, especially related to guilt and shame, intertwined with their sexuality. They often make promises to themselves that they won't act out sexually or look at porn again or chronically masturbate, but they give in easily and repetitively. This represents the least healthy pattern of sexuality among young men and the one most likely to cause them trouble.

Sexually Indulgent

Sexually indulgent individuals are those who have positive emotional associations with sex but have considerable difficulty restraining themselves in line with their own standards and boundaries. These are young men who enjoy sex and find it pleasurable, but find it difficult to keep their own standards. Unlike the compulsives, they are not as saddled with the guilt and shame of their actions, but they frequently find themselves crossing personal boundaries. The sexually indulgent are also those who have no sexual boundaries—defined or undefined.

Sexually Repressed

Sexually repressed individuals are those who have negative emotional associations with sex but tend to have remarkable self-control and restraint with little or no sexual boundary crossing. These are young men who have negative attitudes and negative emotions connected to sex and are able to work very hard to keep their own personal boundaries. They tend to be more anxious or emotionally constricted than others.

Sexually Healthy

Individuals who have positive emotional associations connected to sex and consistently keep their own standards and boundaries are sexually healthy people. These are young men who have positive attitudes and emotions associated with sex and sexuality and are able to stay within their own sexual boundaries and values.

ADDRESSING SEXUAL CONCERNS IN THERAPY

Thinking about where a young man falls among these four quadrants can steer your efforts in therapy. From a helping standpoint, the issue is not whether a young man is sexually active or not, but how his behavior is integrated into his life. A college student who is regularly having sex might be regarded as healthy, while a young man of the same age who has never had sex but compulsively looks at porn and has sexual conversations online against his own moral code would be regarded as unhealthy. This formulation of the four quadrants can be helpful in assessing your client's sexual health along two important dimensions. The central questions are:

- To what degree does he stay within his own boundaries? (And does he even have sexual boundaries?)
- What are his emotional associations and attitudes toward sexuality?

Our three clients actually represent each of the three unhealthy patterns of sexuality. Ricky is clearly compulsive. He has sadness and shame associated with his sexuality, guilt connected to past sexual behavior, and an anxious preoccupation with having sex. He looks at porn Web sites and message boards every day and has had online sexual relationships many times. At the same time, he wants to have monogamous relationships, yet he has cheated and had fairly anonymous hookups. His sexual behavior is a source of tremendous struggle and pain for him.

Gabriel is sexually indulgent, having few qualms or emotional hang-ups about sex or his past sexual behavior. When he was not in a relationship, he felt free to sleep with any girl he found attractive. When he was in a relationship, however, he wanted to stay faithful. Unfortunately, that didn't tend to happen. He cheated on every girlfriend he ever had. In nearly every case, he did it because he got caught up in the moment or had been drinking too much. He wasn't planning it or driven to do it. In his mind, it just happened. Like Travis, another sexually indulgent young man whose story opened the chapter, both are getting to the point where they realize their sexual behavior, as fun as it has been for them, has caused them problems.

Marlon had never talked about his sexual abuse—or sexual content of any kind—before he came into therapy. For him, sex was an uncomfortable subject and one best avoided. He did allow that he had sex with one girl a couple of times, but just let the relationship drop. He tends to avoid close relationships and emotional entanglements and he doesn't put himself in situations where someone might want to get close to him. He is avoidant, emotionally constricted, and fairly repressed in his sexuality.

The goal for each of these guys is to get them into the quadrant of healthy sexuality. Gabriel needs work around defining his sexual values and maintaining his sexual boundaries. Marlon needs work around disconnecting sex from negative emotional associations. Ricky needs both. It would be good for him to work out his shame and guilt; he needs to have healthier attitudes toward his sexuality and less anxious preoccupation with sex. At the same time, he also needs to learn ways to hold to his limits.

Helping Sexually Compulsive Clients

It is estimated that 3%–6% of the general population have clinically significant problems with sexually compulsive behavior, and, not surprisingly, the vast majority of these individuals are men (Kuzma & Black, 2008). Sexually compulsive individuals have the least healthy expression of sexuality among all the four patterns. They have negative associations, usually involving guilt and shame, around their sexuality and sexual behavior. They also have poor internal restraints, feeling driven to act out sexually. To help these clients, you can start on either side of the equation, either by strengthening restraint or changing the associations and emotional connections. I typically prefer to start with the latter, working on attitudes, beliefs, and feelings about sexuality. My goal is not to get a client to conform to my own worldview or my own set of values or boundaries about sex, but I do want to help him get rid of any shame, rage, fear, or other distressing emotion in association with his sexuality. These emotions just serve to strengthen the compulsive aspects of sexual behavior, drive it further underground, and create increasingly more problems.

Many sexually compulsive clients make promises to themselves that they will not act out again, only to see the behavior intensify or worsen. For them, it seems that the more they try to stop it, the worse it gets. Every time Ricky promised himself he would not have an anonymous hookup, it would happen again, and he would be racked with guilt and shame. His resolutions did nothing more than make him feel worse about it. To stop this cycle, therapy needs to strip away the sense of shame from his sexuality. There are many ways to do this, but I would advise starting with *a narrative of sexual history.* Begin by discussing early sexual thoughts, feelings, awareness, and experiences, then move forward. From there, ask about key moments when he felt a sense of shame or guilt or some other intense negative emotion connected to his sexual thoughts, feelings, or actions. Explore where these came from, especially outside messages. Finally, begin to help him reconstruct a healthier view of sex in general and his sexuality in particular by using new learning and the new insights gleaned from this exercise. This healthier view of his sexuality usually involves these 10 key points:

- Everyone is a sexual being.
- Sexual thoughts, feelings, and behaviors are normal.
- Sex and sexuality can be a good, positive, and healthy part of a person's life.
- Negative messages and beliefs about sex can harm healthy sexual development.
- Negative sexual experiences can also harm healthy sexual development.
- Sexually compulsive behaviors are the product of having a normal sex drive coupled with negative messages, beliefs, or experiences related to sex.
- Over time, these struggles can become deeper and cause a person even greater problems.
- Sexual struggles can also negatively affect a person's self-concept and self-esteem.
- It is more helpful and healing to think of these struggles as bad habits and patterns that can be changed than personality traits that cannot.
- The goal is to be in control of and accepting and at peace with your sexuality.

The next step is to build greater restraint and impulse control. One of the ways to do this is by identifying risky situations, thoughts, feelings, and decisions, then planning for how to manage them. I will detail this process in Chapter 9.

Another way to improve restraint can come from teaching specific cognitive skills that help build mental muscle. These skills require practice and rehearsal, but they are helpful.

Detachment

This involves teaching the young man to create distance between himself and his unhelpful thoughts and beliefs. Rather than being fused together with the thoughts, you detach from them and look at them from a slightly different perspective. I use an analogy from video gaming. There are some video games like the *Halo* or *Call of Duty* series, for example, that are called "first-person shooters," where you look through the eyes of the main character. There are other games like *Gears of War* or *Max Payne* that are called "third-person shooters," where you have an over-the-shoulder perspective on the character. Detachment is the psychological equivalent of a third-person shooter. You have the ability to observe your thoughts, feelings, and internal reactions in a way that creates just a little bit of necessary distance. With that perspective, you are better able to see the thoughts and impulses for what they are—merely thoughts and impulses—and can let them go more easily if they are not helpful. A person who practices detachment can become aware of a thought like, "I always give in to this," and see it as just a thought, not a fixed reality. The distance allows you to see a thought for what it really is.

I liken the process of detachment to being a war reporter. You are embedded in the fight, but you step back from it and merely report on it. You don't fight, you don't judge, you don't intervene. You simply report the facts. When there is a battle going on in your head, your first step is just to observe what is happening in language. When Ricky and I did this in a session, he imagined himself online and his internal dialogue was like this:

Go into that chat room. I shouldn't. I really want to. I always do it when I start thinking about it. I can't stop myself. I always do it. I promised I wouldn't do it, but just this once. Just one more time and I won't do it again. My hands are shaking a little. My breathing is a little bit faster, too. And now I'm not thinking anymore. I'm just doing it, like I'm a zombie or something.

I wrote as he talked, trying to recollect what it was like during one of the last times this happened. Afterward, we were able to look at the content together on the page and dissect it. This level of awareness keeps the process from staying so automatic and is likely to keep him out of that zombie, trancelike state that often comes toward the end of a compulsive sequence.

Tolerance

Tolerance is akin to the concept of acceptance found in acceptance and commitment therapy, a third-wave cognitive-behavioral therapy pioneered by Steven Hayes (Hayes, Strosahl, & Wilson, 2003), but I pick the term *tolerance* because it seems to be more fully understood by my clients. Acceptance has to do with coming to terms with something unwanted, whereas tolerance involves enduring something unpleasant. To use an analogy, if you had a drunk relative at your family reunion, acceptance means you come to terms with the fact he is there and don't let it ruin your party experience; tolerance means you endure it and don't let it ruin your party experience. It is essentially the same, but the word *tolerance* tends to sit better with most clients I have seen. They would rather think of themselves tolerating the drunk uncle than truly accepting his presence.

Tolerance is practiced by first becoming aware of the thoughts, feelings, and bodily reactions through the detachment skills, but it builds on this by giving the client a different internal dialogue. In essence, it changes the self-talk about these thoughts and feelings. Going back to the drunk uncle analogy, you can either try to make him leave, stew about it and let it ruin your party, or think about it differently. If you thought about it differently, you might say to yourself, "I don't like the fact that he is here, but that's how it is and we can all deal with it." For Ricky, examples of this tolerance self-talk were internal statements like:

I am feeling really tense, but I can just let myself feel the tension and I don't have to do anything to get rid of it.

My thinking is really preoccupied with this right now, but I don't have to act on it.

I keep telling myself I can't stop it because I've usually failed in the past, but that is just a thought and it doesn't have to be true right now.

His new self-talk now acknowledges that he is feeling tense, preoccupied, doubtful, but it also incorporates the new notions that he doesn't have to act out or even believe the automatic thoughts. It is an internal process that requires a good deal of practice and hard work. I say it is like building mental muscle. However, the effort pays off, and the tolerance skills lay an excellent foundation for being able to have better control of his impulses.

Choice

After the young man gets skilled at stepping back from his internal discomfort and builds greater tolerance for his distress and discomfort, he can move forward with making different choices in the moment than he has before. To make a good choice, though, he needs to have made it ahead of time. In other words, he needs to know what he values and believes before he is in the situation. Ricky has stated that he doesn't

TABLE 8.1   Ricky's Escape Plan

Valued Choice	Derailer	Escape Plan
Faithful in relationship	1. Online sex talk	a. No visiting certain sites at all when surfing (Note: he listed the sites specifically by name in the exercise.)
		b. Calling a friend (Jenna or Noel) when I have the urge to go on the sites.
		c. Play video game to get my mind off of it.
		d. Play guitar to get my mind off of it (backup strategy).
	2. Hooking up	a. Don't go to any party without Colin knowing about it.
		b. Leave immediately if potential hookups are spotted.
		c. Only go to a party (etc.) with someone else; don't ever go alone; make agreement with friend ahead of time to stop me.

think he should be getting into online sexual conversations or encounters. He does not like it when he has impulsive, anonymous hookups with other guys. He has already clarified this, and he knows what choices he needs to make. We start with the valued choice he wants to make, identify the potential derailers that can get him away from this choice, and make an escape plan for each potential derailer. We lay it out as seen in Table 8.1.

Helping a sexually compulsive young man begins by reconstructing his sexual history narrative, examining the roots of his unhealthy sexual patterns. From there, it moves to teaching him skills for managing his well-worn sexual impulses. These skills include *detachment*, which allows a young man to observe his automatic thoughts and internal experiences; *tolerance*, which allows him to sit with his distress and not try to stuff it or act out because of it; and finally, *choice*, which is a process of lining up with his own values by acting in line with what he believes and is consistent with the man he wants to be.

Helping Sexually Indulgent Clients

The essence of sexual indulgence is the belief that sexual desire is the most important consideration in the decision to have sex. Desire supplants boundaries or personal standards. For the sexually indulgent, boundaries are typically determined only by personal preference instead of some value-driven decision. Sexually indulgent clients tend to think sex is great, but they either violate their own loosely formed, poorly reasoned standards (e.g., you should at least know the name of the other person) or they truly have no defined standards. The latter—having no or minimal personal boundaries—is the most common among sexually indulgent individuals.

This was certainly true of Gabriel. Despite the best efforts of priests, youth ministers, coaches, and parents, he had not internalized any of their messages about sex or sexual boundaries. He had no discernible sexual ethic, except "don't get caught" if he was dating a girl and considering a hookup with someone else. He liked sex. He believed it was a natural thing to do. He saw it as little more than fun, like drinking or playing soccer, only better. It has only been recently that he even began to consider the possibility that his sexually indulgent lifestyle might not be the best for him in the long run.

For Gabriel and other sexually indulgent young men, the role of therapy may be to help them establish their own standards and boundaries. From hundreds of therapy sessions over the years, I have heard many standards and boundaries articulated that I have put in an approximate order, starting with the most conservative and moving to the most permissive.

Sex is okay...

- In a marriage relationship
- In a relationship where there is a lifetime commitment (e.g., engaged)
- In a long-term, loving, and monogamous relationship
- In a loving and monogamous relationship
- In a monogamous relationship
- If you know the person well
- If you know the person
- If both partners consent

Clients of certain religious or spiritual backgrounds, along with a few others, may hold the view that sex is reserved for marriage. You will probably find that most young adult clients believe sex is appropriate in the context of some type of relationship. By contrast, most sexually indulgent clients believe a relationship is not necessary for sex, and they will nearly always endorse one of the last three standards on the continuum as their personal standard. The therapist's goal with a sexually indulgent young man is to explore the various standards and boundaries and the rationale behind each one. Using a motivational approach, you guide the client in establishing a personal sexual ethic, then coming up with a plan to keep it. Unlike sexually compulsive individuals who often need months or even years of treatment to manage their difficulties, sexually indulgent young men mostly need work on defining and keeping their own sexual standards, which can often be accomplished fairly rapidly.

Helping Sexually Repressed Clients

Sexually indulgent clients freely and openly talk about sex with their therapists. From the first sessions, they are chatting about sex, both in and out of relationships. Sexually repressed young men, by contrast, hardly ever talk about the topic. In fact, they seem to go out of their way to avoid it. As a result, they represent a big challenge for therapists. On one hand, part of helping them get to a healthier place with their sexuality is to be able to talk about it openly, but on the other hand, the therapist is compelled to respect an individual's unwillingness to talk about a topic.

Sexually repressed young men tend to have good self-restraint but generally negative or functional views of sex. Unlike sexually compulsive individuals who have negative emotions like shame and guilt connected to their sexuality, sexually repressed people tend to see sex mostly as an uncomfortable topic that they would prefer not to think or talk about. The key question is whether his repression of sexual thoughts and feelings represents a problem for him. In some instances, it may not represent the healthiest form of sexuality, but it is not clearly a negative part of his life. In other cases, it may be a source of trouble.

Marlon did not want to talk about sex, and the topic only came up after he referred to his sexual abuse obliquely in a session. Understandably, he felt uncomfortable talking about his abuse, but he also felt uneasy talking about sex at all. I respected his lack of comfort about the topic and did not push it. He was not acting out sexually, and his sexuality was not causing him distress or other problems in his life. We left the topic alone. Sometimes this is the best move therapeutically.

With other clients who were reluctant to talk about a sexual topic but needed to do it for one reason or another, we were able to get to it eventually. We did this by building a rationale for the benefit of discussing it. Once they understood how talking about it could help them, they were typically able to open up about it. One of my clients who had been sexually abused by a family member as a younger child felt guilty and anxious in the presence of children, as if he were doing something wrong by just being around them. In addition, when things with his current girlfriend got rocky, he acknowledged having a sexual relationship with her the way you would confess to having committed a crime. He acted ashamed and embarrassed. By talking about all of this, he was able to work out his feelings of shame, guilt, fear, loneliness, and a tangle of other emotions that were wrapped around his sexuality. Months later, he relayed how he and his girlfriend had worked out a minor conflict about their sexual relationship. I was struck by how at ease he had become in talking about sex. He did it without apparent discomfort or distress. For him, like many other sexually repressed young men, the best intervention is a rationale for why it is healthy to talk openly and then practice having those conversations in therapy when the time is right.

ADDRESSING SEXUAL-IDENTITY
ISSUES WITH YOUNG MEN

Ricky recalls being in middle school, hanging out with a group of guys after lunch. One of them, a guy named Ted, spotted a smaller, slightly effeminate boy sitting alone at the end of a long lunch table. Ted muttered a gay slur with such anger it shocked Ricky. The other boys laughed, but Ricky, who was only then beginning to realize he was attracted to other guys and not to girls, felt a deep sense of sadness run through him. He was going to be one of those boys that guys like Ted seemed to hate. As with many gay young men, this began his descent into a deep sadness and a boiling anger. It is not surprising when you consider the rejections and hostility that gay and bisexual young men often face that they have much higher rates of depression, suicide attempts, drug use, and other mental health problems than their straight peers.

Ricky had the choice of coming out to face the wrath of guys like Ted or keep everything a secret and ache inside. It was an impossible choice, but Ricky decided he was going to hide the truth from everyone for as long as he could. That's exactly what he did for 4 long years until he met a guy named Aaron at a friend's party. Aaron was openly gay and seemed proud of it. He wasn't flamboyant or strident. He was just supremely self-confident. Ricky was instantly attracted to him. He liked how Aaron looked; he liked his personality; he liked his approach to life; he liked everything about him. After a few conversations, it became clear that Aaron liked him back. But Aaron would not be in a relationship with anyone who wasn't fully out. "I can't be with someone who isn't comfortable with who he is," Aaron told him. With that, Ricky was forced to make a choice.

He chose the relationship and began to come out to all his close friends, most of whom greeted his announcement warmly or with little fanfare. Word spread around the school, but no one seemed to treat him differently. He was surprised by how little drama there was about it. Still, he couldn't quite bring himself to tell his parents. To say it was awkward was an understatement. He couldn't imagine telling his father, not because he feared the reaction but because he couldn't conceive of a more uncomfortable interaction. Their relationship had been strained over the past few years, and he felt distant from his dad. Aaron insisted on total disclosure, though, so he knew he had to do it.

The Coming-Out Process

Coming out is an essential part of identity formation for gay young men. Typically, here's how the coming-out process goes: Before age 11 on average, homosexual youths experience same-sex attraction. Just past their 14th birthday, they acknowledge to themselves that they are gay. Just before their 16th birthday, they come out to their families. This is the standard progression for gay youths, but there is much variability, with some young men coming out sooner and some not coming out until their college years or beyond.

The coming-out process is a high-stakes proposition. Gay and bisexual teenagers and young adults who get negative feedback from their parents when they come out are eight times more likely to attempt suicide, six times more likely to experience symptoms of severe depression, and three times more likely to use illicit drugs than their gay or bisexual peers who received positive feedback and support from their parents (Ryan, Huebner, Diaz, & Sanchez, 2009). We also know that younger homosexuals feel worse about themselves and are more prone to engage in high-risk sexual behavior when they don't receive positive support from their parents when they come out (Savin-Williams, 1989).

Parents and other family members are often among the last to know about their son's sexual orientation. In a study of nearly 200 gay/bisexual adolescents (D'Augelli & Hershberger, 1993), the majority first opened up to a friend (73%). Next in line were teachers, counselors, and clergy (all 8%). Only 7% first disclosed to their mothers, 3% to a sibling, and a meager 1% to their fathers. When they did disclose, here's how they perceived the reactions (Figure 8.1):

The majority (55%) of mothers were accepting of their sons, with another 25% expressing tolerant attitudes (i.e., not fully accepting, but not hostile or rejecting). In other words, 8 out of 10 mothers had neutral or positive responses to their son's decision to come out. For fathers, a little more than a third (37%) were fully accepting and another third were tolerant, so about 7 out of 10 fathers had a neutral or positive response (Willoughby, Malik, & Lindahl, 2006). On one hand, this is mostly good news, since the majority of young men get generally acceptable responses from both parents. However, nearly 2 out of 10 young

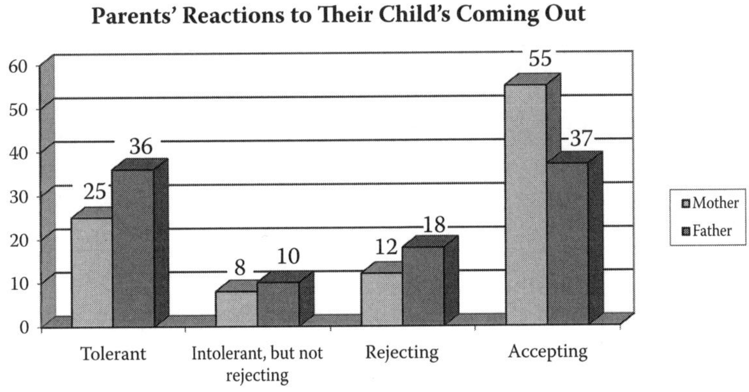

Parents' Reactions to Their Child's Coming Out

Figure 8.1 Perceived reactions of family members after disclosure of sexual orientation by gay/bisexual adolescents.

men get hostile and rejecting responses from their dads and another 1 out of 10 get intolerant (i.e., unaccepting but not rejecting) reactions. Imagine as a teenager facing a 3 in 10 chance of being found unacceptable—or worse—by your parents. Imagine a 2 in 10 chance of being completely rejected. If you can imagine those risks and those stakes, you can understand how hard it is for many gay youths to come out to their parents.

For many gay young men, their fathers represent the biggest risk, at least in their perception of what type of response they are likely to get when they come out. I have heard anecdotal accounts of young men being hit or kicked out of the house after their disclosure, and I know these are true, but I have not heard these extreme parental reactions directly from my gay clients. However, I have had some clients who were rejected by their parents or met with intolerant attitudes.

Willoughby, Malik, and Lindahl (2006) examined family cohesion and adaptability as well as parenting style, as these factors related to parental responses to the coming-out process for young adult gay men. They found that gay men who were in families that were more *cohesive* (i.e., connected, emotionally bonded) and *adaptable* (i.e., able to change in the face of new challenges) received more positive parental reactions than those in less cohesive, less adaptable families. They also found that gay men who had parents with a more *authoritative* style (i.e., having boundaries and structure along with emotional warmth) received a much better reaction than those who had parents with a more *authoritarian* style (i.e., having boundaries and structure but lacking in emotional warmth).

This study has two major implications in our clinical work with gay and bisexual young men. First, therapists who are helping a gay young man through the coming-out process need to assess family variables. Consider asking questions like these with appropriate follow-ups:

1. How close are the members of your family to each other?
2. How much emotional support do family members get from each other?
3. How has your family responded to big challenges or changes in the past?
4. How would you describe your mother and father's parenting styles?

Based on the responses to these questions, you will be better able to advise him on whether or not you believe it is wise to come out to his parents at this time. For most gay young men who come out to their families and receive a healthy, positive response, this can be a healing and healthy experience. It also allows them to take full advantage of their family's support as they move into relationships and other stages of their lives. For those who are likely to receive a negative or hostile reaction from parents, you would be wise to advise caution in the coming-out process.

Second, therapists who have access to the parents of gay clients may want to consider steering them into family therapy that focuses on increasing the emotional warmth and bonding among family members, helping them be more flexible and adaptable in responding to their children, and working on general parenting style as a way of improving their response to their son's sexual-orientation disclosure.

The coming-out process is a highly unique and highly individualized process. There is no one-size-fits-all model for how to do it, when to do it, or with whom. The therapist's job is to help him assess all the variables about his family and make a good decision about the specifics. Your relationship, along with his connection to accepting peers, is likely to provide him with a much-needed sense of safety and stability through this important developmental process.

Rebuilding Self-Esteem

Gay and bisexual young men have often grown up with direct and indirect assaults on their self-esteem since the time they were in middle school or even earlier. They have heard the jokes (and in some cases, participated in them), the hostile comments, and the negative cultural messages, whether aimed at them personally or gay people in general. The wear and tear on their self-esteem in many cases is considerable. By the time they reach young adulthood, they are often angry, depressed, and emotionally battered. It's no wonder gay and bisexual individuals seek mental health treatment at more than twice the rate of heterosexuals (Grella, Greenwell, Mays, & Cochran, 2009).

For some guys, as with Ricky's boyfriend, Aaron, their temperament and social supports and other protective factors come together to make them incredibly resilient and even stronger individuals. For other guys like Ricky, the years of keeping it all in and taking all the negative messages have taken its toll.

Ricky finally came out to his mother. He said it almost in passing when they were riding in a car to a doctor's appointment. She responded by asking him good questions and thanking him for telling her. It was far better than he could have imagined. He told her to tell dad and left it at that, knowing this was easier than facing the man himself. Even after this relatively uneventful and low-key coming out, he still had to sort out the emotional fallout of the past few years. He had felt so bad he had cut himself on several occasions. There had been times he had wanted to die. These negative feelings were somewhat relieved by a positive coming-out experience, but they would not just fade away by themselves. He needed some help with repairing his damaged sense of himself. Using the techniques and strategies that help with identity formation, we began to explore his strengths and unique characteristics. We focused a lot on what was good and healthy about him. Through that process, we discovered he was funny, a good listener, and highly compassionate. We spent time integrating his positive traits into his overall self-concept and into his sexual identity. At the end of that time, I gave him a homework assignment entitled, "What I've learned about being a healthy gay person." It was not to be an essay, but just a list of insights. He came back the next time with this list:

- Being gay is not better or worse than being straight.
- I'm really okay with people who are different from other people.
- Being gay has allowed me to be more sensitive to those who have been mistreated.
- I was hurt by the attitudes of other kids when I was younger, but I don't have to be held back or hurt by that now.
- I want to help younger gay people be okay with who they are.

It was a good list, and it gave us the chance to talk even further about what he had learned about himself. As we talked, he added this comment, "I don't think I would have chosen to be gay, but I'm good with it and I like who I am."

THE PAIN OF PAST SEXUAL HURTS AND NEGATIVE EXPERIENCES

One of the most eye-opening experiences of being a therapist is the realization of how many ways that people can be hurt by sex. I am not even referring just to outright sexual abuse, but rather the much more subtle ways like being ridiculed about a sexual issue or seeing something sexual as a younger child. One of my clients told me that he has harbored anger and mistrust toward women for years after a girlfriend joked to her friends that he was the worst lover she had ever had following their breakup. He felt embarrassed, betrayed, and confused. He didn't know if this was true or just her way of getting back at him for the breakup. If it was true, though, it hit him powerfully and made him feel emasculated and incompetent. He compensated by being more sexually aggressive and less attached. That seemingly small comment had set him on a course of trouble throughout his latter college years.

Sexuality is such a sensitive area for most people. It can be a great source of pleasure and joy, but also an area of tremendous pain. Guys can be hurt sexually in ways big and small. Here are 10 examples of how this could happen:

- Past sexual abuse
- Being taken advantage of sexually by a peer (male or female)
- Being coerced into sex
- Being ridiculed for sexual performance by a partner

- Trouble with sexual performance (e.g., trouble getting or keeping an erection, premature ejaculation, etc.)
- Being ridiculed by peers or sexual partners for physical issues (e.g., penis size, body type, etc.)
- Embarrassment from misreading sexual cues from potential partners
- Being given negative early messages about sex and sexuality
- Being exposed to sexual information or images too early or inappropriately
- Being treated harshly for sexual exploration or curiosity as a child

I have heard guys describe all of these sexual hurts that caused them trouble ranging from embarrassment to deep and enduring emotional difficulties. Guys tend to equate sexual competence and mastery with a sense of masculinity. When they feel inadequate or out of control sexually, they tend to feel weak and vulnerable. As a therapist, there are some guiding principles that can help you in this area:

1. Be aware that guys can have a range of sexual hurts from obvious sources like abuse and less obvious sources like ridicule.
2. For many guys, being able to talk about these sexual wounds can be helpful if the therapist is empathetic and nonjudgmental.
3. Sometimes the sexual hurts of the past affect relationships, thoughts, feelings, and actions in the present, but many young men have not made those connections in their minds. Helping make those connections can be powerful for some clients.
4. Some guys have been hurt in some way sexually, but would prefer not to talk about it. You should respect that.
5. If a client is comfortable discussing the topic, but not good at expressing himself, become more directive and concrete, and ask specific, closed questions to help him clarify and articulate what happened.
6. Validate their feelings and help them make sense of their behavior in light of what they have experienced.
7. Make them feel good, strong, and wise for having shared the information and being willing to talk about it.

Sex is a hugely complex, highly important area in anyone's life. It has the potential to provide the best and worst of human experience. It is also an easy area to get messed up. As a therapist, it's often your job to get it untangled. Many of your young adult male clients will have healthy sexuality with good boundaries and good restraint so that they can operate within those boundaries. There are others who have unhealthy patterns of sexual behavior that will need your help. As you move into this area as a therapist, do so with compassion, humility, and good judgment.

THERAPY TAKE-AWAYS

1. When it comes to discussing sex in therapy with young men, keep your voyeuristic tendencies in check and ask permission first.
2. When appropriate, assess a client's degree of restraint of sexual impulses and the emotional associations he has with sexuality.
3. Identify valued choices, potential derailers, and specific escape plans for sexually compulsive clients.

CHAPTER

9

Skills to Manage Behavioral and Substance Problems

In his brilliant and moving book, *Beautiful Boy*, David Sheff writes hauntingly of his son's addiction to meth: "Nic high is a ghost, a specter, and when he is high, my lovely son is dormant, pushed aside, hidden away in some inaccessible corner of his consciousness" (Sheff, 2008, p. 269). Drug addiction is a horror for the addict and his loved ones alike. In the world of therapy, young men hold a rotten distinction: They have more substance-abuse problems and addictions than any other population. Any therapist who works with this group of guys must be well prepared for a wide range of substance-abuse issues from the occasional pot smoker to the binge drinker to the coke addict. Young men are often no strangers to significant substance-abuse problems.

Not only that, they are more likely to commit violence, act out sexually, get arrested, or be the victim of violence than any other population. This unpleasant reality is coupled with the fact that they are more likely to resist help than their female counterparts. Paving the way with the motivational model is usually essential in your work with these young guys. Despite the obvious implications of their substance and behavioral problems, they still need to be brought on board with the therapy process. Once you get there, however, they will need guidance with how to make those changes. For many guys, the lack of confidence in making a change is well founded. They lack the skills to know what to do next. They simply get stuck with the mechanics of changing well-worn patterns of behavior. Instead, they resort to empty resolutions and vague promises to do better next time.

All three of our guys have done this in the past year.

"Every time I cheated on Kelly, I promised myself it would never happen again. Every single time," Gabriel said, emphasizing every single word of the last sentence.

"I promised my grandma I would stay in school," said Marlon in his session. "I wanted to. I don't know what happened."

"I admit I have a problem with my anger," Ricky told me, his eyes looking anywhere but at me. "I'm just going to start controlling myself better." When I asked Ricky how he might control it better, he gave me the response that I have heard countless times before and since: "I don't know. Just start controlling it."

Of course we know these good intentions will get him nowhere. Ricky, along with the other two guys, needs specific skills to help him manage his behavioral and substance problems.

BUILDING ANGER-CONTROL SKILLS

Ricky told me that he was open to working on his anger, but doubted it would do any good. His previous therapist had told him to "just take three deep breaths," by his report, though I doubt it was said as simplistically as that. He said he tried it a few times, but it didn't help at all. When I told him our work on it might be more detailed and elaborate, he didn't seem fazed. He said he would give it a try.

Teaching anger-control skills may be the most common part of your practice with young men. Poor anger management is the single most common complaint among my clients and those of my colleagues who work with these guys. There are many ways to address anger problems, of course, but I suggest taking a skill-based approach for most of your clients. Built on solid CBT (cognitive behavioral therapy) principles, skill-based anger-control work involves four S's:

1. *Sparks*: knowing what sparks your anger
2. *Signs*: identifying what signs let you know you are getting mad
3. *Sequence*: putting those signs in order from least to most
4. *Strategies*: picking some simple strategies that help derail or contain the angry feelings

Before we started the steps, I needed to make sure Ricky was clear about one common misunderstanding about anger.

"Is anger bad?" I asked him.

"What do you mean?" he asked back.

"Is anger—the feeling of anger—a bad thing?" I asked.

"No, it's just a feeling," he said.

"Exactly," I replied. "Feelings aren't bad. What you do with a feeling may be a problem, but the feeling itself isn't bad. Would you agree?"

"Yes, that's how I think about it," he said.

"How do you know if it is a problem then?" I asked.

"When it hurts someone, I guess," he said.

"Right," I said, then added, "If you hurt someone—physically or in any way—or hurt yourself or lose control of yourself, then I would say that's what you want to keep from happening."

"Yeah, I would agree with that," he said again.

"So here is a key point: our goal is not to keep you from feeling anger. That's just a normal emotion. Our goal is to help you control it when you have that feeling."

"I buy that," he said.

And with that, we were ready to start the steps.

Sparks

Sparks are those things that ignite the young man's anger. It could be when his parents restrict his use of the car. It could be when his girlfriend accuses him of cheating. It could be when teachers single him out in class. It could be anything at all. Whether real or perceived, these sparks are what get his blood boiling.

The reason for identifying a young man's sparks is because the more he is aware of what pushes his buttons, the more prepared he is to control himself. If he knows that his little brother's insults make him furious, he can be more on his guard to take constructive steps to restrain his anger the next time it happens.

Ricky listed five things that sparked his anger. After he listed them, we rated each one from 1 (just a little angry) to 10 (the most angry) to see how they compared:

- When my parents won't let me go out on the weekends (9)
- When my parents ask me a million questions about what I've been doing (8)
- When my parents accuse me of doing drugs when I haven't done it (8)
- When my brother takes my stuff (8)
- When other kids at school gossip about me (6)

He said everything else was, essentially, small potatoes compared to these top five, so I didn't feel the need to ask for more. However, for some clients, the list may be much longer. For other guys, you will be lucky to eke out three. The key is to get as many of the important sparks down on paper as you can.

Signs

The next step is to find out what happens when he gets mad. These are his signs that he is getting mad. As simple as this sounds, this is one of the most important aspects of anger-control work. Rather than asking for him to generate this information cold, I have a worksheet that I use to guide the process. I ask if he ever does any of these things when he gets mad. It doesn't necessarily have to be every time, but just that he has done it "more than once."

For each sign he indicates, I ask him to rate again from 1 to 10. Specifically, on the first checked item I say, "Tell me how mad you would have to be to do this. Give me the lowest number where it might start. For example, you might yell when you are a 4, but you almost might start yelling when you are an 8, so give me the lowest number, 4."

Below is the list of all the signs I consider. Beside each one that was true for Ricky there was a checkmark on the left and his 1–10 rating on the right, but here I have just included the list:

- I break things.
- I clench my fists.
- I clench my jaw.
- I cuss.
- I get an upset stomach.
- I fight somebody.
- I get a headache.
- I think about hurting somebody.
- I hit something hard, like a wall or door.
- I hit something soft, like a pillow or bed.
- I hurt myself.
- I kick something.
- I refuse to do things.
- I run out of the room.
- I say mean things.
- I start breathing fast.
- I tear up things.
- I throw things.
- I yell or raise my voice.

Afterward, I ask him to double-check and make sure all his numbers are correct. This is important because we are going to build on it in the next step. We do all this work in pencil because I want to give us the chance to correct and make changes as we go.

Sequence

Once we are both satisfied that we have accurately identified and rated all the anger signs, we take that information and put the items in sequence from the first signs of anger to the most intense, most out of control. This step and all that happens here is the single most critical aspect of building anger-control skills.

Ricky checked more signs than not, but in a sense, this is good because it lets us build a more elaborate and detailed anger sequence. He held the checklist of signs and I wrote on a separate sheet of paper.

"I remember your lowest sign was a three. Which one was that?" I asked.

"Clenching my fists," he replied.

"Go in that order," I directed. "Start with the lowest numbered signs and go up. If you have a tie, like three things that are all rated a 7, then put those in order starting with what would happen first, then the next, then the third one."

"Alright," he said, grasping the idea right away. Some clients need some additional guidance, but he took off on his own, giving me one sign after another in sequence. I wrote it on a sheet of paper instead of the whiteboard because I planned to give him a copy to take with him if he wanted it.

After we had put the signs into sequence, I wanted to divide the series in half.

"I assume that you are in control of yourself when you are clenching your fists," I said.

He nodded.

"And I am guessing that you feel like you have lost control when you are punching walls or things like that," I said, pointing to the end of the sequence.

Again, he nodded.

"So logically, there is probably a line in here where you lose control," I continued.

"Probably," he said, "I'm not really sure."

"Let's find out," I replied. "Are you still in control when you start to yell or raise your voice?" I asked.

"Usually," he said.

One by one, I went through the list until I found the point where he felt like he lost it. I drew a line between the two halves. On the top half, I wrote "In Control," and on the bottom half, I wrote "Out of Control." For some clients, there needs to be three sections: In Control, Losing Control, Out of Control. For Ricky, there seemed to be a fairly clear line.

There was still one more element to do in order to complete the sequence. I asked him which of the signs above the line—in the "In Control" zone—did he do every time or almost every time. I put stars beside each one that he mentioned.

"Of those four signs we just marked, which of those are your most obvious signs, the ones that would be easiest to recognize?"

"Yelling and cussing," he said. I circled both of those. When we were done, we both studied the sequence for a few moments until he agreed it was accurate.

"This is your anger sequence," I said. "Everyone's anger sequence is so different it's almost like an emotional fingerprint. "The key to anger control is not what you do, it's when you do it. We are going to use those two that you just circled as your big signs, the things you do before you get out of control that let you know you are starting to lose it."

Strategies

There was still one more step to go before we finished our anger-control work. Though there was a lot of ground covered and a lot of details discussed, we still had more than enough time to finish this in one session.

"In psychology, there are three things we focus on: feelings, thoughts, and actions," I explained. "Anger is a feeling. You can use your thoughts and actions to control a feeling."

He sucked his cheeks in and looked like he was considering the notion.

"Remember that the strategy is less important than when you do it, but it is good for you to pick a couple of strategies that work for you," I advised. "Let me start by suggesting some possible strategies and you can choose one or pick your own."

I began by listing out some possible thinking strategies:

- Count backwards from 30 to 0 by 3's.
- Do a word jumble from any word you see around you (for example, from the word "Internet," you could make words like "trite," "nine," or "rent").
- Meditate or pray.
- Use relaxation imagery.

"These all just get your mind off of whatever you were mad about," he said.

"Exactly," I said. "In some ways, it's as simple as that."

He picked the word *jumble*, thinking that was a clever idea. Then I listed some action strategies:

- Do something athletic or physical (run, shoot baskets, lift weights).
- Hit something safe (punching bag, pillow, etc.).
- Take a deep breath and hold it for 10 seconds, then repeat.
- Squeeze something that you carry around with you.

He wasn't especially pleased with any of these options, but he couldn't come up with one on his own, so he chose to hit something safe, specifically the back of a stuffed chair in his room. Some have suggested that hitting something is not a good option for helping clients manage their anger. For many young men, though, they have a need to hit something because their anger is so intense that they will typically either break something or hurt themselves before they get a sense of relief. I've had several clients who have installed punching bags in their garage, one who would hit a dead tree in his backyard with a baseball bat, and another who would go out and dig with a shovel in a garden area. In each case, they had a strong need to do something physically intense because their anger was so powerful. In my experience, these have been effective alternatives to the ways they used to express their anger and made them less—not more—aggressive in other ways.

Once we had done all the steps, I wrote out a lengthy sentence and had him read it. The purpose was to consolidate what we had done over the past hour.

"I get the most angry when my parents won't let me go out on the weekends and I know I am getting mad when I start to cuss and yell," he read, "so when that happens, I need to do a word jumble and hit the back of my stuffed chair."

"That sounds about right," he said.

At that point, we needed to contract to practice using these skills during the coming week and prepare him for what often happens.

"Sometimes we work on anger-control skills like this and the person comes back and says he tried it and it didn't work," I explained. "It's a skill like learning to play the guitar." I chose this example specifically because of his interest in music. Had he been more athletically inclined, I would have likened it to learning to shoot free throws or block goals. "If you took guitar lessons and the teacher taught you a D chord and a G chord and then told you to practice during the week, it would just take work and persistence, but it would eventually pay off.

He clearly understood the point. We agreed he would practice during the week and come back to report how it went. As you might guess, he came back the next session and reported that he had a couple of blowups during the week and had not remembered to cue himself to use the skills.

"I forgot," he told me.

I asked if he still wanted to work on it. He said he did, so we reviewed the steps and then rehearsed scenarios where he might use them. I didn't get discouraged because I knew that, for guys like Ricky, it would take about four sessions of persistent work before we saw solid, sustained improvements. Some clients show improvements in their anger control after the first session; some after six or seven; a few others never show improvements. On average, though, you can expect about four sessions of review, rehearsal, and encouragement before these patterns start to change. Rehearsal can take the form of role-plays or mental imagery. When in doubt, you should over-rehearse, even if it seems a little tedious to the client. This in-session practice makes out-of-session application more likely.

There will undoubtedly be those who don't improve their anger control with this approach. Often, but not always, these are guys with more severe neurological issues. For those young men, you would also want to consider referring to a neurologist or psychiatrist to see if medicine may be helpful to them. Generally speaking, this cognitive-behavioral model will work well, especially if you have addressed the motivational issues sufficiently.

MANAGING OUT-OF-CONTROL BEHAVIORS

Ricky's cutting had started as a way of coping with overwhelming emotions. If he felt so sad or so angry or so anxious that he didn't know what else to do, he would cut himself on the forearm. The feeling was almost indescribable. It was a thrill, a rush, a surge of adrenaline. At the same time, it was peace, relief, almost bliss. His heart rate pounded before he cut, spiked when he first saw the blood, then dropped as he watched it and later cleaned it up. It was a roller coaster ride.

It had become like a drug to him. He couldn't believe it the first time he did it. He wasn't like those crazy cutters at his school, he thought. Then it happened again and again, sometimes more than once a week. He started cutting on other parts of his body—his inner thigh, the top of his arm—to make the scars less visible. It had gotten completely out of control. Now he did it at times when he wasn't even feeling that upset. The last time he did it, he just felt "bored" and did it as if he were on autopilot. Even after doing successful work with helping him manage his emotions, his cutting had subsided but had not gone away. It had become its own freestanding problem.

Young men seem uniquely susceptible to developing patterns of out-of-control behavior. Whether it is drug or alcohol use, pornography addictions, gambling problems, or many other problematic behaviors, their rates of trouble are higher than other groups. Ricky compulsively cuts; Gabriel is a serial cheater; Marlon can't make it through the day without smoking weed. The motivational approach early in therapy had elicited the desire to make the changes from all of them, as well as a decent amount of confidence they could actually make the change. All of them, however, needed some additional skills to get these behaviors under control. Based on well-studied principles of cognitive-behavioral therapy and relapse prevention models, each of these young men can be helped by identifying four aspects of their out-of-control behavior.

Risky Situations

Of our three young men, Gabriel's pattern of out-of-control behavior was the most complex. Ricky only had one risky situation—being in the bathroom with a razor blade and the door locked. And Marlon only had two risky situations—his bedroom in the morning right after he woke up and at night right before he went to bed. But Gabriel could list out no less than six risky situations.

"Describe the situations where you are most likely to cheat," I asked Gabriel.

"That's a lot," he said with a little laugh that looked like pride and guilt at the same moment.

"You say them and I will write them out," I said. After he gave me his list, we went back and rated them from 1 to 5, from very low risk to very high risk. Here was his list:

- Being on campus after midnight (2)
- Drinking heavily around girls at parties (4)
- In a girl's room or apartment at night when no one else is around (5)
- Being alone with a girl in my car (3.5)
- Flirting with a girl in my class (2)
- Being around old girlfriends (4)

Gabriel said none of this surprised him. He had known these occasions were his vulnerable spots for awhile, but he hadn't done much to avoid these situations at all. He knew he kept putting himself in places and in circumstances where there was a pretty big chance of cheating on his girlfriend again, something he had done at least a dozen times in the past year, by his count.

Risky Thoughts

We moved on to an area that was a little tougher for him to identify, so it took us a little longer. When I first asked him what the risky thoughts were that led to his cheating, he said he didn't have any thoughts. He just got caught up in the moment and did it. I gently persisted, and we were able to come up with a list of four thoughts that he had some of the time, but certainly not in every situation:

- I might like her more than my girlfriend (4)
- No one knows I'm here (4)
- My girlfriend is being a bitch right now (5)
- My girlfriend might leave me (5)

These risky thoughts were few but powerful. All three were rated as a 4 or higher, so when he had these thoughts, he was in big danger. It took some work to unearth them, but it was worth the effort.

Risky Feelings

Gabriel was a highly emotional guy, but he wasn't especially skilled at understanding and sorting out his emotions. Every negative emotion felt like anger to him and got expressed as rage. Building on our earlier work on emotional awareness that helped him identify and sort out feelings better, we could revisit that work in this context. Gabriel was able to identify five emotions that put him at a higher risk for cheating:

- Feeling bored (4)
- Feeling lonely (5)
- Feeling depressed (5)
- Feeling really happy (3)
- Feeling worried (4)

This was one area that seemed to take him by surprise. He knew he felt things when he cheated, especially afterward, but he didn't realize how many emotions he felt that led him down this path.

Risky Actions

Years ago, I had a client who was trying to kick a drug habit, but struggled mightily with it. He had a summer construction job and had two routes home, both of which took about 10 minutes. On the surface, there was no difference; it was just a change of scenery. The real difference, though, was that one route took him by his drug dealer's house and the other one did not. On some occasions, he would take the first path and just see if the dealer's truck was in the driveway or see if anyone was on the porch or in the yard. He was not going to stop, he told himself, and, to give him his credit, most of the time he didn't stop; he just kept driving. The problem, of course, was that he was putting himself at a higher and higher risk each time he drove by the dealer's house. Eventually, he was going to stop. When he was honest with himself, he would admit this was true.

In relapse prevention terms, we call this a "seemingly unimportant decision." It's not the relapse itself, but it is putting yourself on the warning track. Another client with a pornography addiction would tell himself he was just going to look at MySpace, but as soon as a picture of an attractive girl appeared anywhere on the browser, he was off to the porn sites. One client with a gambling problem told me he would check the sports section of the paper and read every detail about a big game on days before he would place a huge bet.

In managing out-of-control behaviors, the ability to identify risky actions—these seemingly unimportant decisions—is hugely important. Gabriel had a few that immediately came to his mind and a few others that took some time and patience to identify. Here was his list:

- Driving to campus in the evening when my girlfriend is out of town (4)
- Going by girls' rooms just to visit (3)
- Calling other girls just to talk (2)
- Calling old girlfriends just to see how they are doing (3)
- Drinking at any party (1)
- Talking to a girl at a party when I have been drinking (3.5)

Creating Action Steps

After we finished with this, we looked over all four lists together and felt like we had covered all the important bases.

"So what do we do with this?" he asked.

"Good question," I said. "Our next step is to build a plan of specific action steps on what we just identified."

We both agreed that we would focus on any risk that was rated a 3 or higher. That wouldn't feel too overwhelming and had a very good chance of stopping his cheating behavior altogether. For some clients, the focus needs to be on all identified risks, but for others, it can be only on the areas of greatest risk.

The task becomes to take each focus risk factor and come up with a specific plan for what to do when that occurs. This includes crafting highly specific self-talk or steps of behavioral action. For some, all of this can be accomplished in a single session, but for others, it may take two sessions to do it justice. Gabriel and I spent two sessions working out the details of this plan, but a sample (of just the risks rated 5) is shown in Table 9.1.

For this to work, we will have to review and rehearse it a number of times in subsequent sessions. We will also have to talk about times when he was able to use this in his daily life and times when he forgot all about it, whether he cheated or not. To be effective, it requires a lot of work.

Keep an Eye on Motivation

Again, I cannot overemphasize the importance of doing the motivational work first. All of this work we just completed will be for naught if Gabriel does not see this as important or if he does not feel confident that he can change this behavior. In some instances, you will have a client who appears highly motivated to make the change, but when you begin the harder work or when he is not quickly successful, his motivation may waver. For those guys, our tendency as therapists is to forge ahead, but usually this is a mistake. Instead, it is much better to drop back and work through the motivational issues or importance, confidence, and readiness again. From his vantage point, he probably won't realize that you have switched gears, but you need to be fully aware that you have put the CBT and relapse prevention work on pause for a time and have returned to the motivational work.

In my supervisory and consultation experience, this is one of the areas where therapists have the greatest difficulty. They may become skilled at the motivational work and they may also acquire a big toolbox of CBT skills, but they have a harder time knowing when to toggle back and forth between the approaches. Usually this is because some clients often show significant changes in their motivation by expressing greater readiness, importance, and confidence, yet these gains can erode in subtle and almost imperceptible ways.

The best practice is to monitor readiness, importance, and confidence in an ongoing, dynamic fashion. Near the beginning of the session, it works well to get a read on the client by asking something like, "Last time, we focused a lot on your cocaine use, and I asked you to rate yourself from 1 to 10 about how important it was to change it and how confident you are that you could make that change. Can I ask you those same

TABLE 9.1   Gabriel's Action Steps

Risk	Self-Talk Step(s)	Action Step(s)
Feeling lonely	I should call one of my guy friends.	Call one of my guy friends.
Feeling depressed	It will pass because it always does. Being sad is a normal part of life sometimes.	Go work out. Watch *Family Guy* or another funny show. Go for a drive and listen to music.
Thinking my girlfriend is being a bitch right now	She is under a lot of stress and I need to give her some space. She has the right to be mad at me because of how I acted. Most of the time she is really nice to me.	Send her a nice text message. Write down the things about her I really like or appreciate.
Thinking my girlfriend is going to leave me	She will definitely leave me if I cheat on her. She only talks about breaking up after I have been really rude to her, but we always work it out.	Apologize. Avoid all girls when I am thinking this.
Being in a girl's room at night when no one else is around	I made a mistake and I need to leave right now. When I think I can control myself and be here, I am kidding myself.	Leave immediately. Text Corey before I go anywhere around girls at night.

two questions again to get a sense of where you are with it?" If there are changes up or down in those answers, then it can lead to some good discussion. Sometimes these motivational indicators stay unchanged, but often they fluctuate from session to session. If they move down a point, you may not want to spend too much time on this, but if they drop by two or more points, then it is worth a lengthier conversation before launching back into cognitive-behavioral material.

Because of the nature of out-of-control behaviors—with their push-pull, hate it and love it qualities—motivation waxes and wanes greatly. At times, a client may be highly motivated to change, and at other times, he may want to throw in the towel. This makes it essential that you be constantly monitoring importance and confidence throughout the process and be willing and able to make adjustments to the session and the flow of therapy as needed.

USING CUSTOM CHECKLISTS

One of the more effective interventions I have used in recent years is custom checklists that help a client monitor his own goals, risk factors, or behavioral patterns that concern him. Built from a basic template, these personalized checklists are constructed in the session using the information that has already been captured from earlier sessions. The practice came from having many clients ask for copies of their anger-control sheets or lists of risk factors or other things we had written down, which I was more than happy to give them. I began to think that the information could be given to them in a way that required a little more of them and encouraged them to actively review the information on a regular basis.

These checklists, by their nature, are highly flexible and entirely individualized. They can be designed for daily, weekly, or monthly ratings. They can measure frequency, duration, or intensity of certain targets. They can have weighted items or simply items checked off. In some cases, the checklists can be developed for collateral raters, like parents or tutors. The bigger point is that you are providing a checklist that will keep them focused on their goals after the session.

Therapists with a decent working knowledge of word processing programs like Microsoft Word or Apple Pages can build these checklists on the spot in their office. For those who are not so software savvy, they can be created by hand to be formatted later by support staff or by the client himself.

To demonstrate the flexible nature of this, I'll show you a simple checklist from Gabriel and then a more complex checklist that I developed with Marlon. In both cases, the decision to develop a checklist flowed out of some of the work that we had already done together. Gabriel agreed that it would be a good idea to take his risk factors and convert them into a checklist to serve as a regular reminder for him. He debated about showing it to his girlfriend to let her know he was serious about working on this, but ultimately decided against it because some of the information was a little too revealing. It took us about 30 minutes to make the checklist. You will notice that we decided to round up the half numbers (i.e., 3.5) to be on the safe side. The circled numbers were inserted from the symbols option to make it look a little more fancy, but it could have more easily been done by just writing the number. Table 9.2 shows what it looked like when we were done.

It's better for him to fill it out than just to skim over it, because filling it out requires more active engagement and thought. However, even if he just looks over it on occasion, it is like having a reminder, and it refreshes not only the information, but potentially his resolve to remain faithful.

TABLE 9.2   Gabriel's Custom Checklist

Risk	Score
1. Being on campus after midnight	●
2. Drinking heavily around girls at parties	●
3. In a girl's room or apartment at night when no one else is around	●
4. Being alone with a girl in my car	●
5. Flirting with a girl in my class	●
6. Being around old girlfriends	●
7. Thinking "I might like her more than my gf"	●
8. Thinking "No one knows I'm here"	●
9. Thinking "My gf is being a b* right now"	●
10. Thinking "My gf might leave me"	●
11. Feeling bored	●
12. Feeling lonely	●
13. Feeling depressed	●
14. Feeling really happy	●
15. Feeling worried	●
16. Driving to campus in the evening when my gf is out of town	●
17. Going by girls' rooms just to visit	●
18. Calling other girls just to talk	●
19. Calling old gf's just to see how they are doing	●
20. Drinking at any party	●
21. Talking to a girl at a party when I have been drinking	●
Today's Date: _____ Total (Max of 87):	

Marlon's checklist became a little more complicated. He had bombed out of his adult diploma program at the community college after one semester, having blown off class and assignments. The semester started in mid-August, but he was already sidelined by early October. Earlier, he had practically thrown in the towel with school, but by the time we got to this point in therapy using the sure-and-steady motivational approach, his desire to do school had increased a lot. He reported a high degree of importance (8) when it came to completing the diploma program, but a relatively low degree of confidence (4) that he would actually finish. However, once we started exploring the possibility of having a plan to follow that would keep him on the rails, his confidence shot up (7). We approached this by carefully dissecting what behaviors hurt him with school and what behaviors helped him—or could help him—with school. We took that information and converted it into a checklist, as seen in Table 9.3.

We agreed that he would review the checklist every week and bring it into the session with him. If he forgot to bring it in, we had already

TABLE 9.3   Marlon's School Success Checklist

Date: _____

Things That Help		Things That Hurt	
Set study times	☐	Allowing responsibilities to slide	☐
Keeping room clean	☐	Not doing schoolwork	☐
Staying connected to grandmother	☐	Smoking weed too much	☐
Surrounding self with positive influences	☐	Not going to class	☐
Keeping updated calendar	☐	Lack of physical activity	☐
Be active in class	☐	Excessive videogame playing	☐
Regular contact w/ teachers (1X/wk)	☐	Other (add in):	☐
Getting enough sleep	☐		
Eating healthy	☐		
Total (Max of 35):		**Total (Max of 24):**	

Total of Help – Hurt: _____

agreed that he would review it at the start of the session. Sometimes we would discuss it and sometimes we wouldn't. I was also tracking the information on a spreadsheet that we were able to study after about 6 weeks. Even though it looks involved, this requires a minimal amount of work because the spreadsheet can automatically generate the graph (Figure 9.1).

Visually, we could see a trend that started strong, then dipped, then picked back up again. Marlon and I both agreed that having the checklist

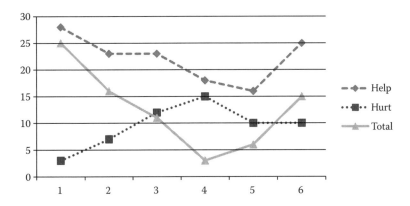

Figure 9.1   Marlon's 6 week progress.

kept the slide from going into the gutter like it had the previous semester. The weekly reminder helped him tighten up when he started to get lax. Seeing the graph a month and a half into the semester let him examine his pattern a little more carefully and strengthened his resolve to keep going.

"By this point last semester, I had already given up," he told me.

"And this semester, you are trending up and not down," I replied.

"I like that," he said, referring to the graph. "Can I have a copy of it to show my aunt?"

IMPROVE DECISION-MAKING SKILLS

I've read many treatment plans that listed something like "improve decision-making skills" as one of the young man's goals. Often these guys are court-ordered or have gotten into trouble with school or parents. Many of them are highly impulsive; some of them are pretty antisocial or otherwise conduct-disordered. The goal is boilerplate for this population.

While I have seen the goal a hundred times, I rarely see specific articulated steps for making this happen. In consultations, it seems that many therapists engage in therapeutic tail chasing, with sessions consisting of gentle lectures followed by the client's assurances that he will not do it again.

I must confess that I have a hard time with this goal myself. Anger control is easier because you usually have salient, recurring signals to latch onto. Managing out-of-control behavior is a challenge because there is such a pleasure drive that is hard to override, but well-motivated clients can make changes in these patterns over time with persistent effort. But decision-making skills are harder to develop. Why? For many reasons:

- There are fewer consistent behavioral signs to identify and use.
- It covers such a wide range of behaviors and contexts that these skills become harder to generalize and use consistently.
- They are often very low-frequency behaviors.
- Young men with serious deficits in decision-making skills frequently have neurological complications that make these skills harder to use.
- Often, the issue is not a skill deficit, but a characterological issue that skill-based therapy will not touch.

Let's take Gabriel as an example. He makes a whole lot of bad decisions: drinking and driving, cheating on his girlfriend, pointless lying, saying things he wishes he hadn't, and so on. There is more than a twinge of narcissism here, where he thinks he won't get caught and the rules don't apply to him, and he is so charming that he can get away with whatever he does. Right now, we have moved past these issues for the most part. He acknowledges things haven't worked out well for him and that he needs to change. His motivation to be faithful to his girlfriend is at an all-time high. His desire never to have another DUI is off the chart. His drive to return to Wake Forest is strong.

Still, breaking these patterns is tough. He cheated on his girlfriend once every 4–6 weeks on average. That sounds like a lot (and it is), but it is also fairly low frequency from a behavioral standpoint. He would drink and drive often, but he would drive impaired about once every two months. That is once every two months too much, but it is still low frequency from a treatment standpoint. He would scream at his girlfriend, call her a bitch or a whore, accuse her of horrible things, and cuss her out on occasion, but sometimes he would go for three months at a stretch without this ever happening. In the daily routine of life, this is nearly an eternity for a 20-year-old. In fact, he was proud of himself for how long he had gone without doing this. When he was in high school, he said, this kind of thing might happen once or twice a week.

Gabriel clearly makes poor decisions in the moment, as do many young men with these problems, but these moments are so infrequent (relatively speaking), so varied, and so unpredictable that it is hard to teach skills that generalize.

With that said, I have developed a basic framework over the years that seems to help many of these guys. To be fair and honest, it is usually slow-going work and requires more rehearsal than even the other interventions described in this chapter to be useful. Still, it is a template that can work well.

We start with three key words: *Past, Present, Future*. Around each of these words we hang images (for more visually oriented guys) or phrases (for the more auditory oriented) that meaningfully relate to that young man's decision-making process.

Past

"Give me a few images or phrases that represent times from the past that you don't want to experience again," I prompted.

He thought for a moment and gave me these four scenes:

- Being sideways in his jeep in the dark.
- Seeing his mother yelling and crying when she found out about the DUI.
- Screaming at his girlfriend.
- Having his girlfriend text him while he was having sex with another girl.

"Do you see these more as images or think of them more in words?" I asked.

"Images. Definitely," he replied without hesitation.

"I am going to suggest that these are the images we should use to help you make better decisions. Are you okay with that?" I asked.

"I don't like thinking about them, but yeah, they would work," he said.

The first start of the decision-making process is to identify clearly defined images or phrases from the past that the client does not want to repeat. By definition, this part of the process is negative in tone and often harder to do because of that. Avoidant guys don't like to think about these things, which, paradoxically, makes them more likely to do them again.

To be most effective, the past images should cover enough territory to allow the process to generalize, but not so many as to be easily forgotten or diminished. I would suggest two to four images as a rule of thumb. For Gabriel, these images covered territory related to drinking, sexual compulsivity, family issues, and relationship conflicts, all of which were agreed-upon areas up for discussion.

Present

After we identified key signifiers from the past, we moved on to the present. The key here is to generate multiple options in each of these situations or in any situation where there is even the potential for trouble. Getting past a mindset of having only two options—do it or don't do it—is an essential part of this skill development process. For example, when Gabriel is drinking at a party, he doesn't just have two options—drive or not drive—he has multiple options. I asked him to list out the choices he could make in that situation. He came up with a few alternatives:

- Give my keys to a friend before I have the first drink.
- Have a friend drive me to the party.
- Ask ahead of time if I can sleep over.
- Tie a note to my keys that says "Never drink and drive" before I get there.
- Tell at least three people at the party to stop me from leaving in my jeep if I have been drinking.

We evaluated each of these and talked about which ones he was mostly likely to do. The point here, however, is less about the specific options themselves as it is about the process. If possible, I would like for him to get in the habit of instinctively generating three or more possibilities in every situation like this. I frame it as a form of creative problem solving, a challenge to see if he can come up with three, four, or even five possibilities each time. If he does this step, the prospects of him making a better decision are significantly increased.

Future

Thinking about the future is the opposite of thinking about the past when working on decision-making skills. Whereas the focus on past is a reflection on what bad things have already occurred, the focus on the present is an anticipation of what good things could be realized if his decision making improves.

To do this, we return to the images from the past and we have corrected images for the future. I structure this process with the client, but he generates the actual wording. Gabriel's corrected images look like this:

- Driving in a new jeep
- Seeing my mother smile at me
- Having a relaxed dinner with my girlfriend
- Walking past another girl's door and knowing I didn't go in

"If this was what your future looked like, how happy would you be?" I asked him.

"Very happy," he said. "All that would be huge."

"How realistic does this seem to you?" I asked.

"Right now, very much," he said.

Rehearsal

The final step, and perhaps the most important one, involves rehearsal—and lots of it. While Gabriel is optimistic and inspired right at this moment, that will quickly fade when he returns to his life of partying. He will forget what we have talked about, or he will think about it too late unless we rehearse.

The rehearsal involves simple cues. The three words—past, present, future—are the anchors. After I coach him on how to do it, I simply say one of the words, and then he does the work.

"Past," I say simply.

"Jeep wreck. Mom freaking out. Screaming at Kelly. Text message," he said, ticking each off one by one.

"Excellent," I replied. "Present: good-looking girl flirting with you at a party. Kelly is out of town."

He hesitated for a moment. His eyes went up as he thought about his options.

"Okay. Tell her I have a girlfriend in the first two minutes of the conversation. Excuse myself and tell one of my bros to keep an eye on me. Leave. Politely refuse to give her my number. Tell her I promised to text message my girlfriend and do it in front of her. How's that?" he concluded, having generated five solid options.

"Good," I said. "Last one: Future."

"New jeep. Happy mom. Dinner with Kelly. Resisting temptation," he replied.

"That's great. You did amazing," I told him. "Say the cue words back to me."

"Past, present, future," he said.

"When do you say those to yourself?" I asked.

"Any time I am around girls or when I am drinking," he said.

"That's right," I said, impressed by how succinctly he said it. "Now this week is all about practice. Make it happen."

"I'll do it," he said.

"I know you will," I told him. "That's the kind of guy you are."

THERAPY TAKE-AWAYS

1. Help guys with anger-control problems identify the 4 S's—sparks, signs, sequence, and strategies.

2. Help guys with out-of-control behaviors identify risky situations, risky thoughts, risky feelings, and risky actions, then come up with specific action steps when these risks emerge. Use custom checklists to help remind them. Custom checklists can also be used to help improve nearly any behavioral problem.

3. Use the past, present, future framework to help a young man improve his decision-making skills.

APPENDIX: ANGER-CONTROL WORKSHEET

Anger-Control Worksheet:

What things make you mad?	How mad do they make you?
1.	10 9 8 7 6 5 4 3 2 1
2.	10 9 8 7 6 5 4 3 2 1
3.	10 9 8 7 6 5 4 3 2 1
4.	10 9 8 7 6 5 4 3 2 1
5.	10 9 8 7 6 5 4 3 2 1
6.	10 9 8 7 6 5 4 3 2 1
7.	10 9 8 7 6 5 4 3 2 1
8.	10 9 8 7 6 5 4 3 2 1
9.	10 9 8 7 6 5 4 3 2 1
10.	10 9 8 7 6 5 4 3 2 1

What happens when you get mad?	How mad would you have to be to do that?
☐ I break things	10 9 8 7 6 5 4 3 2 1
☐ I clench my fists	10 9 8 7 6 5 4 3 2 1
☐ I clench my jaw	10 9 8 7 6 5 4 3 2 1
☐ I cuss	10 9 8 7 6 5 4 3 2 1
☐ I get an upset stomach	10 9 8 7 6 5 4 3 2 1
☐ I fight somebody	10 9 8 7 6 5 4 3 2 1
☐ I get a headache	10 9 8 7 6 5 4 3 2 1
☐ I think about hurting somebody	10 9 8 7 6 5 4 3 2 1
☐ I hit something hard	10 9 8 7 6 5 4 3 2 1
☐ I hit something soft	
☐ I hurt myself	10 9 8 7 6 5 4 3 2 1
☐ I kick something	
☐ I refuse to do things	10 9 8 7 6 5 4 3 2 1
☐ I run out of the room	10 9 8 7 6 5 4 3 2 1
☐ I say mean things	10 9 8 7 6 5 4 3 2 1
☐ I start breathing fast	10 9 8 7 6 5 4 3 2 1
☐ I tear up things	10 9 8 7 6 5 4 3 2 1
☐ I throw things	10 9 8 7 6 5 4 3 2 1
☐ I yell or raise my voice	10 9 8 7 6 5 4 3 2 1
☐ Other: _____	10 9 8 7 6 5 4 3 2 1
☐ Other: _____	10 9 8 7 6 5 4 3 2 1
	10 9 8 7 6 5 4 3 2 1
	10 9 8 7 6 5 4 3 2 1

Anger Pattern: _____

Check at Least One Strategy From Each Column That Will Work for You:

Acting   Thinking

- ☐ Three deep breaths
- ☐ Squeezing something
- ☐ Hitting something safe (punching bag, etc.)
- ☐ Doing something athletic (running, shooting baskets, etc.)
- ☐ Other: _____

- ☐ Word jumble
- ☐ Praying or meditating
- ☐ Counting backward from 30 to 0 by 3's
- ☐ Self time-out
- ☐ Other: _____

Putting It All Together: _____

I get most mad when _____

_____

And I know when I am just starting to get mad, I _____

Or _____

So when that happens I need to _____

And _____

10

Therapy and the Techno-Client

During one session in the middle of our conversation, Ricky's cell phone buzzed in his pants pocket. He grabbed it and flipped it open. A look of frustration swept over his face, and he began to text furiously. He looked up for a brief moment at me.

"Go ahead," he said to me, as if I were in the middle of a presentation.

"I'll wait on you," I said.

"No, it's okay. You can keep going," he replied, continuing to tap away on his keypad. He was more than comfortable having these two conversations simultaneously.

If there is one characteristic that most distinguishes this generation from older generations, it is their use of technology. There has never been a young generation that is so imbued with new technology in their daily lives than this current one. From the time they were preschoolers, these kids knew how to use a computer mouse. From the time they were in elementary school, they could play sophisticated video games. From the time they were in middle school, they could text message with blazing speed. By high school, there was almost no limit to their ability to use technology to solve problems, maintain relationships, have fun, and collect information. This is not merely a generational cycle. Technology use will shape the generations for the foreseeable future.

This reality poses unique challenges to the therapists who treat these adolescents and young adults. Some professionals have ventured to stay on top of the new technologies, with varying degrees of success. Others have become virtual Luddites, refusing to use e-mail, declining to create a Web site, and knowing little about the world of technology that these young adults inhabit on a daily basis. The latter choice is legitimate, but the general posture toward technology does stand the risk of putting therapists significantly out of touch with their clients.

Adolescents and young adults relate through technology in unprecedented ways. Whether it be through Facebook, instant message, XBox Live, MySpace, e-mail, cell phone, text message, or a dozen other ways, this generation keeps in touch with friends and family in immediate, continuous ways. Oftentimes, they have multiple streams of communication happening at once. I have seen high schoolers around a table talking to each other, texting each other, and having outside cell phone conversations all at once. Older generations are distressed by this, but this is second nature and perfectly natural for adolescents and young adults. To be sure, there are dangers and problems with this accelerated and pervasive use of technology, but there are also some good aspects to it.

THERAPY IN THE NEW ERA OF COMMUNICATIONS TECHNOLOGY: EIGHT COMMON QUESTIONS

Regardless of your view of whether all of this is a positive development or not, the unmistakable reality is that this is how life has become for this younger generation. What all of this means for therapists is not entirely clear yet, but it will certainly change much of how we do business in the years and decades to come. As we all wade into these uncharted waters, there are several questions that frequently come up. Here are eight of the most common ones that therapists today are considering, along with thoughts and proposed guidelines for answering them.

How Should We Handle Technology Like Texting and Cell Phone Use in the Session?

Ricky isn't the only client who has texted or taken a call during a session. It has now become commonplace, even with waiting-room reminders to turn off cell phones. Historically, taking phone calls and starting other conversations when you are speaking to someone has been considered rude. Now, younger people think nothing of texting during a conversation or taking phone calls during sessions. I have had at least one client who started texting during an IQ test and several others who have answered calls (though nearly all of them say something like, "Can I call you back? I'm in my therapy appointment"). If these multiple streams of communication are congruent with the norms and values of this generation, then should we permit this to intrude on the session and come to terms with the fact that this is just how these younger people relate and interact?

In a word, no. Therapy is a unique relationship that typically requires a high degree of focus, mindfulness, and the ability to stay in the moment for it to work well. Because of this, I ask my clients to turn off their cell phones when they come in. We counted no fewer than eight small signs in the check-in, waiting, and checkout areas of our practice asking clients to turn off their cell phones. Not everyone complies at first (thus the taking calls and texting on occasion), but when it comes up, it gives us the chance to talk about the reason why it would be best for him to turn the phone off during the session. Nearly all clients understand the rationale for this and shut it down.

Can Therapy Be Effectively and Ethically Delivered Online?

Over the past decade, as therapeutic services have increasingly been delivered online by therapists via e-mail, chat, videoconferencing, and other means, it has opened up a whole new world for therapists and clients alike. Besides the convenience and the "coolness factor," the bigger question is how effective are mental health services when they are delivered remotely? After all, for all the convenience you might gain, you might also lose a lot in translation if the person isn't in the same room with you.

The research, however, seems to be landing solidly on the side of support for online interventions. A meta-analysis of 64 studies of the effectiveness of Internet-based psychotherapeutic interventions involving 9,764 clients found that they were as effective as traditional, face-to-face therapy (Barak, Hen, Boniel-Nissim, & Shapira, 2008). Not only are online interventions judged to be effective by the clients and therapists who use them, but they can also increase access to mental health services, and clients tend to have high levels of satisfaction with the therapy or consultation provided (Beattie, Shaw, Kaur, & Kessler, 2009; Botella, Garcia-Palacios, Baños, & Quero, 2009; Mackinnon, Griffiths, & Christensen, 2008; Monnier, Knapp, & Frueh, 2003; Morgan, Patrick, & Magaletta, 2008; Shepherd et al., 2006). The working alliance between a client and the therapist tends to be rated just as high online as it is in face-to-face interactions. In fact, one study found significantly higher composite scores on the Working Alliance Inventory among the online sample as compared to the traditional client sample (Cook & Doyle, 2002).

So the short answer is that the ratings for these online interventions appear to indicate that online sessions are as effective and satisfactory as face-to-face sessions. That's good news for therapists who are looking to work with young men who will increasingly want to access their mental health services remotely. These young men will want their sessions by videoconferencing, their quick consultations by e-mail, and their check-ins by text.

Not all clinicians will be on board with this, however. A therapist's theoretical orientation seems to have a lot to do with how comfortable he or she is with using online interventions. As you might suppose, cognitive-behavioral therapists were more likely to strongly endorse

Internet-based interventions than psychoanalytically oriented therapists (Mora, Nevid, & Chaplin, 2008). For those with greater levels of comfort and skill with these interventions, they will open up tremendous opportunities to serve young men with therapeutic services in ways that were not available a decade ago.

Recently, therapists at my practice, including me, have been using Skype for clients who are at a distance or who cannot come into the office because of a health or disability issue. It might be a young man who started therapy in town but moved to another city for college, or it might be a guy who contracted mono and finds it very difficult to travel from home. Skype uses low-bandwidth videoconferencing technology that allows you to talk face to face in real time across any distance. Now that many laptops have built-in video cameras and microphones, this type of communication is easier than ever. Skype transmissions are encrypted to protect the security of the interaction, and this makes it functionally as confidential as an office meeting. It is conceivable that someone could eavesdrop on the conversation, but it is also possible that someone could eavesdrop on a conversation in your office if he or she had the means and the motive. Undoubtedly, in the future, there will be other services providing greater refinements and features, but for now, Skype offers low-cost, reliable, and secure communication. In my experience, it is superior to phone sessions and e-mail communication because it gives you the important nonverbal cues that can help you in the session.

As with any new venture, there was a considerable amount of trepidation about the use of videoconferencing. In particular, there were concerns about confidentiality and security, providing services to clients in other jurisdictions, and efficacy. These are all legitimate considerations and concerns that deserved to be addressed, so we spent the better part of a year researching the field. APA's then-president Gerald Koocher laid out four C's that we need to consider regarding the ethics of such practice: contracting, competence, confidentiality, and control (Koocher, 2007). Briefly, here is a summary of the issues he encourages us to take into account:

- *Contracting*: the need to obtain informed consent; the need to work out details of record keeping and storage, fees, and emergency coverage
- *Competence*: the need to ensure that we are well prepared and competent to provide services online
- *Confidentiality*: the need to ensure security and confidentiality of the transmitted information
- *Control*: the need to work out details of who governs and regulates the practice of online counseling, especially when it crosses state lines or across countries

There are some more subtle issues that need to be anticipated as well. For example, what if you are scheduled for a Skype session with a client in his dorm room and he appears on your screen wearing no shirt? (Something like this happened to a colleague.) He may be completely comfortable with this, as he has had other Skype conversations in this very casual state of dress. How should you handle this, though? It's best to be prepared with a mental script for these types of moments before they happen.

One of the practical issues I had not anticipated is that when you are doing therapy online, you are looking at your screen and not the camera, and your client is doing the same thing. What this means is that neither of you are looking each other in the eye. This definitely changes the feel of the interaction. I have begun looking primarily at the camera and occasionally glancing down at the screen for important nonverbal information from time to time. This subtle but important change in the communication has helped, but it definitely makes the interaction feel different than in-person communication

With online therapy, the real issues of confidentiality tend to be much more subtle than the bigger, scarier concerns that are often raised (e.g., the government is eavesdropping, etc.). The more practical issues have to do with things like whether the speaker volume is too loud and might let others outside of the room hear the conversation or the fact that a client's name appears in your list of Skype contacts that must then be shielded from others who see your computer. These concerns can be worked out, but they do need to be addressed if you are to practice ethically and competently.

How Does Being Online Affect a Young Man's Well-Being?

One of the concerns expressed by therapists and others is whether being online negatively affects a young man's social relationships and how he feels about himself. As one counselor told me, "I have these clients who stay on the Internet for hours a day and they don't have any friends in their real life. I'm seeing more and more of that. It can't be a good thing." I've heard this sentiment echoed countless times by teachers, parents, and other concerned older adults.

When we hear accounts of young men staying online playing *World of Warcraft* for six or more hours a day, it is cause for concern. Similarly, when a young person is immersed in *Second Life* to the exclusion of other real-world relationships, we have grounds for worry. Surely this isn't good and healthy. But the truth is that being online is decidedly a mixed bag, with both good and bad features.

It is apparent that being online too much is not healthy. We will define overuse as being online for more than three hours a day, apart from the demands of school or work. It may involve gaming, porn use, checking social networking sites, or just mindless surfing. Those who engage in Internet overuse to this extent tend to have greater depressive symptoms, greater loneliness, fewer face-to-face social interactions, more tendency to feel bored with their lives, and a greater sense that outside people and events control their lives (Chak & Leung, 2004; Fortson, Scotti, Chen, Del Ben, & Malone, 2007; Nichols & Nicki, 2004). It appears that individuals with these traits tend to be online too much, while those who are online too much tend to develop these traits. It is an unhealthy, regressive cycle.

However, low to moderate Internet use can actually be good for most young adults. For example, most of the studies of Facebook have found that it tends to be a healthy force in the lives of people. Facebook users tend to be more willing to engage in face-to-face interactions and relationships rather than less, which challenges the notion that Facebook and similar online social networking sites inhibit real relationships and cause people to be less social in their real-world interactions (Sheldon, 2008). College students use Facebook approximately 30 minutes a day on average, and they spend more time observing content than actually posting their own content. They use their profiles and other parts of their page to share religious preferences, political ideology, and the nature of their work, and they also reveal their media preferences to express their identity (Pempek, Yermolayeva, & Calvert, 2009). Facebook has also become part of the "social glue" that helps incoming freshmen settle into college and build campus relationships. It may also decrease the likelihood that they will drop courses in their first year (Madge, Meek, Wellens, & Hooley, 2009). Contrary to some accounts, there is no strong evidence that Facebook use negatively affects academic achievement in high school and college students. A pilot study had suggested this, but bigger studies have shown no negative impact on grades for the vast majority of students (Pasek, More, & Hargittai, 2009). In fact, moderate use of the Internet is associated with a more positive academic orientation than either nonuse or high levels of use (Willoughby, 2008).

It depends on how much time is spent online, but beyond that, there are some individual differences that make a difference about whether being online is a good thing. One study of over 600 university students found two subsets of Facebook users. One group was more extroverted and had higher self-esteem, while the other was more introverted and had lower self-esteem. The latter group seemed to strive harder to look popular online (Zywica & Danowski, 2008). Researchers found that when a Facebook user had an excessive number of online "friends," others had greater doubts about that person's popularity and social desirability (Tong, van der Heide, Langwell, & Walther, 2008). They were simply trying too hard. Those in that second group with lower self-esteem—who wanted to appear popular online—were also more likely to attempt intimate communication and look for romantic partners online (Dong, Urista, & Gundrum, 2008). For other insecure adults who were already in a relationship, Facebook usage contributed to jealousy in their relationships. When these young adults spent more time on Facebook, they were prone to get more jealous in their romantic relationships. The more jealous they got, the more time they spent searching for other information about their partner that fueled their jealousy and put them into a negative cycle (Muise, Christofides, & Desmarais, 2009). For insecure people, being online a lot is not going to make their lives better. It will likely make them feel more jealous and insecure than they already are.

There is evidence from the research that a person's level of narcissism can be predicted by their Facebook profiles. Those who are more narcissistic tend to have more glamorous, self-promoting profile pictures and far more social contacts or "friends" than those who are less narcissistic. There is no evidence that Facebook users as a whole are more narcissistic than average, however (Buffardi & Campbell, 2008).

Males and females tend to be perceived differently online. If a male's Facebook wall postings had negative comments from others about his own moral behavior, he was seen as more attractive, but females with similar comments on their online walls were seen as less attractive (Walther, van der Heide, Kim, Westerman, & Tong, 2008). Guys were also much less likely to mention a significant other or indicate whether they were in a relationship in their online profiles (Magnuson & Dundes, 2008). This leaves them open to greater risk of online flirting and cheating.

Being online can be good for many young men, but it can also be unhealthy. Guys who spend excessive amounts of time on the Internet and those who are already feeling insecure or have a poorly developed sense of self are not well served by their online time. For the rest, a moderate amount of online time can actually improve their real-life relationships, school performance, and general well-being.

Should a Therapist Accept a Facebook Friend Request From a Client?

If you have a personal page, you realize that the concept of "friend" is so loosely defined in the world of Facebook that it is practically meaningless. A friend could be your spouse, coworker, someone you went to college or high school with, a personal acquaintance, or even someone you've never met but is a friend of a friend. Since it is not ethical to have potentially problematic dual relationships with clients, the therapist should ask whether it is a good idea to be "friends" with a client online, especially when this is so broadly defined as to be meaningless.

Again, the answer here is no. It is not a good idea to be online friends with a current client. When you become Facebook friends with a client, it opens up mutual access to information that could alter the therapeutic relationship in some way. Imagine that you accepted a friend request from a client and now you can view his personal page and see images of him drinking, smoking pot, skinny dipping, or a whole lot of other things. And he can see pictures of you and your family or see your political or religious persuasions. He can post comments on your "wall" or contact you for a personal chat when he sees you are online. As you can imagine, doing so creates a whole range of potential problems. Even if you don't introduce the information into the session, it can change the pattern of interaction for both of you.

Some therapists have asked if it is okay to accept a friend request from a former client, arguing that the therapeutic relationship has ended. This does not pose as many concerns as accepting the friend request of a current client, but it is still potentially tricky. The only time I have ever accepted the friend request of a former client was from a college student who had terminated therapy some months earlier and had moved with his family nearly 3,000 miles away to Seattle. He had no plans to return, and it seemed like a safe bet that I wouldn't see him again. However, a year and a half later, he decided he missed his hometown and moved back across the country to go to school and live in an apartment with some old friends. When he hit a rough spot, he called and asked if I could see him again as a therapist. Of course, I would not deny him this because we had been Facebook "friends," but we did have to talk about it first. We "de-friended" each other and resumed the therapeutic relationship, but it was a lesson learned.

It is a good practice not to accept friend requests from active clients for many reasons, but the decision to accept a friend request from a former client should be made with some deliberation. Some therapists have a general practice of never accepting a friend request from any client, active or inactive. However, there is clearly no ironclad policy or guideline for all therapists with all clients. If you would consider accepting a friend request from a former client, I would suggest asking these questions before making a decision:

1. *Is there a good chance that he may want to resume therapy in the future?* If so, then it is best to pass on the request. However, as you saw from my example, even those who move thousands of miles away and say they have no plans to return to town might end up back in your office. This isn't to say that because anyone has the chance to return to therapy that you must say no to all of them, but the probability of a return to therapy should be a consideration.

2. *Does the client know that the therapy relationship is clearly terminated?* Some clients have a clear termination session or some other communication that lets them know that the therapeutic relationship is done. For others, the relationship is more open-ended, with the client reserving the option of coming back to therapy from time to time. As a rule of thumb, it might be best to accept friend requests only from former clients who are clear that the therapy relationship has come to an end.

3. *Does the client have any personal issues that might make accepting a friend request problematic for you?* Clients who have significant problems with boundaries, antisocial behavior, or other personality concerns will undoubtedly create potential difficulties for you if you accept their friend requests. By contrast, a client you saw

two years ago for a few sessions during a rough period of adjustment following the loss of a parent might be a consideration.

4. *Might accepting the friend request be problematic for him?* There are some clients who might not anticipate problems with the friend request. If he has not anticipated the potential problems, but you have, then you should obviously not accept the invitation.

Most of the time, therapeutic boundaries are important because they protect the client or guard the therapeutic framework. They can also be a consideration for the therapist's protection, as well. However, in those situations where the client initiates the contact, has terminated the therapy relationship, and there are no foreseeable problems that involve the well-being of the client or the therapist, then you could consider accepting the friend request.

All of this raises the inevitable question: Wouldn't it just be easier to say no to all requests? The answer is yes, it would be easier. But easier doesn't always mean better. It is possible that it would be perfectly legitimate and even a good thing to accept a Facebook friend from a former client. With each passing year, the ways that technology is used to connect people to each other, to maintain relationships, and to share information will increase and will become an undeniable part of all of our lives. The reason why it is important to wrestle with these nuanced issues now is because they will become more and more an undeniable, unavoidable part of the daily fabric of our culture.

Should a Therapist Ever Initiate a Facebook Friend Request With a Former Client?

Accepting a friend request from a former client is one issue, but initiating the request is another. In the case of the former, the former client does the initiating; in the case of the latter, it would be the therapist taking the first step. For this reason, it's not a good idea. There may be a situation when it might possibly make sense to take the first step (though I am hard pressed to think of one), but I am confident that these circumstances would be extraordinarily rare and generally not good practice. It puts the person (former client) in an awkward situation, and it is not fair to put him in a situation where he has to make a decision about whether to accept or reject his former therapist. Except in the rarest of circumstances, don't take the first step.

Should a Therapist Check Out Information About a Client Online?

Personal information is so readily available online that it is sometimes tempting to check out clients online. You can see arrest records with mug shots, MySpace profiles, sports records, and a whole lot more. It's all there for you to see. There's a good chance your clients are checking you out online, so is it a good idea to check them out?

Of all the questions, this may be the toughest one to answer firmly. The bottom line is that you must keep the boundary between any information you know from some other source and what the client tells you himself. We might get information about a client from other sources, even when we don't look for it. A mother may send a letter or e-mail describing her perception of her young adult son's struggles. You may have seen a news story featuring a crime committed by an older teenager, then get a call from his family asking for you to be his therapist a few days later. You cannot always control the information that gets to you about a client, even when you don't actively seek it.

Let's take an example where, on more than one occasion, I have been the therapist of a client who has talked about another client in the session, neither of them aware that I had seen the other. In one instance, a client told me about the drug involvement of another guy named Adam, whom I had just started seeing in therapy. He said, "I decided to stop hanging out with Adam. He's a real coke-head. I think he's got a real problem."

Now, Adam had never told me he had ever done cocaine or said he had a drug problem. I can't bring it up with him, and I can't give any indication—overt or subtle—that I know about this. I just have to conduct the next session with Adam as if I had never heard this other important piece of information. As therapists, it's imperative that we have this ability to maintain this separation.

The difference now with Internet searches, however, is not just receiving the information passively, but seeking it actively. Looking up information is different than happening to receive it unintentionally. There are undoubtedly times when you have information that you cannot acknowledge to the client, such as when another client tells you something. However, to actively seek out information and then not tell the client that you have it runs the risk of making you less genuine in your interactions with him. For this reason, I think it is generally not a good idea to actively search online for information about a client.

Another reason not to do the search is that it can often give you information that is actually less valid than what you might get from the therapy session. For instance, I have had more than one parent come to me with reports of their son's MySpace pages that have pictures of marijuana leaves on them or that talk about some anonymous hookup with a girl. In some instances, this information fits with my perception of the young man, but at other times, I would bet that his online persona is very different from how he really behaves in his life. I am fully aware that clients will lie to their therapists, and there is no reason to believe that someone's public MySpace page is any more an accurate reflection of reality than what he is telling you confidentially.

Despite all this, there may be times when it is acceptable to look up someone's information online. I will confess that I have done this a few times, though nearly every time it has been before I decided to see a client. Often it was with individuals who had committed some offense that had been in the news. I looked at the press coverage to get a better sense of whether it was a good referral for me to take. For the most part, though, I do not look up a client's information online after I have begun to see him. I reason that I cannot use anything I discover when I see him in the session, so looking it up would be pointless or just out of curiosity, which is ultimately selfish. My rule of thumb has become not to look up anything on a client unless it serves some clear, constructive purpose that is likely to benefit him. Most of the time, it doesn't, so I don't look up anything.

Should a Therapist Put Personal Information Online?

When we started our practice, we decided that one of the guiding values of our practice would be fun. In keeping with our focus on the positive aspects of psychology, we wanted to create a culture and a presence that was fun and enjoyable. Because of that, our online presence is decidedly nontraditional. The bios on our Web site say that one therapist "suppresses his inner dork" and claims that another is a "princess and occasional loud talker," while revealing that still another "wears black spandex biker pants when mowing his lawn." Linked to my bio is my pop culture blog (called, appropriately, *Shrinkblog*) that covers everything from *American Idol* to *The Arctic Monkeys*. It's become fairly popular and gets thousands of hits from around the world. We have also produced a series of YouTube videos with us doing everything from throwing a computer off a parking deck to parading around a grocery store in superhero outfits.

At a workshop of the American Psychological Association's annual meeting, it became clear to me that the whole issue of online presence is still fairly uncharted territory for many therapists. What also became clear to me was that there was confusion between three overlapping but separate issues: ethics, therapeutic boundaries, and professionalism. What some therapists were referring to as being ethical issues were really boundary issues that have more to do with their theoretical orientation and treatment framework. For example, concerns that a client may see pictures of you and your family are not truly matters of ethics (in the pure sense), but a matter of how personal information may affect the therapy process. The consideration was really how to maintain *therapeutic boundaries* that allow the therapy to move forward. Related to this is the concept of professionalism, the professional manner and persona that you might want to project. When therapists at the conference sniffed in contempt upon hearing that a colleague posted a video of himself singing karaoke on his Web site, the issue at hand was really one of *professionalism*, though some of them regarded it (wrongly) as an ethical issue.

So we have these three overlapping, nuanced issues that need to be teased apart a bit to make a good decision about whether you will post personal information online:

Ethics: protecting the welfare of the client, avoiding harm, keeping the professional in good standing

Therapeutic boundaries: lines around what information the client knows about in order to make the relationship work optimally well within a certain therapeutic framework

Professionalism: what professional image the therapist wants to project and maintain to clients, the public, and other professionals

There is no doubt that these issues overlap to a degree, but they are separate considerations. So how did we decide to post videos of us doing silly things? I will tell you that it wasn't done without a fair amount of deliberation. Here's how we reasoned it out:

1. *Ethics*: We did not see it doing harm to any clients. We also did not see it doing harm to the profession. In fact, we saw it doing the opposite, showing that therapists could be fun, funny, and real. The feedback we have gotten has been overwhelmingly positive, including comments like, "When I saw your videos online, I knew this was the right place for me."
2. *Therapeutic boundaries*: Since we have multiple theoretical models represented at our practice, we give each therapist the option of opting out of any and all videos. They can preview the scripts ahead of time and see rough cuts of the videos before they are posted. If it would interfere with anyone's work, they can take a pass.
3. *Professionalism*: We actually want to project a fun image and work hard to get psychology away from its reputation of being joyless and remote, so the videos fit our vision well. We want our practice to be associated with fun, and we believe that making these videos is a good fit for the professional identity and tone we desire.

The reason for all this discussion and deliberation is to make the point that these issues are subtle, nuanced, and somewhat complex. Another therapist or psychology practice may come to the exact opposite conclusions for perfectly legitimate reasons. With that in mind, I propose that you ask yourself three questions before you post anything online—a video, a blog entry, a picture, a comment on an article—including on your personal Web pages like Facebook or MySpace:

1. Is there a reasonable chance that this will do harm to anyone or to my profession?
2. Could this reasonably compromise my therapeutic work with any present or future client by revealing this information about myself?
3. Is this in line with the professional image that I want to project to others?

These questions can create a filter that lets you decide whether it is wise to post something about yourself online. For some therapists, posting a karaoke video might be detrimental; for others, it may be exactly what you want out there. And, as you know, if it's out there now, it is really out there. Clients and others have access to it at all times.

With the information that is under your control, be wise about what you release out there and have a clear, well-reasoned position before you put anything online. However, while you can make decisions about what you personally post online, you cannot control all the personal information that is out there about you. For example, one therapist recently told me that she was distressed that a past political contribution was listed online in her name. It's even possible that some of what is out there about you isn't even true.

A few years back, one of my clients posted an online blog entry about me entitled, "Keeping It Real At 45." I was 43 at the time he posted it, so that upset me mildly right off the bat. In the entry, he said that I was his hero and used my real name, my real occupation, and the name of my real practice. He also said the following things about me:

- I was his neighbor and had a three-story house with a flower garden in the front and a pool in the back.
- I had a glass-bottom boat and night-vision goggles and kept a large snack-vending machine in my basement.
- I hosted a haunted house in my garage for Halloween and an egg hunt for Easter.
- I have a scar under my left eye that streaks across my face almost to my ear; I will not tell anyone, including my wife, how I got the scar.

I hope you have already figured out that none of this is true (though I wish I had a glass-bottom boat and night-vision goggles). I do have a little scar on my chin from a car accident, but that is the closest to the truth in the four-paragraph story. Except for my real name, real occupation, and real practice name, the entire thing is fabricated and something he wrote for a creative writing class at his university. The problem is that it is also online and can be accessed by anyone with an Internet connection who knows how to get to it.

I cannot control this. There is nothing defaming or slanderous in the story. There is really nothing I can do about it. After he sent me the link, we talked about it in the next session, and he had no thought that this could be uncomfortable or a problem for me. It was simply a creative writing project, and he thought I would be amused and perhaps even a bit flattered because he said in the story that I was his hero, that I was intelligent, and that I seemed well rounded and happy.

The point of this example is that, even if you do not post things about yourself online, others can do as they please. A client can write a story about you; others can post anonymous ratings of you and your services; an old college friend can tag you on a Facebook photo; a neighbor can post a YouTube video of you, and so on. A personal friend told me that she is part of a message board for the parents of children with special needs, and the names of therapists—along with good and bad evaluations of them—pop up there on a regular basis. Your name may be floating out there already. In some cases, it may be invisible to search engines; in other cases, someone's comments may show up on the first page of a Google search.

This is the reality of the world we now live in and will continue to inhabit even more so in the years and decades to come. If you see young adults in therapy, like it or not, you become immersed in their world, which now involves sharing all sorts of personal information about themselves and those in their lives to a wide audience. I have been surprised by some therapists who still believe that not disclosing an e-mail address or not having a Web site protects them from this. There is nothing you can do about it, except come to terms with it and potentially use the new technologies strategically and even therapeutically.

Obviously the discussion here is not about Facebook or Twitter or any other specific site or service per se. New technologies and Web sites will pop up all the time, and our understanding of how they fit into a therapeutic framework will continue to evolve. These are simply some general principles and ways of thinking that can be applied to the next wave of technology that you will face in the coming years of your practice.

Can Online Information and Media Be Incorporated Effectively Into Therapy Sessions?

The Internet is a powerful tool that has reshaped the way we live. Because of this, the reach of the Internet extends into the therapy experience. Clients often want to look up information, such as medication side effects, college acceptance rates, or other statistics. Other times, clients just want to show you something they have found online: a YouTube video of a person talking about his own experience of Asperger's, a Web site devoted to siblings of substance abusers, a cartoon about relationships, and so on.

All of this can be great for the session and should be encouraged. If the client wants to introduce it into the session, then go for it. Similarly, it's also good to share some resources you have found online that might be beneficial to the therapy session. Make sure you choose well-sourced references if you are sharing facts and statistics, and screen all of the media that you share ahead of time to ensure that the content is solid and appropriate.

FINAL THOUGHTS

Therapy with young men will undoubtedly look different in the decades to come, mostly due to the unstoppable impact technology will have on all future generations. It may be that hour-long office sessions may go the way of the dinosaur as videoconferencing and other technologies become more efficient and user friendly and are woven into the daily lives of young people at school, work, and home.

If you see yourself remaining in practice 10 or 20 years from now, I would advise that you begin to consider the ways that newer technologies can be incorporated into the way you do your work. Our practice may not look the same, but change is not always a bad thing. We may find that we can make ourselves more accessible to clients who never would have set foot in a therapist's office before and provide greater continuity of care to others in an increasingly mobile culture. These changes may make therapy and counseling available to more young men than ever before.

I invite you to join me at my new blog called *Therapy with Young Men* at twym.blogspot.com, where you can find further discussion about all of these topics, new content, and downloadable resources. We need to keep pushing each other to get better and better in doing this challenging but highly rewarding work.

THERAPY TAKE-AWAYS

1. Don't become Facebook friends with current clients, and be cautious with accepting friend requests from former clients. Do so only when it is not likely to cause him trouble and when he is aware that therapy is clearly terminated.
2. Consider delivering therapeutic services online, but make sure you take care of the 4 C's—contracting, competence, confidentiality, and control.
3. Incorporate online and interactive media into sessions when they might serve the client's treatment goals.

JUST SO YOU KNOW ...

You've journeyed with these three young men as they struggled with anger, substances, trauma, and relationships, so I thought you might want to know how they turned out.

I saw Gabriel for the better part of a year. During that time, he never got into trouble again with his drinking or his cheating. The last time I saw Gabriel, he had grown his hair back out to chin length and he had added some pounds from working out. He was in town for winter break, having returned to Wake Forest. He and Kelly were still together, and he said he had still not cheated on her or gotten into any more trouble at school. He still drinks, but never drives afterward. His temper is still fiery, by his own admission, but much better managed. It was this improved anger control that had convinced Kelly he had made some genuine changes in his life. He told me, "I'm doing better. She tells me that all the time." The last time I saw Gabriel's mom, she actually smiled. Gabriel didn't get a new jeep, but he got a happy mom, a happy girlfriend, and a fresh start. As he would say, "It was all good."

It's harder to tell you how well Marlon has done. He still smokes weed, but not as much. It's not a necessary part of his day any longer, but he uses it a couple of times a week. He is still in school, having taken—and passed—three classes at the community college over the past year. He still works in the same restaurant and has gotten two small raises this past year. He doesn't like his job and says he wants to get another one, but hasn't made an application anywhere else. I continue to see Marlon periodically. He comes in once every month or two to check in. He says he is happier. He also says he is more confident in himself. On the surface, there haven't been a lot of behavioral changes, but he says his life is better.

Ricky is a clear success story. He is confident, funny, and kind. He has good friends and a good relationship with both parents. The sadness, rage, and self-loathing are all gone. You have the sense he is going to be fine. He is planning to go to college to study psychology. Like several of my former clients, he wants to be a therapist, and it looks like he might be a good one. If he makes it all the way, my hope is that he will never be someone who just takes what he can get from his clients. My hope is that he pushes all of them to be their best. And my hope is that he will have extraordinary fun doing it.

REFERENCES

Ackerman, S. J., & Hilsenroth, M. J. (2003). A review of therapist characteristics and techniques positively impacting the therapeutic alliance. *Clinical Psychology Review, 23,* 1–33.

Arnett, J. J. (1994). Are college students adults? Their conceptions of the transition to adulthood. *Journal of Adult Development, 1,* 154–168.

Arnett, J. J. (1997). Young people's conceptions of the transition to adulthood. *Youth & Society, 29,* 1–23.

Arnett, J. J. (1998). Learning to stand alone: The contemporary American transition to adulthood in cultural and historical context. *Human Development, 41,* 295–315.

Arnett, J. J. (2000). Emerging adulthood: A theory of development from the late teens through the twenties. *American Psychologist, 55,* 469–480.

Arnett, J. J. (2001). Conceptions of the transition to adulthood: Perspectives from adolescence to midlife. *Journal of Adult Development, 8,* 133–143.

Arnett, J. J. (2003). Conceptions of the transition to adulthood among emerging adults in American ethnic groups. *New Directions in Child and Adolescent Development, 100,* 63–75.

Arnett, J. J. (2006). *Emerging adulthood: The winding road from the late teens through the twenties.* New York: Oxford University Press.

Arnold, A. P. (2003). The gender of the voice within: The neural origin of sex differences in the brain. *Current Opinion in Neurobiology, 13,* 759–764.

Barak, A., Hen, L., Boniel-Nissim, M., & Shapira, N. (2008). A comprehensive review and a meta-analysis of the effectiveness of Internet-based psychotherapeutic interventions. *Journal of Technology in Human Services. 26,* 109–160.

Baron-Cohen, S. (2004). *The essential difference: Male and female brains and the truth about autism.* New York: Basic Books.

Beattie, A., Shaw, A., Kaur, S., & Kessler, D. (2009). Primary-care patients' expectations and experiences of online cognitive behavioural therapy for depression: A qualitative study. *Health Expectations: An International Journal of Public Participation in Health Care & Health Policy, 12,* 45–59.

Bellis, M. A., Downing, J., & Ashton, J. R. (2006). Adults at 12? Trends in puberty and their public health consequences. *Journal of Epidemiology & Community Health, 60,* 910–911.

Ben-Shahar, T. (2007). *Happier: Learn the secrets to daily joy and lasting fulfillment.* New York: McGraw-Hill.

Borum, R., & Verhaagen, D. (2006). *Assessing and managing violence risk in juveniles.* New York: Guilford.

Botella, C., Garcia-Palacios, A., Baños, R. M., & Quero, S. (2009). Cybertherapy: Advantages, limitations, and ethical issues. *Psychology Journal, 7,* 77–100.

Brooks, R., & Goldstein, S. (2001). *Raising resilient children.* Chicago: Contemporary Books.

Buckingham, M., & Clifton, D. O. (2001). *Now, discover your strengths.* New York: The Free Press.

Buffardi, L. E., & Campbell, W. K. (2008). Narcissism and social networking Web sites. *Personality and Social Psychology Bulletin, 34,* 1303–1314.

Burton, L. A., Hafetz, J., & Henninger, D. (2007). Gender differences in relational and physical aggression. *Social Behavior and Personality, 35,* 41–50.

Butler, A. C., Chapman, J. E., Forman, E. M., & Beck, A. T. (2006). The empirical status of cognitive-behavioral therapy: A review of meta-analyses. *Clinical Psychology Review, 26,* 17–31.

Carden, R., Bryant, C., & Moss, R. (2004). Locus of control, test anxiety, academic procrastination, and achievement among college students. *Psychological Reports, 95,* 581–582.

Carnegie, D. (1998). *How to win friends and influence people.* New York: Pocket Books. (Original work published 1936)

Carroll, J. S., Padilla-Walker, L. M., Nelson, L. J., Olson, C. D., Barry, C. M., & Madsen, S. D. (2008). Generation XXX: Pornography acceptance and use among emerging adults. *Journal of Adolescent Research, 23,* 6–30.

Castonguay, L. G., Constantino, M. J., & Holtforth, M. G. (2006). The working alliance: Where are we and where should we go? *Psychotherapy: Theory, Research, Practice, Training, 43,* 271–279.

Centers for Disease Control. (2008). Youth risk behavior surveillance: United States, 2007. *Morbidity and Mortality Weekly Report, 57,* SS-4.

Chak, K., & Leung, L. (2004). Shyness and locus of control as predictors of Internet addiction and Internet use. *CyberPsychology & Behavior, 7,* 559–570.

Chandra, A., & Minkovitz, C. S. (2006). Stigma starts early: Gender differences in teen willingness to use mental health services. *Journal of Adolescent Health, 38,* 754.

Chapple, C. L., & Johnson, K. A. (2007). Gender differences in impulsivity. *Youth Violence and Juvenile Justice, 5,* 221–234.

Christopher, A. N., Kuo, S. V., Abraham, K. M., Noel, L. W., & Linz, H. E. (2004). Materialism and affective well-being: The role of social support. *Personality and Individual Differences, 37,* 463–470.

Christopher, A. N., Morgan, R. D., Marek, P., Keller, M., & Drummond, K. (2005). Materialism and self-presentational styles. *Personality and Individual Differences, 38,* 137–149.

Cook, J. E., & Doyle, C. (2002). Working alliance in online therapy as compared to face-to-face therapy: Preliminary results. *CyberPsychology & Behavior, 5,* 95–105.

Cote, J. E., & Levine, C. G. (2002). *Identity, formation, agency, and culture: A social psychological synthesis.* New York: Lawrence Erlbaum.

Cremeens, J. L., Usdan, S. L., Brock-Martin, A., Martin, R. J., & Watkins, K. (2008). Parent-child communication to reduce heavy alcohol use among first-year college students. *College Student Journal, 42,* 152–163.

Cusack, J., Deane, F. P., Wilson, C. J., & Ciarrochi, J. (2004). Who influence men to go to therapy? Reports from men attending psychological services. *International Journal for the Advancement of Counseling, 26,* 271–283.

D'Augelli, A. R., & Hershberger, S. L. (1993). Lesbian, gay, and bisexual youth in community settings: Personal challenges and mental health problems. *American Journal of Community Psychology, 21,* 421–448.

Dean, L. R., Carroll, J. S., & Yang, C. (2007). Materialism, perceived financial problems, and marital satisfaction. *Family & Consumer Sciences Research Journal, 35,* 260–281.

Desai, R. A., Maciejewski, P. K., Pantalon, M. V., & Potenza, M. N. (2005). Gender differences in adolescent gambling. *Annals of Clinical Psychiatry, 17,* 249–258.

Dong, Q., Urista, M. A., & Gundrum, D. (2008). The impact of emotional intelligence, self-esteem, and self-image on romantic communication over MySpace. *CyberPsychology & Behavior, 11,* 577–578.

Eliot, L. (2009). *Pink brain, blue brain: How small differences grow into troublesome gaps—and what we can do about it.* New York: Houghton Mifflin Harcourt.

Erikson, E. H. (1968). *Identity, youth, and crisis.* New York: Norton.

Feder, J., Levant, R. F., & Dean, J. (2007). Boys and violence: A gender-informed analysis. *Professional Psychology: Research and Practice, 38,* 385–391.

Fingeret, M. C., Moeller, F. G., & Stotts, A. (2005). Gender differences among MDMA users on psychological and drug history variables. *Addictive Disorders and Their Treatment, 4,* 43–48.

Finlay, F. O., Jones, R., & Coleman, J. (2002). Is puberty getting earlier? The views of doctors and teachers. *Child Care, Health and Development, 28,* 205–209.

Fortson, B. L., Scotti, J. R., Chen, Y., Del Ben, K. S., & Malone, J. (2007). Internet use, abuse, and dependence among students at a Southeastern Regional University. *Journal of American College Health, 56,* 137–144.

Gale, C. R., Batty, G. D., & Deary, I. J. (2008). Locus of control at age 10 years and health outcomes and behaviors at age 30 years: The 1970 British Cohort Study. *Psychosomatic Medicine, 70,* 397–403.

Garnefski, N., & Diekstra, R. F. W. (1997). Child sexual abuse and emotional and behavioral problems in adolescence: Gender differences. *Journal of the American Academy of Child & Adolescent Psychiatry, 36,* 323–329.

Gladwell, M. (2005). *Blink: The power of thinking without thinking.* New York: Back Bay Books.

Good, G. E., Schopp, L. H., Thomson, D., Hathaway, S. L., Mazurek, M. O., & Sanford-Martens, T. C. (2008). Men with serious injuries: Relations among masculinity, age, and alcohol use. *Rehabilitation Psychology, 53,* 39.

Grella, C. E., Greenwell, L., Mays, V. M., & Cochran, S. D. (2009). Influence of gender, sexual orientation, and need on treatment utilization for substance use and mental disorders: Findings from the California quality of life survey. *BMC Psychiatry.*

Gur, R. C., Gunning-Dixon, F., Bilker, W. B., & Gur, R. E. (2002). Sex differences in temporo-limbic and frontal brain volumes of healthy adults. *Cerebral Cortex, 12,* 998–1003.

Gute, G., & Eshbaugh, E. M. (2008). Personality as a predictor of hooking up among college students. *Journal of Community Health Nursing, 25,* 26–43.

Harrell, Z. A. T., & Karim, N. M. (2008). Is gender relevant only for problem alcohol behaviors? An examination of correlates of alcohol use among college students. *Addictive Behaviors, 33*, 359–365.

Harris, C. R., Jenkins, M., & Glaser, D. (2006). Gender differences in risk assessment: Why do women take fewer risks than men? *Judgment and Decision Making, 1*, 48–63.

Hayes, S. C., Strosahl, K. D., & Wilson, K. G. (2003). *Acceptance and commitment therapy: An experiential approach to behavior change.* New York: Guilford Press.

Hesse, M., & Tutenges, S. (2008). Gender differences in self-reported drinking-induced disinhibition of sexual behaviors. *The American Journal on Addictions, 17*, 293–297.

Hoeft, F., Watson, C. L., Kesler, S. R., Bettinger, K. E., & Reiss, A. L. (2008). Gender differences in the mesocorticolimbic system during computer game-play. *Journal of Psychiatric Research, 42*, 253–258.

Hofmann, S. G., & Smits, J. A. J. (2008). Cognitive-behavioral therapy for adult anxiety disorders: A meta-analysis of randomized placebo-controlled trials. *Journal of Clinical Psychiatry, 69*, 621–632.

Hyde, J. S. (2005). The gender similarities hypothesis. *American Psychologist, 60*, 581–592.

James, B. (1996). *Treating traumatized children: New insights and creative interventions.* New York: Free Press.

Jausovec, N., & Jausovec, K. (2005). Sex differences in brain activity related to general and emotional intelligence. *Brain and Cognition, 59*, 277–286.

Kashdan, T. B., & Breen, W. E. (2007). Materialism and diminished well-being: Experiential avoidance as a mediating mechanism. *Journal of Social & Clinical Psychology, 26*, 521–539.

Kasser, T. (2002). *The high price of materialism.* Cambridge, MA: The MIT Press.

Kasser, T., & Ryan, R. M. (1996). Further examining the American dream: Differential correlates of intrinsic and extrinsic goals. *Personality and Social Psychology Bulletin, 22*, 280–287.

Kimmel, M. (2008). *Guyland: The perilous world where boys become men.* New York: Harper.

Kiselica, M. S. (2001). A male-friendly therapeutic process with school-age boys. In G. R. Brooks & G. Good (Eds.), *The handbook of counseling and psychotherapy with me: A guide to settings and approaches* (Vol. 1, pp. 34–58). San Francisco: Jossey-Bass.

Kiselica, M. S. (2003). Transforming psychotherapy in order to succeed with boys: Male-friendly practices. *Journal of Clinical Psychology: In Session, 59*, 1225–1236.

Kiselica, M. S., & Englar-Carlson, M. (2008). Establishing rapport with boys in individual counseling and psychotherapy: A male-friendly perspective. In M. S. Kiselica, M. Englar-Carlson, & A. M. Horne (Eds.), *Counseling troubled boys: A guidebook for practitioners* (pp. 49–65). New York: Routledge.

Kiselica, M. S., Englar-Carlson, M., Horne, A. M., & Fisher, M. (2008). A positive psychology perspective on helping boys. In M. S. Kiselica, M. Englar-Carlson, & A. M. Horne (Eds.), *Counseling troubled boys: A guidebook for practitioners* (pp. 31–48). New York: Routledge.

Klein, J. B., Jacobs, R. H., & Reinecke, M. A. (2007). Cognitive-behavioral therapy for adolescent depression: A meta-analytic investigation of changes in effect-size estimates. *Journal of the American Academy of Child & Adolescent Psychiatry, 46,* 1403–1413.

Knox, D., Zusman, M., & McNeely, A. (2008). University student beliefs about sex: Men vs. women. *College Student Journal, 42,* 181–185.

Kucian, K., Loenneker, T., Dietrich, T., Martin, E., & Von Aster, M. (2005). Gender differences in brain activation patterns during mental rotation and number related cognitive tasks. *Psychology Science, 47,* 112–131.

Kuzma, J. M., & Black, D. W. (2008). Epidemiology, prevalence, and natural history of compulsive sexual behavior. *Psychiatric Clinics of North America, 31,* 603–611.

Lauer, S., de Man, A. F., Marquez, S., & Ades, J. (2008). External locus of control, problem-focused coping and attempted suicide. *North American Journal of Psychology, 10,* 625–632.

Layard, R. (2006). *Happiness: Lessons from a new science.* New York: Penguin Books.

Levant, R. F. (2008). How do we understand masculinity? An editorial. *Psychology of Man and Masculinity, 9,* 1–4.

Levitt, S. D., & Dubner, S. J. (2009). *Freakonomics: A rogue economist explores the hidden side of everything.* New York: Harper Perennial.

Li, Q. (2006). Cyberbullying in schools: A research of gender differences. *School Psychology International, 27,* 157–170.

Littauer, H., Sexton, H., & Wynn, R. (2005). Qualities clients wish for in their therapists. *Scandinavian Journal of Caring Sciences, 19,* 28–31.

Mackinnon, A., Griffiths, K. M., & Christensen, H. (2008). Comparative randomised trial of online cognitive-behavioural therapy and an information website for depression: 12-month outcomes. *British Journal of Psychiatry, 192,* 130–134.

Madge, C., Meek, J., Wellens, J., & Hooley, T. (2009). Facebook, social integration and informal learning at university: It is more for socialising and talking to friends about work than for actually doing work. *Learning, Media and Technology, 34,* 141–155.

Magill, M., & Ray, L. A. (2009). Cognitive-behavioral treatment with adult alcohol and illicit drug users: A meta-analysis of randomized controlled trials. *Journal of Studies on Alcohol and Drugs, 70,* 516–527.

Magnuson, M. J., & Dundes, L. (2008). Gender differences in "social portraits" reflected in MySpace profiles. *CyberPsychology & Behavior, 11,* 239–241.

Marcia, J. E. (1966). Development and validation of ego identity status. *Journal of Personality and Social Psychology, 3,* 551–558.

Marcus, R. F. (2009). Cross-sectional study of violence in emerging adulthood. *Aggressive Behavior, 35,* 188–202.

Martin, J., Romas, M., Medford, M., Leffert, N., & Hatcher, S. L. (2006). Adult helping qualities preferred by adolescents. *Adolescence, 41,* 127–140.

Maselko, J., & Kubzansky, L. D. (2006). Gender differences in religious practices, spiritual experiences and health: Results from the U.S. General Social Survey. *Social Science & Medicine, 62,* 2848–2860.

Matud, M. P., Rodriguez, C., & Grande, J. (2007). Gender differences in creative thinking. *Personality and Individual Differences, 43,* 1137–1147.

Mavroveli, S., Petrides, K. V., Rieffe, C., & Bakker, F. (2007). Trait emotional intelligence, psychological well-being and peer-rated social competence in adolescence. *British Journal of Development Psychology, 25,* 263–275.

McCabe, S. E., Morales, M., Cranford, J. A., Delva, J., McPherson, M. D., & Boyd, C. J. (2007). Race/ethnicity and gender differences in drug use and abuse among college students. *Journal of Ethnicity in Substance Abuse, 6,* 75–95.

McKelley, R. A., & Rochlen, A. B. (2007). The practice of coaching: Exploring alternatives to therapy for counseling-resistant men. *Psychology of Men & Masculinity, 8,* 53–65.

Meston, C. M., & Buss, D. M. (2007). Why humans have sex. *Archives of Sexual Behavior, 36,* 477–507.

Milani, R. M., Parrott, A. C., Turner, J. J. D., & Fox, H. C. (2004). Gender differences in self-reported anxiety, depression, and somatization among ecstasy/MDMA polydrug users, alcohol/tobacco users, and nondrug users. *Addictive Behaviors, 29,* 965–971.

Miller, W. R., & Rollnick, S. (2002). *Motivational interviewing: Preparing people for change.* New York: Guilford Press.

Monnier, J., Knapp, R. G., & Frueh, B. C. (2003). Recent advances in telepsychiatry: An updated review. *Psychiatric Services, 54,* 1604–1609.

Mora, L., Nevid, J., & Chaplin, W. (2008). Psychologist treatment recommendations for Internet-based therapeutic interventions. *Computers in Human Behavior, 24,* 3052–3062.

Morgan, R. D., Patrick, A. R., & Magaletta, P. R. (2008). Does the use of telemental health alter the treatment experience? Inmates' perceptions of telemental health versus face-to-face treatment modalities. *Journal of Consulting and Clinical Psychology, 76,* 158–162.

Muise, A., Christofides, E., & Desmarais, S. (2009). More information than you ever wanted: Does Facebook bring out the green-eyed monster of jealousy? *Cyberpsychology & Behavior: The Impact of the Internet, Multimedia and Virtual Reality on Behavior and Society, 12,* 441–444.

Ng, T. W. H., Sorensen, K. L., & Eby, L. T. (2006). Locus of control at work: A meta-analysis. *Journal of Organizational Behavior, 27,* 1057–1087.

Nichols, L. A., & Nicki, R. (2004). Development of a psychometrically sound Internet addiction scale: A preliminary step. *Psychology of Addictive Behaviors, 18,* 381–384.

Nolen-Hoeksema, S. (2004). Gender differences in risk factors and consequences for alcohol use and problems. *Clinical Psychology Review, 24,* 981–1010.

O'Boyle, M. W., Benbow, C. P., & Alexander, J. E. (1995). Sex differences, hemispheric laterality, and associated brain activity in the intellectually gifted. *Developmental Neuropsychology, 11,* 415–443.

Oishi, S., Diener, E., & Lucas, R. E. (2007). The optimum level of well-being: Can people be too happy? *Perspectives on Psychological Science, 2,* 346–360.

O'Reilly, S., Knox, D., & Zusman, M. E. (2007). College student attitudes toward pornography use. *College Student Journal, 41,* 402–406.

Orford, J., Hodgson, R., Copello, A., Wilton, S., & Slegg, G. (2009). To what factors do clients attribute change? Content analysis of follow-up interviews with clients of the UK Alcohol Treatment Trial. *Journal of Substance Abuse Treatment, 36,* 49–58.

Page, G. L., & Scalora, M. J. (2004). The utility of locus of control for assessing juvenile amenability to treatment. *Aggression and Violent Behavior, 9,* 523–534.

Pempek, T. A., Yermolayeva, Y. A., & Calvert, S. L. (2009). College students' social networking experiences on Facebook. *Journal of Applied Developmental Psychology, 30,* 227–238.

Pollack, W. (1999). *Real boys: Rescuing our sons from the myths of boyhood.* New York: Owl Books.

Prochaska, J. O., & DiClemente, C. C. (1983). Stages and processes of self-change of smoking: Toward an integrative model of change. *Journal of Consulting and Clinical Psychology, 51,* 390–395.

Prochaska J. O., & DiClemente C. C. (1984). *The transtheoretical approach: Crossing traditional boundaries of therapy.* Homewood, IL: Dow Jones-Irwin.

Rosenbaum, J. E. (2008). Patient teenagers? A comparison of the sexual behavior of virginity pledgers and matched nonpledgers. *Pediatrics, 123,* 110–120.

Rutledge, P. C., Park, A., & Sher, K. J. (2008). 21st birthday drinking: Extremely extreme. *Journal of Consulting and Clinical Psychology, 76,* 511–516.

Ryan, C., Huebner, D., Diaz, R. M., & Sanchez, J. (2009). Family rejection as a predictor of negative health outcomes in white and Latino lesbian, gay, and bisexual young adults, *Pediatrics, 123,* 346–352.

Schaub, M., & Williams, C. (2007). Examining the relations between masculine gender role conflict and men's expectations about counseling. *Psychology of Men & Masculinity, 8,* 40–52.

Selekman, M. D. (2005). *Pathways to change: Brief therapy with difficult adolescents* (2nd ed.). New York: Guilford Press.

Seligman, M. E. P. (2004). *Authentic happiness: Using the new positive psychology to release your potential for lasting fulfillment.* New York: Free Press.

Sells, S. P. (1998). *Treating the tough adolescent: A family-based, step-by-step guide.* New York: Guilford Press.

Sharf, J. (2007). Psychotherapy dropout: A meta-analytic review of premature termination. *Dissertation Abstracts International: Section B: The Sciences and Engineering, 68,* 6336B.

Sheff, D. (2008). *Beautiful boy: A father's journey through his son's addiction.* New York: Houghton Mifflin.

Sheldon, P. (2008). The relationship between unwillingness-to-communicate and students' Facebook use. *Journal of Media Psychology: Theories, Methods, and Applications, 20,* 67–75.

Shepherd, S., Fitch, T. J., Owen, D., & Marshall, J. L. (2006). Locus of control and academic achievement in high school students. *Psychological Reports, 98,* 318–322.

Shepherd, L., Goldstein, D., Whitford, H., Brummell, V., Hicks, M., & Thewes, B. (2006). The utility of videoconferencing to provide innovative delivery of psychological treatment for rural cancer patients: Results of a pilot study. *Journal of Pain and Symptom Management, 32,* 453–461.

Skovholt, T. M., & Jennings, L. (2004). *Master therapists: Exploring expertise in therapy and counseling.* Boston: Allyn & Bacon.

Smith, T. E., Sells, S. P., Rodman, J., & Reynolds, L. R. (2006). Reducing adolescent substance abuse and delinquency: Pilot research of a family-oriented psychoeducation curriculum. *Journal of Child & Adolescent Substance Abuse, 15,* 105–115.

Smits, J. A. J., Berry, A. C., Tart, C. D., & Powers, M. B. (2008). The efficacy of cognitive-behavioral interventions for reducing anxiety sensitivity: A meta-analytic review. *Behaviour Research and Therapy, 46,* 1047–1054.

Stiles, W. B., Glick, M. J., Osatuke, K., Hardy, G. E., Shapiro, D. A., Agnew-Davies, R., et al. (2004). Patterns of alliance development and the Rupture-Repair Hypothesis: Are productive relationships u-shaped or v-shaped? *Journal of Counseling Psychology, 51,* 81–92.

Taylor, G. J., & Bagby, R. M. (2000). An overview of the alexithymia construct. In R. Bar-On & J. D. Parker (Eds.), *The handbook of emotional intelligence: Theory, development, assessment, and application at home, school, and in the workplace* (pp. 40–67). San Francisco: Jossey-Bass.

Tong, S. T., van der Heide, B., Langwell, L., & Walther, J. B. (2008). Too much of a good thing? The relationship between number of friends and interpersonal impressions on Facebook. *Journal of Computer-Mediated Communication, 13,* 531–549.

Van Vugt, M., De Cremer, D., & Janssen, D. P. (2007). Gender differences in cooperation and competition: The male-warrior hypothesis. *Psychological Science, 18,* 19–23.

Van Vugt, M., & Spisak, B. R. (2008). Sex differences in the emergence of leadership during competitions within and between groups. *Psychological Science, 19,* 854–858.

Verhaagen, D. (2005). *Parenting the millennial generation.* Santa Barbara, CA: Praeger Publishers.

Walther, J. B., van der Heide, B., Kim, S., Westerman, D., & Tong, S. T. (2008). The role of friends' appearance and behavior on evaluations of individuals on Facebook: Are we known by the company we keep? *Human Communication Research, 34,* 28–49.

Wester, S. R., Vogel, D. L., Pressly, P. K., & Heesacker, M. (2002). Sex differences in emotion: A critical review of the literature and implications for counseling psychology. *The Counseling Psychologist, 30,* 629–651.

Willoughby, B. L. B., Malik, N. M., & Lindahl, K. M. (2006). Parental reactions to their sons' sexual orientation disclosures: The roles of family cohesion, adaptability, and parenting style. *Psychology of Men & Masculinity, 7,* 14–26.

Willoughby, T. (2008). A short-term longitudinal study of Internet and computer game use by adolescent boys and girls: Prevalence, frequency of use, and psychosocial predictors. *Developmental Psychology, 44,* 195–204.

Zywica, J., & Danowski, J. (2008). The faces of Facebookers: Investigating social enhancement and social compensation hypotheses; predicting Facebook™ and offline popularity from sociability and self-esteem, and mapping the meanings of popularity with semantic networks. *Journal of Computer-Mediated Communication, 14,* 1–34.

INDEX

A

Abuse
  alcohol, 1, 5, 10–11, 21, 43, 68, 69–70, 78
  drug, 3, 10–11, 69–70, 163
  sexual, 160–161
Acceptance and Commitment Therapy (ACT), 107
Accidents, auto, 1–2, 19, 78
Accurate empathy, 62
Achieved identity, 99
Actions, risky, 172
Action stage of change, 44
Action steps for controlling behavioral problems, 172–173
Active listening, 135–136
Adolescence, stages of, 13–17, 42
Adults, emerging, 15–16
Alcohol use, 1, 5, 21, 68, 69–70, 78
  gender and, 10–11
  importance of change and, 43
Alexithymia, 118–121
Alignment, 60–62
Alliance, therapy, 45–47
Anger, 19–20, 122–123. *See also* Behavioral problems
  control skills, 164–169
  -control worksheet, 183–184
  sequence, 164, 166–168
  signs, 164, 165–166
  sparks, 164, 165
  strategies, 164, 168–169
Anxiety, 26
Arnett, J. J., 16

Assessment
  of client needs, 85–88, 89–90
  identity status, 99–100
  of protective factors, 33–34
Attributions, power of, 103–105
Attunement, 61–62
Authority issue, 85
Autism, 7
Auto accidents, 1–2, 19, 78

B

Bagby, R. M., 118, 119–120
Baron-Cohen, Simon, 7
Beautiful Boy, 163
Behavioral problems. *See also* Anger
  actions steps for controlling, 172–173
  custom checklists for controlling, 175–178
  gender and, 10
  improving decision-making skills for controlling, 178–182
  managing, 170–175
  risky actions and, 172
  risky feelings and, 171–172
  risky situations and, 170–171
  risky thoughts and, 171
Ben-Shahar, Tal, 108
Blink, 53
Body work, 125–126
Boss, therapists being the, 67–68
Boundaries, therapeutic, 195–198
"Boy Code," 4
Bragging, sexual, 142–143